IN PURSUIT OF
WORLD ORDER

U.S. Foreign Policy
and International Organizations

Also by the author

STERLING-DOLLAR DIPLOMACY

In Pursuit of
World Order

U.S. Foreign Policy
and International Organizations

RICHARD N. GARDNER

REVISED EDITION

FREDERICK A. PRAEGER, *Publishers*
New York • Washington • London

Published in the United States of America in 1966
by Frederick A. Praeger, Inc., Publishers
111 Fourth Avenue, New York, N.Y. 10003, U.S.A.
77–79 Charlotte Street, London W.1, England

Second printing, 1967

This is an enlarged and completely revised edition of the
book first published in 1964 by Frederick A. Praeger, Inc.

Library of Congress Catalog Card Number: 66–28597

Printed in the United States of America

*For
Danielle*

Contents

Foreword

by Harlan Cleveland

IN EVERY TIME and culture, men have perceived the need to build institutions of cooperation, for safety and for the advancement of the interests they share. But only in our time has this urge become global in extent—witness the fact that 1965 has been celebrated the world over as International Cooperation Year. No one who reads this book can doubt that there is already plenty of International Cooperation to have a Year about.

The trouble is that the thunder and tumult of the cold war has obscured a great spurt in international cooperation in the years since World War II. The polemics of a bipolar world and the awful reality of the nuclear arms race have hidden the foundations of the rising international community. And the notion persists that agreement or disagreement among nations at any given time is total—that you cannot hold opposing views on subject A and simultaneously cooperate on subject B.

This, of course, is nonsense, and the proof can be found between the covers of this book—or wherever else you look.

We disagree with the Soviet Union, for example, on Berlin, Viet Nam, and Cuba. But, at the same time, we cooperate with the Soviet Union in cultural exchange programs, in allocating radio frequencies, in forecasting the weather, in fighting disease, in studying the oceans, and in dozens of other technical ways. We even cooperate, where we can, on the peaceful settlement of our own and other people's disputes.

International cooperation for survival and welfare has become a plain necessity. An increasing number of subjects of importance to our nation can only be dealt with on a world basis. If you like long words, you can call this the technological imperative. Or you can simply repeat the truism—which is every day more true—that it's a small world.

Someone recently put it even better. He defined a "typical American" as a fellow who has just driven home from an Italian movie in his German car, who sits on his Danish furniture drinking Brazilian coffee out of an English china cup, writing a letter on Irish linen paper with a Japanese ballpoint pen—a letter complaining to his Congressman about too much American gold going overseas!

The technological imperative, the need to build worldwide technical agencies, stems, of course, from the headlong pace of scientific discovery. Every time that science chalks up another "success," a new demand is created for a new institution to tame or exploit the new accomplishment. More and more frequently, it is an international institution. Whenever the scientists achieve a break-through in what can be done by man for man, it suddenly seems outrageous not to be channeling the new power that new knowledge confers upon us.

Before we knew how to commit mass murder among the mosquitoes that carry malaria, nobody thought of eradicating malaria from the face of the earth because it couldn't be done. Now that we know it can be done, we are well on

our way to the doing of it—even if the task is proving somewhat longer, and the insects more resistant to our attempts
to poison them, than scientists thought when they proudly
swept every anopheles mosquito from the island of Sardinia
just after World War II.

Before there was radio, we did not need large international conferences to divide up the frequency spectrum.
Before there were airplanes flying across frontiers and
oceans, we did not need an International Civil Aviation
Organization. We are used to the idea that necessity is the
mother of invention. But in the technology of international
relations, the reverse applies as well: Invention is the
mother of necessity.

Nowadays, Congress and the rest of us take international
organizations, and the conferences they spawn, as part of a
familiar landscape. The United States belongs today to
fifty-three international organizations. We contribute more
than a third of a billion dollars to them and to twenty-two
international operating programs, mostly sponsored by
these same organizations—and that does not count the activities of international lending agencies. In the past two
years, the United States has participated in more international conferences than we attended in our entire history
from the founding of the Republic to the beginning of
World War II.

International organizations exist simply because they are
needed; we belong to them simply because it serves our
national interest to belong—and because it would damage
our national interest to remain aloof. So while nations
cling to national sovereignties and national purposes, science is creating a functional international community
whether anyone likes it or not.

It is certainly good that, within the frontiers of special
areas like agriculture, health, or the physical sciences, we
are beginning to demonstrate that men can get along with
each other without an intolerable amount of friction and

confusion, just as we are beginning to demonstrate within the frontiers of nations that men can get along with each other without an intolerable amount of bloodshed. It is good that scientists can "speak the same language," even through an interpreter; that physicians can cooperate with each other in a global war on disease; that farmers can teach each other how to get higher yields without politics getting too much in the way.

All this is good, but it is not enough. The spawning of new technologies is not always or necessarily beneficent. The technology of nuclear fission and fusion can provide electric power for national development; it can also incinerate all life in the Northern Hemisphere.

The parochialism of each major field of knowledge is not necessarily an improvement on the more familiar parochialism of nation-states, *unless* the demonstration that experts can work with each other on food and health leads in fact to nations working with each other to keep the general peace.

A civilization that guarantees people enough to eat and a longer life—and then exposes them to lethal radioactivity —is not moving onward and upward. It is moving sideways toward a precipice. If a workable pattern of peace must be constructed patiently by building first its component parts, the parts must in the end add up to international organizations that work for peace and freedom as well as health and welfare.

Beyond the technological imperative, therefore, is a political imperative. It stems from our basic value-system: the kind of safe and open world we want to live in, the kinds of rights and opportunities we want to see secured to every human being. So we naturally are working toward a world of peaceful change under a system of order based on consent in which cooperation is an international way of life. Our belief in diversity and our need for safety together define the goal of American foreign policy: "to make the world safe for diversity."

The first requirement of a foreign policy so defined is to avoid the cataclysm of nuclear war. That is why the Administrations of John Kennedy and Lyndon Johnson have invested so much Presidential time and attention on the attempt to wrap the new-born weaponry of fission and fusion in the swaddling-clothes of social constraint and political responsibility.

The United States, the Soviet Union, and the United Kingdom—joined now by nearly a hundred other nations—have confirmed by formal treaty that they have a common interest in not polluting the common atmosphere with radioactive particles, and a common interest in putting a brake on the nuclear arms race. They have agreed that this common interest requires such a treaty *despite* irreconcilable ideologies, incompatible values, and antithetical ways of organizing political power.

What is new and hopeful here is the dawning realization that national rivals can remain rivals and still agree on what is in the interest of both. Mutual suspicion and mistrust are certainly not dispelled, but the nuclear weapons are not poisoning the atmosphere while negotiations proceed on their control and inspection.

Perhaps we are learning that national rivals do not have to kiss and make up before they agree not to annihilate each other. International politics is not what the "war-game" men call a "zero-sum game": A foot gained on one side does not necessarily mean a foot lost on the other.

Perhaps the world is beginning to fumble its way toward a pragmatic modern approach to the ancient dream of peace, toward a manageable, workable system of order based, as President Kennedy said at American University, "not on a sudden revolution in human nature but on a gradual evolution in human institutions—on a series of concrete actions and effective agreements which are in the interest of all concerned."

Beyond the control and reduction of arms, a world safe for diversity requires a wide range of international institutions and procedures to deter the resort to war, and encourage the resolution of conflict without war.

The United Nations is sometimes called a safety-valve, a place to let off steam. Much steam is in fact let off there, and the valve has a certain value. It is good that a building exists on the East River in which every nation, large and small, can grumble for the record about his neighbor—and provide his neighbor equal time to grumble about him.

But the Security Council and the General Assembly are not at their best when they are adding heat to an already overheated dispute. They function at their best as devices for recording solutions arrived at by honest—which is to say, quiet—negotiation.

The growing value of the U.N., as peacekeeper and peacemaker to the world, lies not so much in its public debates as in its operating machinery—its mediators, its observers, its inspectors, its truce supervisors, and its emergency peacekeeping forces.

In spite of our great power, the United States cannot alone be policeman to the world. The rest of the world would not like it, and the American people would not stand for it—which is reason enough to build international peacekeeping machinery to take on the sometimes unhappy policeman's lot.

Thus we share with most of the rest of the world an interest in spreading the risk and the responsibility for international peacekeeping. Important as this has been in the past, especially in Korea, Kashmir, the Middle East, the Congo, and Cyprus, it is likely to be much more important in the future. For the nuclear stalemate appears to have loosened the inhibitions that kept the lid on incipient disputes. Having concluded that we may not after all die of a nuclear thrombosis, the world seems to have broken out in a rash of smaller local disputes, each carrying the virus of general war.

How much further can—or should—the U.N. develop its peacekeeping capacity? It is a fair question, but no answer today is certain to make sense tomorrow.

For the U.N. has whatever capacity its members can agree to endow it with, at any given time for any given purpose. Until one knows the nature of a future emergency and then plumbs the will of the U.N.'s majority to act in the face of common danger, one cannot say what the "capacity" of the U.N. is to act in defense of the peace.

The day before the Korean invasion, the day before the Suez crisis, the day before the army mutiny in the Congo, nobody would have dreamed that the U.N. could or would take on the peacekeeping tasks it did in fact assume. The capacity of the U.N. is the sum of the wills of its members to act together.

Dag Hammarskjöld said it well, in remarks which Prime Minister Pearson of Canada quoted in his Hammarskjöld Memorial Lecture: "The basic policy line for this Organization is that the United Nations simply must respond to those demands which must be made of it. . . . The United Nations should respond and should have confidence in its strength and capacity to respond."

Obviously, there is always the question of how great an administrative load can safely be taken on. Obviously, too, there is the sticky and contentious problem of finance, and the always difficult matter of recruiting and training first-rate people capable of doing unprecedented jobs in a fog of controversy and frustration. The U.N.'s small operations in Greece, Palestine, and Kashmir helped to put it in training to climb what Hammarskjöld called "the very steep hill of Suez"; in turn, the operation in the Gaza Strip served as calisthenics for the Congo; and what was learned in the Congo deeply affected the mandate, the strategy, and the tactics of the Cyprus operation.

Yet if there is one lesson to be drawn from the thirteen alarms to which the U.N. has responded, it is that each peacekeeping task is unprecedented, that the U.N.'s resources are never fixed or exhaustible, that being busy in one place must not preclude being busy in another.

So the measure of future United Nations actions for peace, here and there around the world, is not some predetermined quantum of "capacity to act," but rather the complex circumstances under which the requisite majority of its members can agree to pool their strength and act together for the Charter's purposes. This is the real variable in the equation—not the age or experience of the Organization, not the state of its bank account, not the level of its current workload.

The U.N.'s future capacity to act will be deeply affected by the outcome of issues that are unresolved as this is written. To be an effective instrument, its members will have to develop a way of financing peacekeeping operations that does not create a constitutional crisis over each half-billion dollars. The Organization will also have to find some way to reflect the political facts of life in the United Nations where equal votes are endowed with unequal influence and unequal responsibility for the consequences of inaction.

This does not imply that the stronger members must lead the less strong around by the nose—any more than that the "one country, one vote" principle subordinates the U.N.'s big-power minority to its small-power majority. It implies, rather, that in a responsible organization, the less strong must have the realism to know the U.N. depends on its stronger members for its capacity to act—and the good sense to know that when the most powerful members can agree, the less powerful are often protected by that agreement.

All this is to say that the United Nations is and will continue to be a political body, and anybody who has worked in a legislature or on a school board or even on a student council knows the limitations imposed by the politics of consent.

International cooperation is uphill work all the way. Nuclear arms—clashing ideologies—conflicting ambitions —contradictory principles—economic interests—territorial disputes—racial, religious, and tribal animosities—personal greed—the lust for power: These, too, are realities. And so is the stubborn addiction of the human race to the ways of the past, its adamant resistance to change, its persistence in prejudice, bias, and hatred.

International cooperation must push against all the traditional, provincial, reactionary instincts of the human race. And if it seems hard for us, let us keep in mind that it is even more difficult for those nursed on dogma, weaned on historical determinism, and schooled on the "inevitability" of, say, the class struggle.

But we are in a very early stage of the journey toward world order. Both the technical and political pressures for international cooperation will not diminish but rise.

These are some of the reasons why our enthusiasm for what we call "international cooperation" must be grounded in reality and focused on practical expectations. International cooperation does not just happen. It is not an ideal, a spirit, a principle, a wish, or a policy. It is represented by institutions, treaties, laws, negotiations, agreements, and actions—hard, concrete realities that often are difficult to come by.

Peace is not an abstraction: It is an organized system for the peaceful resolution of difference and the peaceful management of needed change. The alternative to missiles is not merely the absence of missiles: The alternative is the presence of workable, reliable institutions—governed by accepted laws and agreed procedures, administered by flesh-and-blood men and women.

A decent world order will only be built brick by brick. Those who wish to help build it, and not merely to talk about building it, will concentrate on the next brick—on how it can be fashioned, where it belongs, how it will fit, when it should be added to the structure.

This book describes some of the main bricks, and indicates where the United States thinks they belong. Its author, Richard Gardner, helped to fashion most of them during his four years as part of the Kennedy and Johnson Administrations. He understands the process of international institution-building as clearly and deeply as any American of our time.

IN PURSUIT OF
WORLD ORDER

U.S. Foreign Policy
and International Organizations

Those who live in the emerging community of nations will ignore the problems of their neighbors at the risk of their own prosperity. . . . To commemorate the United Nations' twentieth birthday, 1965 has been designated International Cooperation Year. I propose to dedicate this year to finding new techniques for making man's knowledge serve man's welfare. Let this be the year of science. Let it be a turning point in the struggle—not of man against man, but of man against nature. In the midst of tension let us begin to chart a course toward the possibilities of conquest which bypass the politics of the cold war.

—PRESIDENT LYNDON B. JOHNSON

Let us focus instead on a more practical, more attainable peace, based not on a sudden revolution in human nature but on a gradual evolution in human institutions—on a series of concrete actions and effective agreements which are in the interest of all concerned. . . . For peace is a process, a way of solving problems.

—PRESIDENT JOHN F. KENNEDY

Introduction

NOT LONG AGO, Secretary of State Dean Rusk was asked in a television interview whether the United States was pursuing a "no-win" foreign policy. The answer was delivered in the closely reasoned phrases that are his trademark:

> Well, I would not agree with this. What we are trying to accomplish in this world—the American people and most people in most other countries—is a victory for freedom, for the independence of states and the freedom of peoples . . . a victory for a decent world order under conditions of law. . . .
>
> Now we know that this struggle for freedom is constant, it is implacable, and it is necessary to win it. But you would not win it by a vast military orgy which would bring into jeopardy the existence of the Northern Hemisphere. . . .
>
> The problem here is to make it very clear that the vital interests of the free world will be defended with whatever is necessary. But the problem also is to defend these by peaceful means if possible. . . . The easiest thing in the world to think of is to expand a war. . . . But the human race needs something else if we can find it.

A central purpose of United States foreign policy under the Kennedy and Johnson Administrations has been to find this "something else"—something that could lead to victory without war, a victory of human dignity not just for Americans but for all men everywhere.

It has been said many times but it bears repeating: Such a victory will not be won through the subjugation of any people. It will not be won by force of arms—although the free world must have adequate military strength and the will to use it in defense of freedom. It will be won by painstaking efforts to build the foundations of peace and the general welfare of mankind. Moreover, it will never be finally won—it will have to be fought for and earned, every day, by ourselves and our posterity.

Mankind is now divided by two competing concepts of world order—one based on coercion, the other based on consent. Because of the kind of society we are at home, because of the kind of order we seek abroad—we cannot simply impose our views on other peoples. Our method of building a world order is much more difficult than the Communist method, but it is also much more durable. It is through free association with other nations in bilateral, regional, and global diplomacy.

Much is heard these days about the protection of national sovereignty. But if sovereignty is more than a sterile legalism, if it means the real power of a nation to assure by itself the security and welfare of its citizens, then it is obvious that no nation is any longer truly sovereign. It is one of the great paradoxes of our time, and undoubtedly a major source of public frustration, that the most powerful nation in the world is less able to employ its power alone, in pursuit of national ends, than at any previous point in history. Compared to the destructive power the United States possesses today, all the destruction wrought in previous wars is, in President Johnson's words, "like a firecracker thrown against the sun." Yet the achievement of minimum security for the American people depends in part upon cooperation from other countries—even from our greatest adversaries.

What is true of security is true of other essential goals of our national policy. We can no longer assure the material well-being of American citizens by acting alone. The cooperation of other nations is now essential to protect our balance of payments, to assure us of access to raw materials and markets, to maintain the safety of our air and ocean transport, to enjoy the full benefits of space technology in communications and weather forecasting, and generally to bring about the kind of world environment congenial to our continuing prosperity.

All this is obvious. What is less obvious is that to encourage the cooperation of other nations which is necessary for our security and welfare, we have had to develop a new arm of diplomacy. This new diplomacy is carried on through international organizations. That is why President Johnson has pledged this country "to do its full share to assist in the development of sound, efficient international organizations to keep the peace, to resolve disputes, to promote peaceful change, to conduct a world war against poverty, to exchange technology, and for other purposes."

Someone once said that all revolutions seem impossible before they occur and inevitable after they occur, an observation that applies well to the diplomatic revolution of the last generation. At the beginning of World War II, it would have been difficult to conceive of the vast array of important functions now being discharged through international institutions. Today, it is hard to imagine a world without them.

This book is about the use of international organizations in our efforts to achieve a victory without a war—a decent world order in the interests of all mankind. It is not concerned with regional organizations in the North Atlantic Community, the Americas, or elsewhere—important as these are as stepping stones toward our global objective. It concentrates instead on the major world-wide organizations, mainly the United Nations and its Specialized and Affiliated Agencies, most of which comprehend not only our allies but also uncommitted and Communist nations.

A realistic appreciation of the work of these agencies is not a distinguishing feature of the contemporary scene. Discussion of whether or not we should be in the United Nations is about as useful as discussion of whether or not we should have a United States Congress. What we really need is to accept the fact that international organizations are here to stay and to turn to the much more difficult question of how we can use them better to promote our national interest. We need to discuss the U.N. and other international organizations in operational rather than in symbolic terms. We need to consider in professional detail just what these agencies do and how they could do it better.

Both the uncritical admirers of the U.N. and its uncritical opponents do a disservice to the institution and to U.S. foreign policy. One group regards any criticism of the U.N. as profanation of a religious shrine; the other never fails to point out the yawning chasm between U.N. aspirations and U.N. accomplishments. Neither group looks at the U.N. for what it is—a reflection of a turbulent and divided world, an arena for the interplay of national power, a limited instrument for the voluntary association of nations in areas where the interests uniting them are stronger than the interests dividing them. All too few of those forming judgments about the U.N. bring to the subject even a fraction of the professional attention they apply to local or national politics—not to speak of the conduct of their private affairs. This is unfortunate, for the path to world order will not be found by those who are negligent of details, indifferent to obstacles, and hell-bent on "final solutions"—whether in the form of a military show-down or instant world government.

Those who would make a responsible contribution to foreign policy—particularly to the field of multilateral diplomacy—should combine a passionate dedication to long-term goals with a sober appreciation of the difficult tasks of institution-building that lie along the way. Technological and political imperatives are pressing the United States and other nations more and more to work through international institutions to promote their basic interests. Yet we also live in a era of resurgent nationalism which places severe limitations on what can be done in the short run.

President Johnson asked that 1965—which the United Nations officially designated International Cooperation Year—be used to take stock of the international cooperation already under way in international institutions and to examine the ways in which it could be strengthened. This book was designed as a contribution to that effort. It is natural, therefore, that it should emphasize the positive more than the negative side of the equation—the constructive ways in which we and other nations have pursued our common interests and the new possibilities we have for doing so in the future. It is all too evident what international organizations have *failed* to do; the story of what they have *succeeded* in doing is largely unknown and therefore needs telling. Besides, we can usually get better results in dealing with the shortcomings of international organizations by working to correct them through quiet diplomacy than by denouncing them from the rooftops.

Emphasis on the positive contribution of international organizations does not mean we are uncritical. It would do no service to U.S. foreign policy—or to the United Nations—to hug that organization to death. We must continue to view the U.N. at a distance sufficient to permit a realistic look at its strengths and limitations and a clear appreciation of where and how it touches our national interest. Our approach to the United Nations and other international agencies is therefore pragmatic. In determining whether to pursue a particular foreign-policy interest in international agencies, we weigh the disadvantages as well as the advantages.

Law in our society has been well defined as consisting of "the wise restraints that make men free." In the international community, some restraints on the use of national power are obviously required in the common interest. Other restraints may be undesirable or impractical because common interests do not exist. International institutions require exchanges of mutual restraints and reciprocal concessions by the participating countries. And in each case, it is right and proper for the United States, as well as other countries, to ask whether the restraints and concessions undertaken by others are adequate compensation for the restraints and concessions undertaken by ourselves.

The central thesis of this book is that the pragmatic balancing of the advantages and disadvantages inherent in this system is yielding positive results over a widening range of subject matter. But not all governments share this conclusion. This is not because the national interest of their countries would not be furthered by the continued strengthening of international organizations. On the contrary, as this book argues, the long-term interest of all countries in survival and welfare requires a steady build-up of international institutions. Yet for one reason or another, the leaders of some countries do not share this concept of the national interest or are not prepared to act upon it. Not only are they reluctant to undertake bold new reforms in the direction of closer international cooperation; they are resisting some of the forms of international cooperation we already have.

This situation helps to explain why the U.S. Government has been unenthusiastic about proposals for a conference to review and amend the United Nations Charter. Some of the proponents of this idea believe such a conference would help to transform the U.N. into some kind of world government; others believe it would at least strengthen the organization in fundamental respects. But amendment of the Charter requires approval not only of two-thirds of the member states but specifically of the Soviet Union, France, and other permanent members of the Security Council. If one examines carefully the attitude of U.N. members toward specific proposals for strengthening the organization, one quickly discovers that the most likely consequence of wholesale revision of the Charter would be to diminish rather than enhance the strength of the organization.

The Charter of the United Nations, like the American Constitution, is a framework for organic growth in response to new demands and changing realities. The United Nations has been able, within the context of the Charter, to assume ever greater responsibilities in the service of its members' long-term interests. An attempt to rewrite its constitution would arrest the continued growth of the United Nations, for some of the members would be reluctant to give explicit endorsement to some of the implicit powers that have been granted to the organization over the years. The fact is that the Charter is a better instrument for the achievement of U.N. purposes than any that could be negotiated today. The same is true, by and large, of the constitutions of other major international agencies.

It is a very large question whether the impressive growth in the responsibilities of international institutions recorded in the last two decades and analyzed in this book can continue in the years ahead—or whether we are in for serious disappointments in our efforts to achieve a decent world order. "Crisis" has become an overworked word, but it is no exaggeration to say that the system of international institutions of which the U.N. is the center is now in crisis. The future of that system, and the pace of progress toward world order, will be determined to a large extent by what takes place in the years immediately ahead. The members of the United Nations face many questions of unprecedented difficulty. They will have to deal with the United Nations' financial problem caused by the refusal of the Soviet Union and other countries to pay their assessments for U.N. peacekeeping operations—and with the consequences of not applying Article 19 of the United Nations Charter, which provides for loss of vote in the General Assembly to members that are more than two years in arrears in their assessed contributions. They will seek to develop new arrangements to insure that future peacekeeping operations can be initiated and financed without provoking another financial and constitutional crisis. And they will try to find some reasonable balance in the control of these operations between the large and middle powers which carry the principal burden of supporting them and the small nations which now comprise a majority of the General Assembly.

But the years ahead will be a time for decisions not only about peacekeeping operations, but also about cooperative endeavors for the general welfare of mankind. The members of the United Nations will try to make a success of new U.N. organs dealing with industrialization and with problems of trade and development. They will seek to strengthen the recently merged U.N. institutions providing preinvestment aid to less developed countries. They will review the world population problem and consider how United Nations agencies can help to develop programs for limiting population growth. They will seek to increase the volume of financial aid flowing to the developing countries through bilateral and multilateral channels. They will examine pressing issues of human rights and the adequacy of existing machinery to deal with them. And, outside the U.N. itself, decisions will be made in the most ambitious negotiation ever undertaken to reduce trade barriers and on new measures for strengthening the world's monetary system.

These problems and prospects are considered in detail in the following chapters. It may be appropriate at this point to underline the critical importance of the decisions facing the U.N. in the peacekeeping field. Will the U.N.'s financial difficulties arising from past peacekeeping operations be resolved in a satisfactory manner? Will improved procedures be found for initiating and financing future peacekeeping operations? The answer to these questions cannot fail to have a decisive influence on the future of the United Nations not only as an instrument for peace and security but also as an instrument for the promotion of the general welfare. The work of the United Nations system in economic and social development is not likely to prosper if the countries that bear the principal burden of supporting it lose confidence in the financial and constitutional integrity of the system.

How the United Nations survives this emerging crisis will be determined by the response of four groups of members:

The first group includes the Soviet Union and other Communist countries. In recent years, Soviet leaders have said uncommonly generous things about the importance of strengthening the peacekeeping work of the United Nations. Yet the Soviet Union has refused to pay its share of past and present peacekeeping costs or to negotiate meaningfully on new procedures for future peacekeeping operations. In the final analysis, the peacekeeping work of the United Nations must continue—in the future as it has in the past—even without the cooperation of the Soviet bloc. Yet it is obvious that Soviet cooperation is greatly to be desired and that continued Soviet opposition will make progress more difficult.

The second group includes those countries from Africa and Asia which have recently achieved independence. Many of these countries describe themselves as "uncommitted." This term causes no problem if it means uncommitted as between parties, for rigorous adherence to an independent stance often serves the cause of freedom as well as choosing sides in the cold war. But the term is dangerous if it means uncommitted as to values, if it means that on any given subject, a country or a person takes a position that is halfway between the positions of the United States and the Soviet Union. Such a policy is the very negation of independence, for it makes the country or person applying it a dependent variable whose position on any given subject is determined by where the great powers stand. The day the members of the United Nations decide to be uncommitted to the principles of the Charter, the organization will cease to exist.

If the Soviet Union fails to alter its policy on U.N. peace-keeping operations in the months ahead, it will test as never before the attitudes of the newly independent nations. The very future of the United Nations may be decided by the determination with which these countries implement their commitments to the Charter in the face of Soviet opposition. If they respond to this new crisis as they have responded to similar crises in the past, they will rally to support the organization, out of a recognition of their basic interests in a stronger United Nations working in pursuit of freedom and economic advancement for all nations.

The third group includes the countries of Latin America and the older nations of Africa and Asia. In past years, they have helped to encourage a responsible dialogue between the industrialized countries and the new members of the United Nations. Much depends on how they play this role in the future.

The fourth group includes the United States and the other countries of the North Atlantic Community, together with Australia, New Zealand, and Japan. These countries have provided the main material support for the United Nations and other international organizations. The unusual obstacles that now obstruct the path to world order demand of them a much more unified and effective effort in the future. Such an effort will require a broader consensus than now exists on the ways in which the North Atlantic nations and their Pacific partners can employ international institutions to promote the common interest in peace and welfare. The development of this consensus should be an urgent item of public business for all these countries.

As anyone familiar with government knows, the making of policy is a corporate rather than an individual effort. While the author, during his service in the State Department from 1961 to mid-1965, helped to shape the policy of our government on most of the subjects discussed in this book, he was but one small part of a very large enterprise in which many others have shared. This volume is the result of a personal effort and the responsibility for any shortcomings in exposition or argument rests solely with the author, yet it must be emphasized that the final manuscript draws greatly on the suggestions of many government colleagues.

Every book reflects the particular perspective of its author. The character of this book would have been different had the author never left Columbia University for the State Department. In government, the view is different (not necessarily better or worse) from what it is in private life. Moreover, subjects must be handled differently on the printed page. The government official benefits from inside knowledge, but he also observes restraints that are vital to the conduct of modern diplomacy.

John F. Kennedy liked to quote the ancient Greeks' definition of happiness—"the exercise of vital powers in a life affording them scope." Those who came to Washington in the spring of 1961 were blessed with an extraordinary opportunity to enjoy that kind of happiness. It was a particular joy for one whose central professional interest has been the development of international law and organization to find himself with a broad mandate to assist in the development of U.S. policy in the United Nations and other international organizations. It was still a greater privilege to be associated with a group of men and women dedicated to the same concerns and embodying the best combination of thought and action—thinkers and doers in the best sense of both words.

The person responsible for bringing me to Washington and the guiding force in the development of the ideas contained in this book has been Harlan Cleveland, Assistant Secretary of State for International Organizations Affairs from 1961 to 1965. My indebtedness to him, intellectual and otherwise, is infinite. I owe a similar debt to Ambassador Adlai Stevenson, whose life was an inspiration for all those beating paths to world order. I should also like to mention the other leading members of the team who helped to shape U.S. policy in international organizations in the Kennedy and Johnson Administrations and whose contributions are reflected here—my former colleagues Joseph Sisco, now Assistant Secretary of State for International Organization Affairs, Elmore Jackson, and Thomas Wilson. And it is difficult to overestimate the continuing contribution to policy made by the extremely able members of the career service in the Bureau of International Organization Affairs—surely one of the most extraordinary concentrations of talent in this or any other government.

Special thanks must be given to Mrs. Mary Frances Keyhoe, who discharged with her usual good nature and efficiency the difficult assignment of preparing this manuscript.

Grateful acknowledgment is hereby made to *Foreign Affairs, The Saturday Review,* and *The New York Times Sunday Magazine* for permission to use material originally published in those periodicals.

R. N. G.

New York City
June, 1966

PART I

In Pursuit of Peace with Justice

Chapter **1**

The United States and
the United Nations

UNITED STATES PARTICIPATION in the United Nations is
now, more than ever, a subject of national debate. To be
sure, there has always been a small minority of Americans
hostile to policies of international cooperation which has
opposed United States participation in the United Nations
as a matter of principle. What makes the present situation
different is that a number of citizens who accept the necessity for far-reaching overseas commitments as well as membership in the United Nations are now raising questions
about the place of the U.N. in U.S. foreign policy. They
are asking whether the U.N. can survive as an effective
international organization and whether present U.S. policy
toward the U.N. serves the interest of the United States
and the free world.

This new situation is understandable. The United Nations today is a very different organization from the one
which was created in 1945 and to which most Americans
have become accustomed. It has grown from a Western-
oriented institution of fifty-one countries to a parliament

of more than double that number in which the new countries of Africa and Asia hold about half the seats. Even more significantly, it has evolved from being mainly a forum for discussion to an executive instrument with an increasing capability for promoting economic progress and keeping the peace. As a consequence, it has been plunged into controversy in the Middle East, the Congo, and Cyprus, and into a financial and constitutional crisis of unprecedented dimensions.

The fact that participation in the U.N. has become a subject of intense national interest and even controversy is not necessarily a cause for concern. It was easy for people to pay lip-service to the United Nations as long as it was regarded merely as a sentimental abstraction, a symbol of the international good society. But human institutions, like the human body, develop muscle only painfully. The Congress, the Executive, and the Supreme Court of the United States all achieved greater strength only in the stress and strain of national controversy. That United Nations actions and the United States' relationship to them are subjects of national concern reflects the fact that the United Nations is doing things that really matter. Far from dying, the United Nations has become a significant mechanism of international politics—one of the important arenas for the exercise of national power.

With these facts in mind, let us turn to the central question: Does present U.S. policy toward the United Nations serve the national interest?

There are some who may take exception to the form in which this question is put. They may feel that the American commitment to the United Nations should be a matter of faith, and that questions of "selfish" national interest are not involved. But a responsible official of the U.S. Government cannot accept this view. All those who serve in Washington—like their counterparts in the other capitals around the world—are under an obligation to further the national interest of their country. There can be no other test in national decision-making.

In fact, the difference between thinking that support of the U.N. should be a matter of faith and thinking that it should be contingent upon the national interest is probably more apparent than real. There is a profound sense in which idealism is realism. When we say that the United States is "committed" to the support of the United Nations, we really mean, or ought to mean, that the United States is determined to help make the United Nations a success, out of conviction that the enlightened long-term interest of our country requires the development of a civilized system of collective security.

Before we can decide whether our present policy toward the United Nations serves the national interest, we must consider carefully just what the United Nations is, and how we presently use it in the promotion of our foreign policy. This may seem to some an unduly elementary exercise, but such a return to fundamentals is essential. Listening to much of what is currently said about the United Nations and our relation to it, one gets the impression that there is a good deal of misunderstanding about United States policy toward the organization whose headquarters is located at Forty-second Street and the East River in New York City.

What, then, is the United Nations, and what is our national strategy for making use of it? The United Nations is really three institutions in one, and each of them has a unique value for the United States—as well as for other member countries.

First, the United Nations is a place for debate—a center for publicity, education, and persuasion—a forum in which the weak as well as the strong can make their case.

It is fashionable in some quarters to denigrate this aspect of the United Nations. It is said that the U.N. is a "cave of winds," a mere "debating society." Yet our history and tradition in the West emphasize the value of free and open discussion, of commerce in the market-place of ideas. Our parliamentary institutions place great emphasis on debate and are not notably more disciplined than the General Assembly. Most of us believe—and rightly so—that, in the long run, free debate works against error and for truth and justice. Those who deplore the United Nations as a "debating society" appear to have little confidence in the capacity of the United States to present its case successfully in the councils of nations.

Of course, no one claims that "world opinion" is self-enforcing or that U.N. debates can work miraculous changes in the behavior of nations. The Soviet Union has demonstrated its contempt for what the rest of the world thinks on numerous occasions, notably in its brutal suppression of Hungarian freedom. But it would be absurd to conclude from this that "there is no such thing as world opinion," or that U.N. debates are utterly futile.

The fact of the matter is that, starting with the Security Council debates that led to the Soviet withdrawal from Iran in 1946, the United Nations has served as a useful instrument to throw the spotlight of publicity on acts of injustice, or, to vary the metaphor, to "blow the whistle" on breaches of the peace. This function of the U.N. has real vitality where small powers are concerned—the disputes in the Middle East are notable examples—and also, though to a lesser extent, in moderating the behavior of larger powers, even of the Soviet Union. The Soviet posture on issues such as the Congo, Cyprus, disarmament, outer space, and aid to less developed countries has been influenced by concern with its "public relations" both in the West and in the so-called uncommitted countries, particularly as reflected in the United Nations.

As a place for debate, the U.N. provides us with a useful instrument to build support for our national policies. We use debates in the General Assembly, the Security Council, and other U.N. organs to defend and explain our positions on a range of subjects from disarmament to economic development. If we fail to persuade all U.N. members of the justice of our positions, it is not the fault of the U.N.—we would have to take account of the views of other countries in any case. The point is that the existence of the U.N. has enabled us in case after case to influence the opinions of foreign governments.

Second, the United Nations is a place for negotiation—a standing diplomatic conference where the peaceful settlement of disputes can be sought through quiet diplomacy. This aspect of the United Nations is still only dimly understood. It is the seven-eighths of the iceberg below the surface of the water. Diplomats and historians schooled in the arts of old-fashioned diplomacy continue to deplore the "glass house" on the East River where there are "open disagreements openly arrived at." Such criticism is justified when public debates contribute to more rigid positions rather than to mutually acceptable solutions. Nevertheless, the United Nations can provide significant opportunities for quiet diplomacy. It is a place where the representatives of more than one hundred sovereign states can meet on an informal and continuing basis, rubbing elbows at countless conferences and social occasions, from formal dinners and receptions to amiable chats in the delegates' lounge.

To be sure, we shall continue to rely heavily on our relations with the diplomatic corps in Washington and on our embassies around the world as the principal channels of quiet diplomacy. But the United Nations does have advantages which make it of particular usefulness in certain situations. It is a convenient forum for a multilateral negotiation involving the interests of many countries. It is a place where diplomatic encounters can be easily managed on an informal and quiet basis—with the special advantage that there is a "third man" present in the person of the Secretary-General to get negotiations started when neither side is willing to take the first step.

The United Nations as a facility for negotiation has demonstrated its value on countless occasions. One famous example occurred seventeen years ago, when a series of informal meetings between American Ambassador Philip C. Jessup and Soviet Ambassador Jacob Malik led to an agreement that settled the Berlin crisis of that day and made it possible to terminate the Berlin airlift. Many times since then, quiet negotiations under U.N. auspices in New York and elsewhere have helped to promote peaceful settlement or reduce international tensions in such far-flung places as Bizerte, Kuwait, and West New Guinea. Even in the crisis precipitated by the emplacement of Soviet missiles in Cuba, the U.N. served as a useful channel of communication between the United States and the Soviet Union.

Third and last, the United Nations is a place for action—an international executive—a place for doing things rather than merely talking about them. It is this third function of the United Nations—its capacity to act—that is now the subject of particular controversy. Does the strengthening of the United Nations as an action agency serve our national interest?

The answer to this question must be in two parts, in accord with the two-pronged nature of the U.N.'s executive contribution. One part—which we shall consider later in more detail *—has to do with the work of the United Nations in promoting the general welfare of nations through action in the economic and social field. This function is by far the greater in terms of the money and personnel involved. It is much less controversial than the U.N.'s political and military role, but by no means beyond controversy. Although it seldom makes the headlines, its importance to the United States and other members is considerable. The

* See Chapters 5–10.

U.N. and its Specialized Agencies together are spending some $300 million a year on programs for economic and social betterment around the world. The United Nations is at work in dozens of countries healing the sick, feeding the hungry, teaching the illiterate. It is setting standards for workers in factories, for air and ocean transport, for peaceful uses of atomic energy. It is building governmental services in less developed countries and helping these countries to draw up rational development plans. It is training the human resources of the future in the manifold tasks required to make a reality of independence, a success of self-determination.

How does this aspect of the U.N.'s work serve our national interest? Some of the work of U.N. agencies—for example, in the allocation of radio frequencies for communication—helps the United States directly. No less important, the work of the U.N. in promoting the economic and social development of other nations contributes to our own prosperity and security. Although U.N. assistance programs are a small fraction of total bilateral aid efforts, their significance cannot be measured solely in quantitative terms.

The case for using the United Nations as an instrument for promoting economic and social development rests primarily on one fundamental point. The less developed countries badly need advice and financial aid from the United States and other industrial countries in building healthy economies and free institutions. But political leaders in some of these countries do not wish to depend for aid and advice entirely upon the United States or even upon a group of Western countries. Such dependence would render them too vulnerable to domestic charges by nationalists or neutralists that they were becoming tools of Western policy or compromising their neutrality in the cold war. Such leaders can, however, accept aid and advice when it comes under a United Nations umbrella. Thus the

United Nations often provides a useful bridge from the United States and the North Atlantic Community to developing nations in the Southern Hemisphere. In the bargain, we also benefit by being able to tap the skills and talents of U.N. experts from many countries. And we encourage other countries to share the aid burden to an extent that would not otherwise be possible.

The other aspect of the United Nations as an action agency is its wide range of peacekeeping activities. At one end of the spectrum are the Secretary-General's diplomatic efforts in mediation, conciliation, observation, and fact-finding. The disputes involving the Yemen, the Federation of Malaysia, and Cyprus were important instances where the Secretary-General played a mediating role in trying to bring about a peaceful settlement. Beyond the personal efforts of the Secretary-General and small numbers of individuals acting on his behalf are the more substantial U.N. "presences" such as the United Nations Truce Supervision Organization policing the armistice lines between Israel and her Arab neighbors. At the other end of the spectrum are the peacekeeping operations involving large numbers of troops such as those established in connection with the Suez, Congo, and Cyprus crises.

In disputes between small powers, or in situations where the withdrawal of a colonial regime has left a dangerous power vacuum, action by the United Nations at one point or another along the peacekeeping spectrum may be the best means of preventing violence that is acceptable to the specific parties involved and to the world community as a whole. And the United Nations can help even the great powers disengage from dangerous confrontations (such as in Cuba) and prevent brush-fire conflicts from triggering a thermonuclear war. It is often said in criticism of the United Nations that it has failed to keep the great powers together. The point is that the U.N. has been able on numerous occasions to keep them apart.

The Middle East, Congo, and Cyprus crises reveal a basic truth about the peacekeeping operations of the United Nations—namely, that in *some* situations in *some* parts of the world, they represent the lesser of several evils, the least undesirable course of American action. When critics complain about the use of the United Nations in situations of this kind, they have the obligation to answer the question: What is the alternative? Indeed, to form mature judgments as to the real value of the United Nations, we *must* consider alternatives; we must ask questions that challenge the imagination to answer what might have happened if the United Nations had not been there at all. For example:

Would the Communists have fared better or worse in their efforts to divert the independence movement into a Communist mold—the supreme opportunity for them to extend their power—if the United Nations had not existed?

Would the prospects of peace be better or worse—in Iran, in Greece, in Korea, in Kashmir, in the Middle East, in the western Pacific, in central Africa, in Cyprus—if there had been no United Nations at work during the past two decades?

Would the crises in the Congo and the Caribbean have been better or worse without a United Nations during the past few years?

Would the North Atlantic countries have greater or fewer resources for communicating effectively with the less developed countries, with the countries of Eastern Europe, and with the Soviet Union if the United Nations did not exist?

There is no need to dwell on these rather frightening alternatives: The questions answer themselves.

This, in summary form, is the case for the proposition that the United Nations has been and continues to be an asset rather than a liability for the United States—as well as for other countries of the free world. But the United

Nations has not been, and should not be, beyond criticism. In recent years, a number of questions—some specious, some fundamental—have been raised about our relation to the United Nations. Let us examine in detail some that are heard most frequently.

1. *The United Nations is a failure because it has not brought peace.* This is one of the most popular, and least substantial, of the criticisms. The United Nations is not a guaranteed patent remedy for all the ills of our unhappy world. It has failed to do a number of things—free Hungary or defend Goa, for example—but since neither the United States nor anyone else was willing to take responsibility for these things, it is hardly logical to blame the failures on the U.N. The U.N. has no more solved all the world's problems than foreign aid has cured political instability and economic stagnation, yet both institutions have brought measurable improvements in the state of the world. The test of the United Nations is not whether it has solved every problem but whether on balance the world is better off than it would have been if the United Nations had never existed.

It is probably true that the United Nations, like most new institutions, was "oversold" at its inception. To some people, it heralded the dawn of a new era in which power politics would vanish and the rule of law would be achieved. We know now that this view was hopelessly inadequate, not merely because it failed to forecast the cold war, but also because it misconceived the true nature of international relations. The United Nations cannot be a substitute for power politics or the clash of national interests. It merely provides a new arena for the play of politics and the adjustment of interests—and, hopefully, a substitute in some situations for the use of force.

Lord Gladwyn employed a useful metaphor to answer the objection that the United Nations had not brought peace to the world. "The United Nations is a mirror of the world we live in," he liked to say, "and if the reflection is ugly, it is not the mirror which is to blame." Unfortunately, there are still a number of people who are prone to blame the mirror. Public support for the United Nations has tended to fluctuate in accordance with the way a particular operation—in Cyprus or the Congo, for example —is going during a particular week. When an outbreak of violence occurs or the prospects for settlement worsen, the stock of the United Nations falls; when order is restored and progress is made in achieving a satisfactory solution to the problem, the stock of the United Nations rises.

Surely support of the United Nations must be based on a more solid and enduring foundation than this. Our opinion of our family doctor does not go up and down in accordance with the temperature of his patient. If we have confidence in the doctor, we support his best efforts and understand that sometimes people sicken and even die in spite of everything he can do to help them. We can fairly criticize the United Nations, like our family doctor, only if it is disappointing reasonable expectations that it improve the situation.

2. *The United Nations costs too much for the United States.* To evaluate this charge, it is necessary to see the U.N. financial picture in broad outline. There are four kinds of United Nations operations toward which the United States contributes:

First, there is the regular assessed budget of the United Nations. In 1966, this totaled $115 million; the United States' share was 31.91 per cent, or about $36.7 million.

Second, there are the regular assessed budgets of the Specialized Agencies. In 1966, these totaled $127 million, of which the United States contributed $37.9 million. The U.S. share in these budgets is the same as or less than its share in the regular U.N. budget.

Third, there are the voluntary economic programs—the

Expanded Program of Technical Assistance, the United Nations Special Fund, the United Nations Children's Fund (UNICEF), and the United Nations Relief and Works Agency for Palestine Refugees—in which each country puts up what it wishes to contribute. In 1966, these programs totaled $249 million, of which the United States contributed $108 million.

Fourth, there are the peacekeeping activities—which may be financed on an assessed or on a voluntary basis, or on some combination of the two. These vary substantially in cost from year to year. In the early 1960's, peacekeeping expenses totalled about $140 million per year—$120 million for the Congo, and $20 million for the United Nations Emergency Force in the Gaza Strip (UNEF). In 1966, the U.N.'s Congo operation had long since been phased out, and UNEF costs had been reduced to $15 million, of which the United States' contribution was $6.8 million. The Cyprus operation was running at an annual rate of about $23 million, of which the U.S. share was about $9 million. Thus, the two peacekeeping operations not covered from the regular budget were running at an annual rate of $38 million in 1966, of which the U.S. share was approximately $15.8 million.

With the expansion of United Nations activities, the total annual budget of the U.N. family is about $500 million, of which the U.S. share is not quite $200 million. Is this too expensive for the United States? It amounts to about one dollar a year for every man, woman, and child in our country. It is less than what the war in Vietnam cost the United States during one week in the summer of 1966. In terms of the net return to world peace and welfare and therefore to our national interest, this can hardly be termed unreasonable. One dollar spent on preventive diplomacy and on the redressing of economic and social grievances can save many dollars that might otherwise be consumed in sterile and tragic conflict. This point seems obvious enough—but it is a lesson that we have had to relearn over and over again in international as well as domestic affairs.

Of course, the objection to U.N. financing is often not that the cost of the United Nations is too great but that the United States bears too great a share of it. The United States has pressed successfully over the years for a reduction in its share, in recognition of the growing prosperity of other countries and also of the desirability of maintaining the multilateral character of the institution. Our share in the regular budget has been reduced from 40 per cent to 32 per cent; in technical assistance, from 60 per cent to 40 per cent; in UNICEF, from 72 per cent to 40 per cent; in the Middle East and Congo peacekeeping operations, from 49 per cent to 37 per cent. The present U.S. share in U.N. costs is not unreasonable when one bears in mind that the United States accounts for nearly 40 per cent of the combined national incomes of U.N. member states and that our standard of living is twice the average of other industrialized countries and some twenty times greater than the average in less developed countries. And in evaluating the justice of the U.S. financial share in peacekeeping operations, it is well to bear in mind that since the Korean War, the American contribution has been in money and logistical support, while other countries have supplied troops in addition to their financial contributions.

The question of the U.S. share in U.N. costs is related to the controversy over how to deal with the U.N.'s present financial crisis. This crisis does not derive from the regular U.N. budget, from the regular budgets of the Specialized Agencies, or from the voluntary programs. Although some of the poorer countries are occasionally slow payers to the regular budgets as well as to the voluntary programs, the United Nations has no major problem of arrearages on account of these three sets of operations. The major problem arises because of the failure of the Soviet bloc, France, and certain other countries to pay their peacekeeping assessments. Some of these countries, such as the Soviet Union, argue that there is no legal obligation to pay for the Middle East and Congo operations; others contend that they have difficulty in making payments of this size. As a result, the United Nations is now owed more than $120 million in overdue assessments.

To deal with this predicament, Secretary-General U Thant presented, in December, 1961, a three-part financial plan which was approved by the General Assembly. It provided for another assessment to carry forward the Middle East and Congo operations to July 1, 1962. It called for an advisory opinion of the International Court of Justice to settle the question of whether the obligation to pay for such assessments was binding on all members. And it authorized the issuance of $200 million of United Nations bonds bearing 2 per cent interest and repayable over twenty-five years. The proceeds of the bond sales made it possible to finance the Middle East and Congo operations from July 1, 1962, until June 30, 1963. In May and June, 1963, a Special Session of the General Assembly adopted general principles to govern the financing of peacekeeping operations, and voted funds—a combination of assessments and voluntary contributions—to continue the Congo and Middle East operations from July 1 to December 31, 1963. The 18th General Assembly in October, 1963, voted funds to finance these operations in 1964.

On July 20, 1962, the International Court of Justice, in an advisory opinion, confirmed that the expenses incurred by the U.N. in its Middle East and Congo operations were "expenses of the organization" under Article 17 of the Charter. This opinion was accepted by the General Assembly by a vote of 76 to 17, with 8 abstentions. It thus decided that the assessments levied by the General Assembly to defray these expenses were binding on all U.N. members, and that the amounts were due and payable. The continued refusal of the Soviet Union and other bloc countries to pay their peacekeeping assessments made them more than two years in arrears in their total contributions and subject to loss of vote as of the 19th session of the General Assembly which opened at the end of 1964. Since France boycotted only the Congo operation, it was not subject to the loss-of-vote provision until 1965.

Pending efforts to find a negotiated solution to this problem, the 19th General Assembly suspended normal operations and transacted only such minimal business as could be done on a no-objection basis. These efforts collapsed when the Soviet Union insisted that it would not even contribute to a voluntary fund to restore the U.N. to solvency until the General Assembly had set aside Article 19 of the Charter. The members of the General Assembly were reluctant to reverse their acceptance of the International Court's decision. But it also became clear that they were unwilling to apply Article 19 to the defaulting members. To break the impasse and to enable the General Assembly to resume its normal business, the United States announced in August, 1965, that it would accept the majority will and the *de facto* situation thus created: It would agree to permit the Assembly to resume its normal business with voting by the delinquent members. "At the same time," Ambassador Arthur J. Goldberg added, "we must make it crystal clear that if any member can insist on making an exception to the principle of collective financial responsibility with respect to certain activities of the Organization, the United States reserves the same option to make exceptions if, in our view, strong and compelling reasons exist for doing so. There can be no double standard among the members of the Organization."

3. *The voting procedures of the General Assembly are unreasonable and work against American interests.* With the rapid influx of new U.N. members in recent years,

there has been increasing criticism of the principle of one-nation, one-vote in the General Assembly. Some critics have urged that the United States now insist on weighted voting to protect its interests.

Naturally, it is easy to criticize the system of one-nation, one-vote, just as it is easy for critics of American domestic institutions to fault the principle of having two Senators from each state or to pick flaws in the electoral college. But in criticizing international as well as domestic institutions, the critics have the obligation once again to answer the question: What is the alternative?

Any system of weighted voting in the General Assembly would have to weight population as a major factor. It is questionable whether such an arrangement would suit a country like ours, which has only 6 per cent of the world's population and which, together with its NATO allies, has only 16 per cent. If population were a primary criterion, India, with its 450 million people, might well end up with more votes than the United States. Of course, it is always possible to imagine a system of weighted voting that would offset the population factor with such factors as literacy, per-capita income, and military power. But the establishment of any weighted-voting system would require Charter amendment—and therefore the approval not only of the Soviet Union, France, and the other Permanent Members of the Security Council, but also of two-thirds of the members of the General Assembly. There is therefore no possibility of getting the necessary agreement on the kind of weighted-voting formula the critics have in mind. Indeed, the most likely consequence of pressing for a Charter review conference to achieve weighted voting, which some have urged, would be to provide a golden opportunity for the Communist countries and others to press for amendments diminishing the powers that the United Nations has developed under the Charter during the last twenty years and that have generally promoted the objectives of U.S. foreign policy.

We should not overlook the fact that as between the free world and the Communist bloc, the present system of voting in the General Assembly is far from unfavorable. To the critics of the present arrangement, we should put the question: Can you show us a politically possible alternative that would confine the Communist bloc (not counting Yugoslavia) to what it has now—less than 10 per cent of the votes in the General Assembly?

The Department of State recently conducted a study of various weighted-voting formulas based on population and contributions to the U.N. budget. When these formulas were applied to 178 key votes that took place in the General Assembly between 1954 and 1961, it was found that, while they would have somewhat reduced the number of resolutions passed over U.S. opposition, they would have reduced much more the number of resolutions supported by the United States and passed over Communist opposition. The same conclusion was reached in projecting these formulas to 1970, having regard to further increases in membership. The conclusion was that any system of weighted voting taking population substantially into account (and no weighted-voting system would be negotiable that failed to do this) would help Communist countries more than ourselves, by making it easier for them to achieve a blocking one-third vote on U.N. actions for peace and welfare that are in the interest of the United States and other nations of the non-Communist world.

The results of this study reflect the fact that the desire for political independence and economic progress has put most U.N. members on the same side as the United States on most important matters—particularly those where action was involved as well as talk.

To be sure, the United States has not been in the majority on every vote, nor have the resolutions it supported always reflected its views in every detail. In a world in which there are substantial differences of opinion between nations, this could scarcely be expected. But when one looks at the record as a whole, as distinguished from the votes on individual items, one finds little to support the charge that voting procedures in the General Assembly, combined with the inflation of its membership, have made it impossible for the United States successfully to prosecute its interests in the United Nations.

Ambassador Adlai Stevenson summed up the matter in testimony before the House Foreign Affairs Committee on June 27, 1962:

We have heard fears expressed that the United Nations might be perverted to serve Soviet purposes in this situation —namely, to unite the Soviet bloc with Africa and Asia in a majority against the West, under the banner of anticolonialism. But in practice this has not happened. Usually when the Soviets have proposed extreme anti-Western resolutions on colonial issues, such as Angola or the Congo, they have found little support among the Afro-Asian members. I believe this will continue so long as our diplomacy is active and our policies are in harmony with the legitimate aspirations of the African and Asian countries for independence and development.

Moreover, the members in the General Assembly may have equal votes, but they are far from having equal influence. Dag Hammarskjöld made this point five years ago in his annual report to the General Assembly:

"The criticism of 'one nation, one vote,' irrespective of size or strength, as constituting an obstacle to arriving at just and representative solutions, tends to exaggerate the problem. The General Assembly is not a parliament of elected individual members; it is a diplomatic meeting in which the delegates of member states represent governmental policies, and these policies are subject to all the influences that would prevail in international life in any case."

Anyone who believes that United States influence in the United Nations is measured by the fact that it has less than one-hundredth of the votes in the General Assembly fails completely to understand the realities of power as they are reflected in the world organization. These realities include the fact that the U.S. is the principal contributor to the U.N.'s regular budget and by far the largest supporter of the U.N.'s peacekeeping and development programs, and that the U.S. is making by far the largest individual contribution to the defense and development of the non-Communist world. On U.N. decisions of vital importance to the United States, the voting of other countries has been considerably influenced by U.S. views.

This is not to say that the present voting procedures are entirely satisfactory or that they need not be adapted in certain respects. Weighted voting, or any other system requiring Charter amendment, is not a practical possibility in the foreseeable future. But, without amending the Charter, procedures in the United Nations could be modified in certain areas, in the light of the U.N.'s expanded membership and the need to insure that its decisions take due account of the special responsibilities certain members have for implementing them. Secretary of State Dean Rusk made this a major theme of his Hammarskjöld Lecture at Columbia University in January, 1964. Since then, the United States has begun negotiations with other member states on proposals that would give the large and middle powers a greater voice in initiating and financing substantial peacekeeping operations that involve military forces. These proposals seek to strengthen the Security Council's primary responsibility for peacekeeping by requiring that the General Assembly cannot launch a substantial peacekeeping operation unless the Security Council has been unable to act. They also provide that all decisions on the financing of such operations be approved by a special committee of the Assembly on which the substantial contributors would have a greater proportional representation than they do in the Assembly as a whole.

The United States has also sought to strengthen the voice of the major contributors in budget and program decisions of the United Nations and the Specialized Agencies. It is now technically possible in U.N. agencies for countries paying only 5 per cent of the total to muster a two-thirds majority in support of increased budgets. In practice, this does not happen, since the heads of the agencies and most of the members recognize the political limitations on voting budgets over the determined opposition of the larger contributors. Moreover, since increased assessments bear heavily in relative terms on small as well as large countries, there is some built-in discipline concerning budget levels. Nevertheless, recent experience suggests that these elements of discipline now need to be strengthened. The United States and other substantial contributors have therefore been concerting their views more effectively on budget and program issues and bringing them to the attention of the secretariats of the U.N. agencies in time to influence budget proposals.

Efforts to bring greater responsibility into U.N. decisions are being made in the field of trade as well. The United Nations Conference on Trade and Development recommended to the General Assembly, in June, 1964, the establishment of new institutions to deal with the special problems of less developed countries. At the initiative of the United States, general agreement was reached that any new institutions for this purpose would require special procedures to encourage conciliation rather than voting on issues that divided developed and less developed countries.

The United Nations will be able to assume greater responsibilities for the peace and welfare of mankind only if its procedures adequately reflect the world's power realities. This will not be achieved by proposing Charter amendments that have no possibility of adoption or that

will not serve the long-term interests of the United States
and other countries of the free world. It will be achieved
by continuing the efforts already under way to modify procedures to take account of the different responsibilities of
member states, efforts that require no amendment of the
Charter and that have reasonable prospects of success.*

4. *The Afro-Asian "bloc" is irresponsible on colonial
issues, and our desire to please them in the United Nations
has divided the NATO Alliance.* There are three main
points to be made about this charge. In the first place,
there is no such thing as a cohesive Afro-Asian bloc with a
unified view on every question. There are more than fifty
U.N. members from Africa and Asia. So far as the Asian
countries are concerned, even a casual examination of the
record will show that a large number of these countries
often find themselves voting with the United States. The
same has been the case with respect to the African countries, which are often divided on issues in the U.N., even
though they seek to adopt common positions wherever
possible as members of the Organization of African Unity.

In the second place, it is true that there is a large degree
of cohesion among U.N. members from Africa and Asia on
colonial and racial issues. In particular, there is a growing
sense of frustration and impatience with the lack of progress toward the elimination of *apartheid* in South Africa
and toward self-government in Portuguese African territories. There is also much concern over continued white
dominance in Southern Rhodesia and the extension of
apartheid to South West Africa.

The United States has deplored the failure of Portugal
and South Africa to undertake adequate measures in the implementation of their Charter obligations to promote self-
determination and human rights and has supported reso-

* For a more detailed analysis of recent and proposed procedural reforms, see the Appendix, "Adapting U.N. Procedures To Reflect Power
Realtities."

lutions calling on them to do so. At the same time, we have also opposed certain resolutions supported by the great majority of U.N. members, including most African and Asian members, calling for punitive measures or mandatory sanctions against Portugal and South Africa, because we do not think such resolutions would facilitate a solution of these problems, and because they are appropriate under the Charter only when there is a threat to or breach of international peace.

Since the end of World War II, some fifty nations have achieved their independence. For the most part, this independence has been gained without large-scale violence, and not one of these new nations has joined the Communist bloc. The existence of the United Nations has helped to fill the power vacuum created by the withdrawal of old colonial regimes, and it has greatly assisted orderly progress toward independence and responsible self-government. While the record is far from perfect, it is undoubtedly a good deal better than it would have been had the United Nations never existed.

With all but 2 per cent of its population now freed from colonial rule, the world finds itself confronted with the last, "hard-core" colonial and racial problems, of which the Portuguese African territories and South Africa are the outstanding examples. These problems would be with us even in the absence of the United Nations, but the fact that the United Nations exists greatly increases the prospects for a constructive solution. For, just as it has helped to guide orderly progress to self-government in the past, so the United Nations offers a resource for dealing with these "hard-core" problems. As between the advocates of a peace based on rigid maintenance of an inequitable *status quo* and the advocates of change without regard to order and stability, the United States will continue to seek ways in which the U.N. can assist in *peaceful change*—by maintaining the pressure of world opinion on Portugal and

South Africa, by using the good offices of the Secretary-General for fact-finding and conciliation, and by trying to convince U.N. members to avoid a resort to violence.

The United States, of course, also has an interest in maintaining and strengthening the NATO Alliance. So far as the majority of NATO members are concerned, the pursuit of this objective is not inconsistent with an interest in promoting orderly progress toward self-government for those relatively few peoples around the world who have not achieved it. Indeed, the record of the General Assembly in the years 1961–63 reveals one startling fact: *The majority of NATO countries voted with the United States on thirty-seven out of forty colonial issues that came to a vote.*

5. *The United Nations makes U.S. foreign policy.* U.S. foreign policy is not made by the United Nations, nor is U.S. foreign policy made by the United States Mission to the United Nations. The center of decision-making on all questions of United States foreign policy is Washington, D.C. To be sure, the facts and recommendations received from the U.S. Mission receive considerable weight, as do the facts and recommendations received from within the State Department, from our embassies around the world, and from other executive agencies. But on any question that arises in the United Nations, U.S. foreign policy is determined in Washington on the basis of a total appreciation of the national interest.

6. *The United States should rely on the Atlantic Community rather than the United Nations to promote its national interest.* Both supporters and critics of the United Nations should avoid an either/or philosophy. Despite the affirmations of some of its uncritical enthusiasts, the United Nations is by no means the only instrument of our foreign policy. We have many important institutions for the promotion of our national interest. We have the Strategic Air Command. We have Polaris submarines. We have

NATO. We have the Organization for Economic Cooperation and Development. We have the Alliance for Progress. We have the Peace Corps. We have programs of foreign aid, technical assistance, and cultural exchange. We have the Organization of American States. We have the United Nations. There is no inconsistency in our use of all these and other instruments of national policy. As Ambassador Stevenson told the Democratic Platform Committee on August 17, 1964:

> In the second half of the twentieth century, the U.N. is a plain necessity, a primitive but essential beginning of a system of world order. It is not a substitute for a strong defense, for a strong Atlantic Community, for alliances, or for bilateral, nation-to-nation diplomacy. But it is indispensable as one of the mutually reinforcing instruments of peaceful change in a world that is bound to change and had better do it in peace.

We should be on our guard in particular against thinking that there is a necessary conflict between the building of the North Atlantic Community on the one hand, and effective participation in the United Nations on the other. What we see emerging today are two concentric circles. At the core, in the inner circle, are the regional organizations of Western Europe and the North Atlantic Community such as the Common Market, NATO, and OECD. In the outer circle are the institutions of the United Nations family. These two circles are complementary, not competitive. The outer circle, the United Nations family, needs the inner circle of North Atlantic institutions whose members offer an impressive concentration of experience, power, and wealth. But the inner circle also needs the outer circle, as a bridge to the less developed countries and the Communist bloc. *Our task today is to build a concert of free nations, not in one of those circles alone, but in both of them at once.*

The North Atlantic institutions can be invaluable to the interests of their member countries if they are used not as an alternative to the U.N., but to concert the industrialized countries' policies in the United Nations and to strengthen their contributions to U.N. programs in both money and personnel. On the other hand, there may be cases such as Cyprus where the U.N. can significantly contribute to prevention of conflict within the Atlantic Community.

7. *The development of the U.N. peacekeeping role is dangerous because it might be used against us.* Certainly there are risks in any human endeavor, but there are several good reasons why we have much more to gain than to fear from the development of the U.N.'s peacekeeping capacity.

First, the Charter of the United Nations is an eloquent restatement of the values that lie at the center of our national policy. It embodies the concept of an open world society of independent states that stands at the opposite extreme from the Communist pattern of standardization and coercion. The United States can pursue its interests in the world within the framework of Charter principles.

Second, the United Nations capacity to act in peacekeeping as well as economic programs depends crucially on our support. The Soviet bloc plays little or no part in the main executive operations of the United Nations. The U.N. acts in the name of global universality, but the U.N. in action is largely the free world in action. The United States and other members of the North Atlantic Community, Japan, Australia, and New Zealand pay for three-quarters or more of the economic and peacekeeping operations of the United Nations. Without the support of these powers, the U.N. would very largely lose its capacity to act.

Third, the procedures of the United Nations provide us with important defenses against peacekeeping actions that we do not approve. The United States has a veto in the

Security Council. The General Assembly has the residual authority to launch voluntary peacekeeping operations not involving enforcement action, but such operations can be recommended by the Assembly only if two-thirds of the members present and voting vote in favor. It would be extraordinary if the United States could not muster a "blocking third" in the Assembly against a peacekeeping action contrary to its vital interests, considering all the abstaining votes that would result in such a situation.

Of course, there is no ironclad guarantee for the United States in the present procedures of the United Nations. All one can say with assurance is that the procedures are extremely favorable to our country and that the authorization of a peacekeeping action against our vital interests is difficult to imagine, *assuming always that the American position is reasonably founded in justice and the United Nations Charter.*

The conclusion of this analysis of the U.S. interest in the United Nations is not that the United Nations is perfect. We are *not* wholly satisfied with the U.N. as it now exists. We want to make it better. We are now engaged with other nations in a number of practical efforts to improve the U.N.'s capacity to act for peace and welfare. These efforts are directed toward achieving:

—new procedures for the initiation and financing of peacekeeping operations that take adequate account of the interests of the large and middle powers;

—the advance earmarking and training of national military contingents to enable the U.N. to cope more effectively with peacekeeping emergencies;

—increased and more effective resort to peaceful settlement and peaceful change;

—an equitable and sound solution to the United Nations' financial crisis, and the application, so far as it is possible, of collective fiscal responsibility for U.N. expenses;

—special procedures in new U.N. trade institutions to promote conciliation and a reasonable consensus on issues dividing developed and less developed countries;

—centralized management of U.N. pre-investment programs and other reforms to assure greater efficiency and the focusing of U.N. assistance on priority tasks;

—a greater influence for larger contributors in budget and program decisions;

—more effective recruitment of able Americans for key posts in international organizations; and

—maintenance of the efficiency and integrity of the international secretariats.

Progress in these areas has required and will require a maximum effort on the part of the United States. This effort will be aided by frank and constructive criticism of U.N. shortcomings. But, to be successful, it must also be founded on a broadly based American conviction that, with all its shortcomings, the United Nations remains a valuable asset for the United States and the entire free world. Such a conviction is justified not merely as a matter of faith but as the result of a careful scrutiny of the recent record, in the hard light of our national interest.

As the United Nations embarks on its third decade of existence, there comes to mind the remarkable prophecy which Beardsley Ruml made in 1945:

> At the end of five years you will think the U.N. is the greatest vision ever realized by man.
>
> At the end of ten years you will find doubts within yourself and all through the world.
>
> At the end of fifteen years you will believe the U.N. cannot succeed. You will be certain that all the odds are against its ultimate life and success.
>
> It will only be when the U.N. is twenty years old that . . . we will know that the U.N. is the only alternative to the demolition of the world.

Chapter **2**

The Soviet Union and
the United Nations

AFTER A RECENT SPEECH by a State Department official on U.S. policy toward the United Nations, someone got up in the question period and declared: "You have argued that the United Nations serves the national interest of the United States and other countries of the free world. But how, according to your own analysis, can it also be said to serve the interest of the Soviet Union?"

This perceptive and difficult question is asked in one form or another in all serious discussions of the United Nations. To help find an answer, it may be useful to take a brief look at the record of Soviet participation in the U.N., and at the prospects for the future suggested by recent developments in Soviet foreign policy.

When we look at the record of the Soviet Union in the United Nations, we see a striking contrast between word and deed, between Communist ideology and Charter principle. In word, the Soviet Union has often found it expedient to support the U.N. In 1947, for example, André Vyshinsky, then Deputy Minister for Foreign Affairs, had this to say:

> The policy of the U.S.S.R. with regard to the United Nations calls for strengthening that body, extending and reinforcing international cooperation, unfaltering and consistent observance of the Charter, and the implementation of its principles.

The Soviets have hardly lived up to these fine words. Why not? Putting it bluntly, the ideological "baggage" that the Soviet Union brought with it into the United Nations has made it difficult, if not impossible, to accept the full obligations of membership. Indeed, it is hard to escape the conclusion that there is a fundamental incompatibility at almost every point between traditional Communist doctrine and the principles of the U.N. Charter:

—Communist doctrine looks forward to a monolithic world of Communist states. The United Nations Charter looks forward to a world of diversity, where each country can develop differently in accordance with the different characteristics and aspirations of its people.

—Communist doctrine seeks to build a Communist world through coercion. The United Nations Charter seeks to assure a world of free choice.

—Communist doctrine sees a world divided into hostile camps—Communist and Capitalist. Even its slogan of "peaceful coexistence" was defined by Khrushchev as "a form of intensive economic, political, and ideological struggle" whose only outcome can be the triumph of Communism and the burial of Capitalism. The Charter sees one world in which the interests that unite nations are stronger than the interests which divide them. As Alexander Dallin has put it, the Soviet Union is "a state with a 'two-camp' world view trying to operate in a 'one-world' organization." *

—Communist doctrine—like all totalitarian doctrine— distrusts international organizations that the Communist leadership cannot control. The U.N. Charter establishes an international organization beyond the control of any state or party.

—Communist doctrine denies the possibility of impartial men rendering disinterested judgment in the service of international institutions. The United Nations was founded on this very assumption.

—Communist doctrine, and the narrow interests of the Communist elite, demand a closed society in which the population is sealed off from exposure to alien ideas. The United Nations looks to an open world in which the free play of ideas can build a community of values and attitudes.

But we do not need further illustrations of the clash between Communism and the Charter on the level of principle. What is more relevant is the collision between the Soviet Union and the United Nations in actual practice. In two decades of U.N. history, this collision has occurred in eight principal areas:

1. *Communist Coercion.* The most obvious area in which Soviet policy has collided with the Charter has been in the systematic attempt of the Soviet Union to promote its political and ideological objectives by the use of force. This collision was not unprecedented. In 1939, the Soviet Union had been expelled from the League of Nations only a few years after its admission for its unprovoked invasion of Finland. Those who hoped that the creation of the United Nations would bring fundamental changes in Soviet foreign policy were quickly disappointed. Indeed, many of the major crises that have beset the U.N. since its inception—in Iran, Greece, Korea, Hungary—have resulted

* *The Soviet Union and the United Nations* (New York, 1962), p. 6.

from the attempt of the Soviet Union to impose its system by force in violation of the U.N. Charter. The fact that the Soviet Union has found it necessary to cast more than 100 vetoes in the Security Council gives one measure of the extent of the problem.

The United Nations operation in the Congo provides a recent example of how the U.N. stood in the way of the historic Soviet thrust for world domination. The Soviet Union counted on filling the power vacuum created by the withdrawal of colonial rule in Africa and elsewhere. The Congo offered a particularly good opportunity: Here was the strategic key to sub-Saharan Africa, possessed of great wealth, in a chaotic condition after independence. The Soviet Union voted for the initial Security Council resolutions on the Congo—perhaps in the mistaken belief that the U.N. would confine itself to preventing the re-entry of Belgian troops. It soon began to oppose the operation when it became clear that the U.N. would act to protect the new Congolese nation against the intervention of outside forces—including those of the Soviet Union—and to preserve a unified state. By controlling the key airfields and other points of entry into the Congo, the United Nations was able to prevent the extensive intrusion of Soviet personnel against the wishes of the Central Government and thus helped to avert the transformation of that country into a cold-war battleground. It was inevitable that the U.N.'s attempt to implement its mandate to protect the Congo's territorial integrity and political independence would provoke the violent opposition of the principal member that was working in the other direction.

2. *Constitutional Development.* The Soviet Union has always seen the United Nations Charter essentially as a contract between rival states rather than as a constitution capable of organic growth in the service of a world community. The collision between the pursuit of Communist goals by coercion and the U.N.'s defense of national inde-

pendence based on free choice has with growing frequency been manifested in constitutional arguments about the interpretation of the U.N. Charter.

The central element in the controversy has been the authority of the United Nations to carry on peacekeeping activities that could frustrate the pursuit of Communist aims. The Soviet Union has insisted on the so-called "principle of unanimity"—the doctrine that no peacekeeping action can be undertaken except through agreement at every step of the way of all five Permanent Members of the Security Council.

The overwhelming majority of U.N. members have refused to accept so restrictive an interpretation of U.N. power. Through the Uniting for Peace Resolution, they established procedures by which the General Assembly could exercise its residual authority contained in the Charter to deal with threats to international peace and security in the event that the Security Council was unable to carry out its primary responsibility in this field. And in instances such as the Congo crisis, when the Security Council initially voted a peacekeeping operation, they supported the broad exercise of authority by the Secretary-General to assemble peacekeeping forces through voluntary arrangements with individual members. The refusal of the Soviet Union to accept the legality of these procedures and of the operations they made possible thrust the United Nations into its most serious constitutional crisis.

3. *Financing.* Directly related to the conflict between the Soviet Union and the United Nations over constitutional interpretation has been the conflict over U.N. financing. In the face of the veto power of Security Council members, the United Nations had no legal right to require that the Soviet Union supply troops or logistic support for operations it opposed, but it did have the legal right to assess the Soviet Union for its fair share of the cost of peacekeeping forces voluntarily supplied by others. The

exercise of this right in the Middle East and Congo operations led to the clash over Article 19 of the Charter, which provides for the loss of vote in the General Assembly of any country more than two years behind in its total assessments.

The Soviet position in this matter has been very clear: It will not pay for U.N. activities it does not like—at least insofar as the expenditures support functions it regards as beyond the normal administrative activities of the organization. As a result, the Soviet Union has even gone so far as to declare its intention not to pay the portion of its regular budget assessment going to the U.N. field service, the Korean cemetery, and the repayment of interest and principal on the U.N. bonds. Obviously, the collision between the Soviet Union and the United Nations on financial matters is but another manifestation of the Soviet Union's restrictive view of the U.N. Charter, and of its determination to pursue its foreign-policy goals free of any possible interference from the independent activity of international organizations.

4. *International Civil Service.*   Still another manifestation of the Soviet attempt to hamstring the independent operation of the United Nations has been the conflict between Soviet and Charter concepts of the international civil service. This conflict came to a head in 1961, when the Soviet Union mounted a frontal assault on the independence of the U.N. executive. Having failed to paralyze the U.N. through the exercise of its veto in the Security Council and its refusal to pay its peacekeeping assessments, the Soviet Union unveiled its Troika demand. This proposal to replace the Secretary-General by three Secretaries-General (representing the Communist states, the so-called Western states, and the so-called uncommitted states) would have given the Soviet Union the very veto over U.N. operations that it had failed to achieve by other means. This fact was very clearly perceived by the other

U.N. members, and they rejected the Troika overwhelmingly.

Article 100 of the United Nations Charter represents the most modern expression yet given to the concept of the international civil service:

1. In the performance of their duties the Secretary-General and the staff shall not seek or receive instructions from any government or from any other authority external to the Organization. They shall refrain from any action which might reflect on their position as international officials responsible only to the Organization.

2. Each Member of the United Nations undertakes to respect the exclusively international character of the responsibilities of the Secretary-General and the staff and not to seek to influence them in the discharge of their responsibilities.

The Soviet Union has accepted this Article neither in principle nor in practice. At the time of the Troika controversy, Walter Lippmann wrote that Khrushchev told him he "would never accept a neutral administrator. Why? Because, he said, while there are neutral countries, there are no neutral men. You would not accept a Communist administrator and I cannot accept a non-Communist administrator." *

In expressing these views, Khrushchev was not developing any new Soviet policy. His remarks are consistent with the Soviet Union's traditional philosophy toward the international civil service going back to League of Nations days. The concept that an individual from any country can serve an international institution in a disinterested manner rather than carry out the policies of his nation, party, or class is alien to traditional Communist doctrine. Indeed, the attitude that the Fascist countries took on the

* *The New York Herald Tribune*, April 17, 1961, quoted in Dallin, *op. cit.*, p. 162.

same issue in the League of Nations days indicates that the
concept is equally incompatible with any totalitarian philosophy.

Soviet practice reflects precisely this traditional philosophy. The Soviet Union normally hand-picks its senior
nominees for the U.N. Secretariat from its Foreign Ministry and does not permit direct recruitment of U.N. staff
within the Soviet Union. It does not permit its citizens to
undertake careers with the United Nations but rather ro-
tates them in and out of the Secretariat every two or three
years. Most important of all, it does not permit its citizens
to serve as truly independent members of the Secretariat.
Newspaper accounts of the senior Soviet official in the Secretariat passing notes to the Soviet representative on the
Security Council and of the espionage activities conducted
in the United States by Soviet citizens in the Secretariat
have dramatized the problem for all who are willing to
face the facts. It is only in technical and relatively nonpo-
litical assignments with the U.N. and the Specialized
Agencies that Soviet citizens seem to live up fully to their
responsibilities under the Charter.

The Troika demand was defeated. But the battle still
goes on. Continued vigilance is necessary to protect the international civil service from these Soviet practices. Moreover, United Nations agencies continue to be threatened
by "creeping Troika"—the simplistic concept not confined
to the Communist bloc that the world is divided into three
groups and that every individual must be regarded as the
servant of one of these groups.

5. *International Adjudication.* The Soviet Union has
consistently resisted the settlement of disputes by international courts or arbitral tribunals. It was obliged to accept
the statute of the International Court of Justice as the
price for membership in the United Nations. But it never
accepted the compulsory jurisdiction of the Court—i.e., the
obligation to submit to the jurisdiction of the Court in an

international legal dispute at the behest of another country accepting the same obligation. By itself, of course, this fact would not be conclusive: A large number of non-Communist countries have also declined to accept the Court's compulsory jurisdiction, and some of the countries that have accepted it in principle—such as the United States—have attached important qualifications. What is more significant is that the Soviet Union has steadfastly refused to submit individual cases to the Court. And it has usually declined to accept provisions in bilateral or multilateral agreements calling for compulsory jurisdiction of the Court in disputes over their interpretation.

The Soviet Union has also consistently opposed requests by U.N. organs for advisory opinions from the International Court. In the assessments case, however, the Soviet Union did participate for the first time in oral argument before the Court—in the person of Grigory I. Tunkin, the Legal Adviser of the Soviet Foreign Ministry. Having participated, the Soviet Union nevertheless did not consider itself estopped from continuing to challenge the validity of the advisory opinion as accepted by the General Assembly.

6. *Economic and Social Cooperation.* The Soviet Union has taken a highly restrictive view of the economic and social as well as the political activities of international organizations. At the outset of the United Nations, indeed, the Soviet attitude was even more negative on the economic than on the political side. In his opening speech at the San Francisco Conference in 1945, Foreign Minister Molotov emphasized the need for an "international security organization" and failed entirely to mention any economic and social functions.

Soviet policy in the early years of the United Nations reflected this negative attitude toward the development of international organization in the economic and social field. The Soviet Union turned up at the Bretton Woods Conference at the last moment but failed to join either the

International Bank or the International Monetary Fund. It declined to participate in the drafting of the Charter for the International Trade Organization despite the elaborate state-trading provisions which were included to facilitate its membership. It never adhered to the General Agreement on Tariffs and Trade.

The pattern was the same with other international organizations in functional and technical fields. Of the Big Five nonfinancial Specialized Agencies, the Soviet Union never joined the Food and Agriculture Organization or the International Civil Aviation Organization, and for some years it would not take part in UNESCO, the International Labor Organization, and the World Health Organization. While it has not failed to exploit meetings of these institutions for propaganda purposes, its participation in their field operations has been marginal, and the Soviet Union has consistently opposed substantial increases in their budgets and programs.

The pattern has been the same in the case of voluntary programs of the United Nations. The Soviet Union at first declined to participate in the Expanded Program of Technical Assistance when it was created in 1949; although it joined the program in 1953 and also joined the U.N. Special Fund when it was created in 1959, its participation in both institutions has been unenthusiastic. In 1966, the Soviet contribution to the two programs amounted to $3 million out of some $155 million—which is about 2 per cent of the total—as compared to its 17 per cent share of the regular budget. Even this modest contribution is paid in rubles, the employment of which is subject to so many restrictions that the U.N. has difficulty in making full use of them. Soviet experts participating in these programs in 1965 totaled only 161 out of 5,633.

The niggardly Soviet financial contribution to the U.N.'s economic and social work scarcely bears out Soviet claims of superior economic performance. Observers at the

U.N. General Assembly are always amused to hear Soviet delegates boast in the Economic Committee that the Soviet Union will soon overtake the United States in gross national product and living standards while pleading in the Budgetary Committee that its stringent economic circumstances and balance of payments difficulties require modest contributions to the United Nations.

It is not difficult to explain why executive action by international agencies should be anathema to the Soviet Union in economic as well as political affairs. Traditional Soviet policy has sought to maintain the maximum freedom of action in both areas. Only in recent years has the Soviet Union begun to emerge from a policy based on economic autarky to play an increasingly active role in international economic relations. It is clearly determined to play that role for high political stakes—to use trade and aid as political and ideological instruments. So far, there has been little room in such a strategy for large-scale cooperative programs through international organizations in trade and aid.

The negative Soviet attitude toward economic cooperation has been reflected in another area of U.N. activity—the promotion of human rights. The Soviet bloc joined the Union of South Africa in 1948 in abstaining in the vote on the Universal Declaration of Human Rights. In the early years of the United Nations, it took a wholly negative and defensive posture in the discussion of human-rights questions. While later it began gradually to exploit the propaganda opportunities in this field—as it did in economic relations—its objection to the development of any executive functions for the United Nations continued unabated. The Soviet Union has consistently resisted any proposals for the international implementation of human-rights standards, even comparatively modest measures involving fellowships, research, and the reporting of national human-rights practices. It has opposed the implementation provisions in the draft Human Rights Covenants for bringing disputed situations to a Human Rights Committee or to the International Court. As might be expected, it has also opposed any role for nongovernmental organizations in the submission of information in the field of human rights.

7. *Information Activities.* It is implicit in the Charter of the United Nations that the informed citizenry in member states, knowledgeable about the purposes and activities of the U.N., will encourage the responsible behavior of their governments in conformity with Charter standards. This assumption has considerable validity in many countries of the free world. In the United States, for example, public opinion is highly sensitized to activities of the United Nations. Thanks in part to the work of a national organization—the United Nations Association of the United States of America *—information about the United Nations and other international organizations in universities, high schools, and adult organizations is extensive and well presented. Most important, the work of this organization and the widespread coverage of events in New York by the press, radio, and television insure that those who determine U.S. policy on issues before the United Nations are conscious at every step of the way of the pressures of American opinion. While there is a powerful anti-U.N. lobby, there is also an important constituency pressing for affirmative U.S. policies in the political and economic work of the organization.

No such influence affects Soviet policy in the United Nations. Few United Nations activities take place in the Soviet Union. The Soviet equivalent of the U.N. Association is largely ornamental and does not act independently of the government to influence public attitudes. United Nations documents are not readily available to Soviet citizens. The U.N. Information Center in Moscow is located in three rooms of an apartment house in a modest residential

* This private organization is the result of a merger of the American Association for the United Nations and the U.S. Committee for the U.N.

section, and foreign visitors describe it as one of the loneliest places to be found in the city. There is only perfunctory mention of the United Nations in the schools and only limited and self-serving coverage of United Nations activities in the Soviet press.

8. *Peacekeeping and Disarmament.* A central element in the disarmament plans advanced by the United States and other Western countries has been the building up of the United Nations as a peacekeeping agency—specifically, the creation of a U.N. peace force and more effective procedures for pacific settlement of disputes. The reason for this is obvious: Nations will never be willing to eliminate or even radically reduce their arms until they have some other way to maintain their security and protect their vital interests.

Here again, hopes for building up the U.N. as an executive agency have run squarely into Soviet opposition. While the Soviet Union has sometimes paid lip service to the concept of a U.N. peacekeeping role, its proposals on this subject have been devoid of substance. Moreover, Soviet-bloc representatives at the Geneva disarmament conference have depreciated the peacekeeping issue as an undesirable distraction from the subject of disarmament.

One cannot fail to be impressed with the consistency of Soviet behavior on constitutional issues during two decades of participation in the United Nations. Yet Soviet tactics have not been static. They have changed with the general change in tactics of Soviet foreign policy that became evident in the early 1950's and are generally associated with the death of Stalin.

During the last decade, Soviet diplomacy in the United Nations has become more sophisticated. The Soviets recognized that the old hard line was not working and that a softer approach might yield political dividends. And they were encouraged to believe that the influx of newly independent countries from Africa and Asia would change the balance of forces in the United Nations in their favor. In recent years, Soviet publications have ceased to speak of "automatic majorities" of Western nations in the U.N. and have suggested instead that on key issues, the United States and its allies will eventually be reduced to a minority position.

The fundamental element in the change of Soviet U.N. tactics was the recognition that the new nations arriving in the U.N. offered a tempting and available opportunity to influence important and, hopefully, susceptible political figures. Anticolonialism, disarmament, and trade became the central themes in the Soviet Union's new approach, which culminated in Premier Khrushchev's dramatic visit to the 15th General Assembly in 1960. The more sophisticated Soviet policy was also evident in some of the Specialized Agencies and in economic forums such as the Economic and Social Council. Perhaps the most dramatic example of the shift in the Soviet line came in the field of trade. The same nation that had ignored international economic problems entirely at San Francisco and had boycotted the negotiations on the ITO and GATT suddenly turned around in the mid-1950's and started calling for an International Trade Organization with a broad mandate to promote and regulate international commerce, particularly between countries with different economic systems.

Yet the shifts on all these issues were essentially tactical ones. The Soviet Union had come to appreciate the possibilities of the U.N. as a propaganda vehicle, but it continued its negative approach to U.N. operations. During his famous visit to the 15th General Assembly, Khrushchev declared:

Experience of the work of the United Nations has shown that this body is useful and necessary, because in it are represented all the States which are called upon to solve, through negotiation and discussion, the pressing issues of international relations so as to prevent them from reaching a point where conflicts and wars might break out. That is the positive aspect of the work of the United Nations. That, indeed, constitutes the main purpose of the creation of the United Nations.

Notably missing from this Soviet benediction of the U.N. was any reference to its function as an operating agency—as an instrument for building free nations and keeping the peace. This is not surprising. The Communists have been concerned by the prospect that the United Nations might achieve a greater operational capability to carry out a charter full of dangerous thoughts about freedom of choice for all men—a capability that could bury the Communist version of history without the necessity of a major war.

This record of Soviet participation in the United Nations is not encouraging. But it is no occasion for hopelessness or despair. We must not fall into the habit of thinking that nothing can be done to strengthen the U.N. as a force for peace and welfare without the cooperation of the Soviet Union. The whole history of the United Nations—in Korea, the Congo, and the Middle East, in technical cooperation and aid to less developed countries—proves that the contrary is the case. This will continue to be so as long as the United States and other free nations work together to maintain and strengthen the U.N.'s capacity to act on the basis of the common interest recognized by the large majority of its members.

Moreover, the position of the Soviet Union may not be frozen for all time. Recently, we have seen some hopeful stirrings in Soviet foreign policy. For various reasons—the confrontation over Cuba, the increase of Western military strength, the split with Communist China, and domestic economic difficulties—the Soviet Union has come to acknowledge and in certain cases to act upon the fact that, despite national and ideological conflicts, nations may share common interests in survival and welfare.

With this modification in Soviet attitudes, there has developed what some have described as a "limited adversary relationship" between ourselves and the Soviet Union—a relationship in which fundamental differences remain but do not preclude limited forms of cooperation based on mutual restraints and reciprocal undertakings that serve the national interests of both sides. Among the more significant manifestations of this new relationship have been the agreements that have helped somewhat to slow down the arms race—the partial ban on nuclear testing, the communications link between Washington and Moscow to help prevent accidental war, and the General Assembly resolution against the placing of weapons of mass destruction in outer space. Other examples have been the agreements on international cooperation in the peaceful uses of outer space and the policy of mutual example in which both countries have announced cutbacks in the production of nuclear materials.

There have also been some straws in the wind on Soviet policy toward the U.N.—the fact that the Soviet Union invited U Thant to Moscow for the signing of the test ban treaty, that it has made special efforts at some recent U.N. meetings to avoid polemics and facilitate the orderly disposition of major issues, and that it voted affirmatively in the Security Council on the resolution establishing the U.N. peacekeeping force in Cyprus and on the one authorizing the deployment of U.N. military observers to implement the cease-fire between India and Pakistan over Kashmir. We have been disappointed too often in the past to assume that these are more than tactical shifts. Whether they herald really fundamental changes in attitude, only time will tell.

Certainly, there was much in what Khrushchev was saying in 1964 that sounded unusually congenial to American ears. The most celebrated example was his advice to Hungarian comrades that goulash and ballet were more important than revolution. Less widely quoted, but no less interesting, were some of the observations in his message to foreign heads of state at the beginning of the year. Among other things, Khrushchev noted that in our interdependent world, "a collision which may occur in any place and would, seemingly, have a purely local character, can quickly involve many other countries." To avoid the danger of such "collisions," Chairman Khrushchev proposed the conclusion of a treaty for the peaceful settlement of territorial disputes. In explaining this proposal, the Soviet leader appeared to modify somewhat the line that Soviet delegates had been taking in the disarmament negotiations —that the problem of peace could be solved automatically by general and complete disarmament without the concomitant improvement of peacekeeping machinery. He asserted that measures of peaceful settlement would make it "far easier" to make progress in disarmament:

> When states need not worry about their borders, when any plans for their alteration by force are prohibited by general international law, a considerable part of the motives which prompt states to increase their armed forces will disappear.

Chairman Khrushchev's New Year's Message also had some sympathetic and moderate things to say about the United Nations:

> The peaceful settlement of territorial disputes is also favored by the fact that in the practice of international relations there has already been a growth and improvement in the

very methods of settling disputes by peaceful means, namely, direct negotiations between the interested states, the use of good offices, appeal for help to international organizations, etc. Although I am far from convinced that the United Nations in its present form is an ideal instrument of peaceful cooperation of states, it too can, given an objective approach, make a positive contribution to the peaceful settlement of territorial and boundary questions.

The Soviet Union developed this theme further in a note sent in July, 1964, to the United States and other U.N. members. The note went beyond the specific reference to territorial disputes in the New Year's Message and urged "wider use . . . of the peaceful means of settling international disputes provided for in the Charter." It said an "understanding" among U.N. members on "the strengthening of the organization's effectiveness in safeguarding international peace and security" would "help in further easing international tension, in strengthening mutual trust in relations between States and in normalizing the international situation." Stressing the potential contribution of the U.N. to world peace, it warned of "certain circles that have no interest in preserving peace" and of "some countries" that are "still endeavoring by force to maintain their dominion over peoples waging the just struggle for freedom and independence." Some observers felt that these last references may have been intended to apply to a certain large Asian power as well as to Soviet adversaries in the West.

For all its interesting preambular language, however, the July note represented no progress from the traditional Soviet line when it came to details. The note restated the old Soviet position that all U.N. peacekeeping must be subject to the exclusive jurisdiction of the Security Council and therefore to great-power veto. It also proposed to introduce the Troika into peacekeeping operations by requiring the participation of contingents from "socialist" as well as Western and uncommitted countries. The note was particularly disappointing since it came as a response to new proposals handed to the Soviet Union in March by the United States and the United Kingdom. It was poorly received by the large majority of U.N. members who are not prepared to surrender the General Assembly's residual powers to initiate peacekeeping operations.

In the face of these developments, diplomatic observers could only regard Soviet professions of interest in a stronger U.N. peacekeeping role with continued skepticism. Obviously, Soviet expressions of support for the U.N. can only be meaningful if the Soviet Union embraces not merely the *principle* of peaceful settlement but the *machinery* for peaceful settlement embodied in the United Nations—and does so in deeds as well as words in application to specific disputes.

In the months ahead, there will be at least two critical tests of Soviet policy in the U.N.—in addition to the outstanding difficulties between us on Cuba, Berlin, and Southeast Asia. The first test will come in the constitutional crisis that has been precipitated by the refusal of the Soviet Union to pay its dues for U.N. peacekeeping operations. The U.N. cannot work to full advantage as an instrument for peaceful settlement of international disputes until its financial crisis is resolved. If the Soviet Union is really concerned about the contribution that peaceful settlement can make to disarmament and the avoidance of war, it will make a substantial contribution to restore the U.N. to solvency—a contribution it promised to make in consideration for the setting aside of Article 19. Hopefully, the Soviet Union will also abandon, sooner or later, its refusal to pay peacekeeping assessments, and will drop its refusal to pay its share of continuing items in the regular budget for the U.N. field service, the maintenance of the Korean cemetery, and the repayment of interest and principal of the U.N. bonds.

The second major test of Soviet policy will come in the current re-examination by U.N. members of procedures for initiating and financing future peacekeeping operations. The improvement of present procedures could serve the interests of all members of the U.N. The members of the U.N. will never accept the Soviet Union's traditional position that no peacekeeping operation can ever take place without its consent, but they might accept adaptations in General Assembly procedures to give large and middle powers a greater voice than they have under present arrangements. Here again, if the Soviet Union is genuinely concerned to improve the international climate and strengthen the machinery of peaceful settlement, it will join with other members in developing rational decision-making procedures for future U.N. peacekeeping operations.

How will the Soviet Union respond to these and other tests of its U.N. policy? Seasoned diplomats and Kremlinologists, recalling past shifts in Soviet policy and innumerable disappointments of previous expectations, will be properly skeptical of the possibilities. We shall have to wait and see.

Yet there is one factor that gives us the right to be hopeful for the long run. Soviet foreign policy ultimately reflects Soviet national interest—and the real long-term interest of the Soviet Union, as well as of other countries, would be served by a stronger U.N. that could help the great powers disengage from dangerous confrontations and that could prevent brush-fire conflicts between small states from triggering a nuclear war. By "real long-term interest," of course, we mean the interest of the Soviet state and people and not the interest of an elite in promoting world Communism by force. The Soviet Union will play a more constructive role in the U.N. only as the former interest takes precedence over the latter.

As Secretary Rusk pointed out in his Hammarskjöld Lecture at Columbia University:

> As long as a member possessing great power was intent on promoting conflict and upheaval—the better to coerce the world into its own image—that member might well regard the United Nations as a threat to its own ambitions.
>
> But suppose it is agreed that all members, despite their deep differences, share a common interest in survival—and therefore a common interest in preventing resort to force anywhere in the world. Then the peacekeeping capacity of the United Nations can be seen realistically for what it is: an indispensable service potentially in the national interest of all members—in the common interest of even rival states.

Chapter 3

Two Tests of the United Nations: Cuba and the Congo

FOR INSTITUTIONS NO LESS than individuals, performance in a crisis is the acid test of strength and reliability. How did the United Nations perform in the two most serious crises brought before it in this decade—Cuba and the Congo? A review of those two episodes may help to illustrate just what the U.N. can do, and what it cannot do, in the service of world peace.

The attempt of the Soviet Union to install missiles in Cuba in October, 1962, and thus to achieve a radical alteration in the world balance of power, precipitated the most dangerous crisis of the nuclear era. The principal factor in the resolution of that crisis was not the United Nations; it was the power of the United States and the determination to use it. But the decision to apply American power was synchronized carefully with bilateral, regional, and U.N. diplomacy, and thus, as Harlan Cleveland has put it, "was enveloped from the very outset in a plan for widening the communities of the concerned." *

In his television address to the American people on Monday, October 22, President Kennedy announced the deployment of a full range of military and diplomatic instruments to meet the threat to American and hence free-world security posed by the Soviet missiles in Cuba: He initiated a strict quarantine of shipments of all offensive military equipment to Cuba; directed close surveillance of Cuba and its military build-up; declared that the United States would regard any nuclear missile launched from Cuba against the Western Hemisphere as an attack by the Soviet Union on the United States requiring a full retaliatory response upon the Soviet Union; reinforced the U.S. base at Guantánamo; called for a meeting of the Council of the Organization of American States to invoke the Rio Treaty in support of hemispheric security; and requested an emergency session of the United Nations Security Council.

The O.A.S. Council met on the morning of Tuesday, October 23. Sitting as the U.S. Representative, Secretary of State Dean Rusk described the nature of the threat to this hemisphere and the countermeasures that the United States considered it essential for the inter-American system to take. He told the Council that:

> The Soviet intervention in this hemisphere with major offensive weapons challenges as never before the determination of the American governments to carry out hemispheric commitments solemnly assumed in inter-American treaties and resolutions for the defense of the peace and security of the nations of this hemisphere against extracontinental aggression or intervention.

He proposed that the Council take action pursuant to the Rio Treaty and call for the immediate dismantling and

* "Crisis Diplomacy," *Foreign Affairs,* July, 1963, p. 646.

withdrawal from Cuba of all missiles and other weapons of offensive capability. He further asked the Council to recommend that the member states of the O.A.S. take the measures necessary to insure that Cuba did not continue to receive additional offensive weapons and to prevent the offensive capacity already acquired by the Castro regime from being used to destroy the peace and security of the hemisphere.

The Secretary of State noted that the United States was simultaneously asking the U.N. Security Council to act in the matter. He observed:

> The threat is to our hemisphere, and we have the primary responsibility and duty to act as we are now doing as a hemisphere. But the threat originates from outside the hemisphere, and it is appropriate that the extracontinental power which challenges our inter-American commitments . . . be dealt with in that forum in which the power participates. It is therefore fitting in this case that the Security Council of the United Nations be requested to call upon this member to refrain from his aggressive actions against us and to seek to enforce upon him its decisions.
>
> Meanwhile, without awaiting the outcome of the United Nations approach, we must insure that our hemisphere is effectively quarantined against any further additions to Soviet offensive nuclear military power in our midst.

In the mid-afternoon of October 23, the Council, now constituted as the Organ of Consultation, took its historic decision. It called for "the immediate dismantling and withdrawal from Cuba of all missiles and other weapons with any offensive capability," and recommended that:

> The member states, in accordance with Articles 6 and 8 of the Inter-American Treaty of Reciprocal Assistance, take all measures, individually and collectively, including the use of armed force, which they may deem necessary to ensure that the Government of Cuba cannot continue to receive from

the Sino-Soviet powers military material and related supplies which may threaten the peace and security of the Continent and to prevent the missiles in Cuba with offensive capability from ever becoming an active threat to the peace and security of the Continent.

The resolution also expressed "the hope that the Security Council will, in accordance with the draft resolution introduced by the United States, dispatch United Nations observers to Cuba at the earliest moment."

Following the meeting of the Council and pursuant to the recommendations contained in the second paragraph of the resolution it had adopted, President Kennedy issued the Presidential proclamation interdicting the delivery of offensive weapons and associated material to Cuba, to commence at 2 P.M., Greenwich time, on October 24.

Simultaneously with the call for a meeting of the O.A.S. Council, Ambassador Adlai Stevenson had requested the President of the U.N. Security Council—that month it was Soviet Ambassador Valerian Zorin—to call an urgent meeting of the Council "to deal with the dangerous threat to the peace and security of the world caused by the secret establishment in Cuba by the Union of Soviet Socialist Republics of launching bases and the installation of long-range ballistic missiles capable of carrying thermonuclear warheads to most of North and South America."

"The United States," Ambassador Stevenson wrote, "now has incontrovertible evidence that the U.S.S.R. has been installing in Cuba a whole series of facilities for launching offensive nuclear missiles and other offensive weapons and installing the weapons themselves." The establishment of these bases "constitutes a grave threat to the peace and security of this hemisphere and of the whole world." It should be the purpose of Security Council action, he concluded, "to bring about the immediate dismantling and withdrawal of the Soviet missiles and other offensive weapons in Cuba, under the supervision of United Nations observers, to make it possible to lift the quarantine which is being put into effect." He also expressed the willingness of the United States to confer with the Soviet Union "on measures to remove the existing threat to the security of the Western Hemisphere and the peace of the world."

The Security Council held its first meeting on Tuesday afternoon, October 23, just as the O.A.S. was concluding its session. The United States submitted a draft resolution that called for the immediate dismantling and withdrawal from Cuba of all missiles and other offensive weapons and that authorized the sending to Cuba of a U.N. observer corps to assure and report on compliance with the resolution. The draft resolution called for an end to the U.S. quarantine of military shipments to Cuba when the above terms were complied with and recommended that the United States and the U.S.S.R. "confer promptly on measures to remove the existing threat."

Ambassador Stevenson's memorable address to the Council that afternoon made three principal points:

1. The Soviet action in sending thousands of military technicians to a nation of the Western Hemisphere, supplying jet bombers capable of delivering nuclear weapons, installing missiles capable of carrying nuclear warheads and preparing sites for additional missiles with a range of 2,200 miles, and doing these things through deceit and under the cloak of secrecy, constituted a manifest threat to this hemisphere and to the whole world.

2. The action and policy of the United States in this matter were in consonance with the United Nations Charter and had the unanimous backing of the Organization of American States.

3. The Security Council should remove the threat by calling, as the draft resolution proposed, for the immediate dismantling and withdrawal from Cuba of all missiles and

all offensive weapons; by authorizing and requesting the Secretary-General to dispatch to Cuba a U.N. observer corps to assure and report on compliance with this resolution; by calling for termination of the quarantine upon U.N. certification of such compliance; and by urgently recommending that the United States and the Soviet Union confer promptly on measures to remove the existing threat to the security and the peace of the world and report thereon to the Security Council.

During this first encounter, while avoiding direct reference to the presence of Soviet missiles or bombers in Cuba, Ambassador Zorin declared that accusations to the effect that the Soviet Union had "set up offensive armaments in Cuba" were false, and he officially confirmed the statement already issued by the Soviet Union "that the Soviet Government has not directed and is not directing to Cuba any offensive armaments." He also recalled the statement made by the Soviet Minister for Foreign Affairs, Andrei Gromyko, in the General Assembly a month earlier, that "any sober-minded man knows that Cuba is not . . . building up her forces to such a degree that she can pose a threat to the United States . . . or else a threat to any State of the Western Hemisphere."

The next day, Wednesday, October 24, Secretary-General U Thant addressed an urgent appeal to President Kennedy and Premier Khrushchev which proposed "the voluntary suspension of all arms shipments to Cuba and also the voluntary suspension of the quarantine measures involving the searching of ships bound for Cuba." U Thant believed that such voluntary suspension for a period of two to three weeks would greatly ease the situation and give time to the parties to "meet and discuss." He offered to "make myself available to all parties for whatever services I may be able to perform." In addition to this appeal to President Kennedy and Premier Khrushchev, the Secretary-General took the occasion of the Security Council meeting to address an urgent appeal to the President and Premier of Cuba, declaring that "it would also contribute greatly to the same end if the construction and development of major military facilities and installations in Cuba could be suspended during the period of negotiations." He then appealed to "the parties concerned" to enter into negotiations immediately, "even this night," irrespective of other procedures, with the first subject to be discussed being the "modalities" to achieve his suggestions.

Within the next few hours, reports reached the United Nations that Soviet ships bound for Cuba had turned off course and that Khrushchev had accepted U Thant's proposals. By the end of the week, the Soviet Union had agreed also to withdraw its missiles and other offensive weapons from Cuba.

Looking back on this historic week, one can see that the United Nations rendered useful service in each of its three main functions:

As a place for debate, the United Nations enabled the United States to build support for its Cuban policy in the most rapid and effective way. One need only recall the dramatic confrontation between Ambassador Stevenson and Ambassador Zorin in the Security Council on October 25, the televised recording of which must have been witnessed by millions of persons around the world. Ambassador Stevenson had described in detail the Soviet missile sites in Cuba, a description that he was shortly to supplement by showing the actual photographs in the Security Council chamber—evidence sufficient to satisfy even the most skeptical of U.N. members. Yet Ambassador Zorin persisted in evading the issue, declaring that the Soviet Union had no need to put missiles in Cuba and that photographs of the missile sites were forgeries manufactured by the U.S. Central Intelligence Agency.

It was this brazen piece of duplicity that triggered the unforgettable exchange in the Council chamber:

AMBASSADOR STEVENSON: . . . Well, let me say something to you, Mr. Ambassador: We do have the evidence. We have it, and it is clear and incontrovertible. And let me say something else: Those weapons must be taken out of Cuba. . . . Finally, Mr. Zorin, I remind you that the other day you did not deny the existence of these weapons. Instead, we heard that they had suddenly become defensive weapons. But to-day—again, if I heard you correctly—you say that they do not exist, or that we have not proved they exist—and you say this with another fine flood of rhetorical scorn.

All right, Sir, let me ask you one simple question: Do you, Ambassador Zorin, deny that the U.S.S.R. has placed and is placing medium- and intermediate-range missiles and sites in Cuba? Yes or no? Do not wait for the interpretation—yes or no?

AMBASSADOR ZORIN: I am not in an American courtroom, Sir, and therefore I do not wish to answer a question that is put to me in the fashion in which a prosecutor puts questions. In due course, Sir, you will have your reply.

AMBASSADOR STEVENSON: You are in the courtroom of world opinion right now, and you can answer yes or no. You have denied that they exist, and I want to know whether I have understood you correctly.

AMBASSADOR ZORIN: Will you please continue your statement, Sir? You will have your answer in due course.

AMBASSADOR STEVENSON: I am prepared to wait for my answer until hell freezes over, if that is your decision. I am also prepared to present the evidence in this room.

This public exposure of Soviet deception had a tremendous impact, and helped to build support for the quarantine and other components of the American response to the situation in Cuba. Even though the debate on Cuba took place in the Security Council, it affected the course of events in the General Assembly, and it turned foreign opinion in favor of the United States on a number of other subjects. The United States could not have achieved these results with anything like such success if it had been obliged to show its pictures of the missile sites and explain its response to them separately in more than 100 different countries. In addition, the United Nations provided a forum in which the American republics could impress on the world their solidarity on this issue.

As a place for negotiation, the United Nations was scarcely less important. The Secretary-General served as a useful point of contact in the tense days at the onset of the crisis. To begin with, he helped to avert a direct confrontation at sea between the Soviet Union and the United States, when his proposal led to the formula under which Soviet ships stayed clear of the American quarantine fleet. If the Soviet Union needed an "out"—a face-saving explanation for its behavior—it could find it in the U.N. appeal, in responding to which it could avoid admitting publicly that it was responding to United States power.

Lastly, as a place for action, the United Nations demonstrated its peacekeeping potential for the future. Khrushchev agreed to U.N. inspection on the spot. By refusing to allow this, Castro branded Communist Cuba as unwilling to cooperate with the world peace organization. The fact that the United Nations was willing and able to perform the inspection task in Cuba and that this was agreed to between the United States and the Soviet Union had a twofold value: The United Nations demonstrated its potential as an organization able to provide machinery for the critical task of inspection and verification; and Castro was put in the position of defying not just U.S. inspection but U.N. inspection. His refusal to accept the latter made it both necessary and appropriate for the U.S. to carry out inspection of the island through aerial reconnaissance.

The Congo crisis was of a different order than the crisis over the emplacement of Soviet missiles in Cuba. There was no direct confrontation of Soviet and American power.

An East-West confrontation was latent in the situation, however, and the potential and actual involvement of outside forces posed a serious threat to international peace. The Congo crisis thrust the United Nations into the most difficult and controversial operation in its history. Almost from the very beginning of the operation, serious questions were raised about what the United Nations was doing in the Congo and why the United States was supporting it—questions that were revived by developments in the Congo after the withdrawal of U.N. troops in the summer of 1964.

To answer these questions, it is necessary to recall the choice that confronted the United States in the Congo some four years earlier. Belgium had granted the Congo independence suddenly and, as soon became apparent, prematurely. Almost immediately after this event, Congolese troops rebelled against their Belgian officers; looting, killing, and general disorder followed; and the Belgians began to send back their troops and personnel to protect the Congo's European population. At this point, the two leaders of the Congo, President Joseph Kasavubu and Prime Minister Patrice Lumumba, together appealed to the United States to send American troops and other assistance to protect the Congo against Belgian "aggression."

President Eisenhower declined this appeal for direct U.S. aid. It was apparent that for the United States to airlift thousands of American soldiers into the Congo would have the gravest domestic and international political implications. President Eisenhower told the Congolese leaders that if they wished American assistance, they would have to get it through the United Nations acting in the name of the world community. Kasavubu and Lumumba then sent a second appeal—this time to the United Nations. At that point, they also issued a public warning that if United Nations assistance was not forthcoming, they would look for help elsewhere. There is not the slightest doubt that "elsewhere" meant the Soviet Union.

The alternatives open to the United States, therefore, were clear:

It could do nothing—in which case the new nation would be submerged in disorder and bloodshed, its future as an independent unit perhaps fatally compromised, with the Soviet Union free to move in and gain a strategic foothold in central Africa.

It could intervene directly with large numbers of American troops and trigger a confrontation in the heart of Africa between the great powers—a confrontation that could be the prelude to a wider conflict.

Or it could do what in fact it did—propose that assistance to the Congo be given through the United Nations.

No one pretends that the United Nations operation in the Congo was an unqualified success. How could it have been, when 20,000 troops from about thirty different countries, speaking different languages and following different military traditions, sought to keep order in a country one-third the size of the United States, with inadequate public administration and basic services? In carrying out this task of unprecedented difficulty for an international organization, the United Nations made many mistakes. But the test of the Congo operation is not whether it achieved some imaginary standard of peacekeeping excellence. It is whether the operation resulted in a situation better than would have occurred through the use of any available alternative. On this question, the judgment of history will surely confirm that the use of U.N. forces in the Congo was the least dangerous of the three risky alternatives confronting the United States and the world in the summer of 1960.

Most people recognize the merit of these arguments. Yet a number of specific questions continue to be asked—and the answers to them provide important insights into the nature of the United Nations as well as its operations in the Congo.

To begin with, some have asked whether the United Nations was not responsible for the fact that the people of the Congo achieved independence without having been adequately prepared for it. It is certainly true that the Charter of the United Nations commits its members to work for the self-determination of all peoples, including those in non-self-governing territories under colonial rule—an objective that forms an important part of the foreign policy of the United States and of most other countries. It is also true that the United Nations has been the scene of unrealistic demands for immediate independence, some expressed in the form of General Assembly recommendations. But the record does not support the charge that the U.N. was responsible for the birth of the Congolese nation in such a state of unpreparedness. Belgium decided precipitately to give independence to the Congo after rioting broke out in Léopoldville and other cities in 1959. The Congo was left at independence with hardly any Congolese university graduates, without a single Congolese doctor, lawyer, or engineer. The responsibility for this situation cannot reasonably be laid at the doorstep of the world organization.

Of a different kind, but no less persistent, is the question: What was the legal basis for the U.N.'s action in the Congo? The answer can be summarized in this way: First, the Government of the Congo asked for the United Nations to come in. Second, the Security Council authorized the U.N. to respond to this appeal. It gave the U.N. forces a mandate to maintain law and order—which it subsequently expanded into a mandate to prevent civil war, protect the Congo's territorial integrity, and remove foreign mercenaries. Third, the military actions of the U.N. force were taken in pursuit of these mandates and in self-defense.

It is well to remember that the fighting that culminated in the ending of Katanga's secession began when Katangese soldiers attacked a U.N. command post on Christmas Eve of 1962. This attack was the last in a long series of harassments of U.N. soldiers designed to cut them off from one another and from their supplies and communications. The principle is well accepted in both domestic and international law that a policeman who is lawfully on the beat has the right to defend himself against attack.

As a part of the question of the legality of the U.N.'s presence in the Congo, there is also the question: Was this not intervention in the internal affairs of a sovereign state? The answer is no, for at least two reasons:

First, the Congo asked that the U.N. come in—specifically, it asked for U.N. military assistance "against the present external aggression which is a threat to international peace." Second, this was not solely a domestic matter—there was a clear threat to international peace and security because of the actual or potential involvement of outside powers.

Another question often raised is whether the United Nations action in the Congo did not violate the principle of self-determination. This complex question requires a detailed answer.

To begin with, the principle of self-determination, like many other valuable principles, provides no automatic solution to complex human problems. A judgment has to be made on the unit to which the principle should apply. The United States fought a civil war to deny self-determination to the South. Carried to its logical extreme in the Congo, the principle of self-determination could be used to justify the creation of dozens of tribal states—a recipe for certain chaos.

Secondly, even if applied to Katanga, the principle of self-determination could not justify Tshombe's attempted secession. Tshombe's mandate to speak for the whole of Katanga was questionable. He was the leader of the Lunda tribe, one of several tribes in Katanga, and one that is a minority in numbers and that occupies less than half the land area of the former Katanga Province. Tshombe was strongly opposed by the Baluba tribe in the north. In the only popular election in Katanga, his party gained only twenty-five seats in a sixty-seat Assembly. The parliamentary group that supported him was a rump parliament lacking adequate Baluba representation. And it should not be forgotten that the United Nations forces were greeted with open arms when they entered Jadotville and Kolwezi—towns in the heart of Tshombe's tribal area. Third, Tshombe was estopped from pleading the principle of self-determination when he agreed to accept a single Congolese state. He did this at the Brussels round-table conference of January, 1960, prior to the time when the Belgians left and the Congo actually became independent. He did it on numerous occasions thereafter—notably in the fall of 1962, when he accepted the conciliation plan of the United Nations.

There are people who will concede all these things, but say: Very well, but where will this United Nations business stop? Isn't the Congo a precedent for the U.N. going into Mississippi? The answer is no again, since the United States would not ask the United Nations to come into Mississippi, and by no stretch of the imagination could the situation in Mississippi be regarded as a threat to international peace and security.

Then there are those who are satisfied on these legal and moral questions, but ask: Wouldn't the national interest of the United States have been served better by supporting Katangan secession? The answer again is no, because Katangan secession, in addition to being opposed by the Central Government of the Congo, was generally opposed in Africa, and it had no official support either in Europe or elsewhere; no country ever recognized Katangan separatism. Moreover, the Congo is not a viable economic unit without Katanga, and its secession under Tshombe would have ended moderate government in the new republic and would have precipitated the disintegration of the country into tribal groupings, with maximum opportunity for Communist penetration.

The appearance of Tshombe as head of the Central Government of the Congo in the summer of 1964 provided an ironic postscript to the four-year United Nations operation. The designation as Congolese Premier of the very man whose actions in Katanga the United Nations had opposed with U.S. assistance was cited by some as evidence of the failure both of U.N. and U.S. Congo policy. But this judgment confuses personalities with issues. The United Nations and the United States opposed Tshombe in 1961 and 1962 not because he was Tshombe but because he was leading Katanga's secession—a policy that was fraught with the most dangerous consequences for the Congo and for world peace. The return of Tshombe as head of a unified Congolese state in 1964 represented not a repudiation but, if anything, a vindication of the purpose of the U.N. operation.

The renewed disorders and threats of secession that beset the Congo even as the U.N. forces withdrew led to the most ominous question of all: Had not the U.N. operation failed in its essential purpose?

The answer to this question must take account of the fact that the United Nations is an organization with limited powers. To vary a metaphor used earlier, one does not blame a doctor who delivers a baby if the infant catches pneumonia several years later. The United Nations was not established and is not equipped to provide the Congo or any other country with a stable government. What it was established and is equipped to do is to deal with certain kinds of threats to international peace and security. Such a threat attended the Congo's achievement of independence in the summer of 1960. Despite all the disappointment of subsequent Congolese history, that particular threat was met successfully. The U.N. could not and did not bequeath to the Congo a tranquil or easy existence —only a lease on life.

What can fairly be argued is that the United Nations was obliged to leave the Congo before its job was finally completed. Unfortunately, four years of work against heavy odds sorely strained the U.N.'s financial resources and the political will of its members. It clearly would have been better if the U.N. had assisted in training the Congolese Army and stayed in that country until the Congolese Government was able to maintain security. It is unfortunate that there was not an adequate consensus between the Government of the Congo and other members of the United Nations to permit this to be done.

The withdrawal of U.N. troops in the summer of 1964 did not, in any case, mark the end of U.N. involvement. The U.N.'s Congo mandate concerned nation-building as well as peacekeeping. The U.N. and the Specialized Agencies have helped the Government of the Congo to man posts in schools, hospitals, airfields, telecommunications, and in key government departments—and to train Congolese for these jobs. U.N. experts have helped the Central Government to integrate its tax system with those of the provinces; experts from the International Monetary Fund have helped to reform and unify the currency. But eventually, the people of the Congo will have to maintain their basic services by themselves. The job of training them to do so can be usefully continued through the U.N. system, as well as through bilateral aid.

The United Nations did not solve all the problems of Cuba or the Congo. To have done so, it would have to have been a world government—something its members clearly do not want it to be. What it did do in each of these cases was provide the community of nations with a useful facility to cope with a grave threat to international peace. Considering the magnitude of the Cuba and Congo crises, this was not an inconsiderable achievement for an international organization.

Chapter 4

The Future of
the United Nations as
a Peacekeeping Agency

IN HIS PROVOCATIVE BOOK, *Thinking About the Unthinkable,* Herman Kahn imagines a nuclear war with "millions, perhaps tens of millions of people killed," which is suddenly called off when President Kennedy sends Chairman Khrushchev a copy of *World Peace Through World Law,* by Louis Sohn and Grenville Clark, and proposes that they adopt the book's proposals forthwith.

Kahn has the President say to Khrushchev, "There is no point to your reading this book; you will not like it any more than I did. I merely suggest you sign it right after my signature. This is the only plan which has even been roughly thought through; let us therefore accept it." Thereupon, Kahn has Chairman Khrushchev "accepting the offer and signing."

Like this charming allegory, much current discussion about the control of violence in the nuclear age is at once apocalyptic and utopian. We are told that unless a particular brand of world order is accepted—whether it be called "world peace through law" or "general and complete disarmament"—we are doomed to incineration in a nuclear holocaust. Too often the advocates of a particular brand of world order are satisfied merely to state the stark alternatives. Few of them stop to answer the question: How do we achieve world order?

If there is any answer to this question, it is surely composed of a number of elements—among them, the maintenance of our deterrent capacity, the building of the material basis of freedom through investment and trade, and the development of the political cohesion of the free world.

The time has come to devote increasing attention to another element of the answer—the development of the peacekeeping capacity of the United Nations.

There are two sides to the U.N.'s peacekeeping coin: preventive diplomacy—measures of pacific settlement to keep disputes from erupting into violence; and, international policing action—to contain violence and prevent it from widening into a global conflict.

How do these peacekeeping functions of the United Nations help us to achieve world order? They do so in two principal ways: In the first place, they help us to prevent and contain conflict and thus to live somewhat more safely in a world of deep political divisions and vast national armaments. This contribution of the U.N. in the present stage of world politics—made through debate, negotiation, and action—needs no further elaboration. In the second place, and beyond these immediate benefits, the peacekeeping functions of the United Nations are an indispensable element in any plan to escape from the balance of terror and to create a disarmed world under law.

This value of the U.N. as a peacekeeping agency is less well understood. But in helping to achieve world order, it is scarcely less important. If general and complete disarmament is ever to be achieved, there will have to be a major build-up in the U.N.'s peacekeeping powers—its capacity for peaceful settlement and for controlling international violence by all means, including the employment of international peace forces. For nations will never agree to eliminate their arms unless they have some other means of protecting their territorial integrity and vital interests. As President Kennedy told the U.N. General Assembly in September, 1961: "To destroy arms . . . is not enough. We must create even as we destroy—creating world-wide law and law enforcement as we outlaw world-wide war and weapons."

The United States draft outline of a disarmament treaty recognizes the inescapable relationship between peacekeeping and disarmament. It specifies a number of measures for the development of the U.N.'s peacekeeping role —among them, the acceptance of the compulsory jurisdiction of the International Court of Justice, the improvement of nonjudicial methods of peaceful settlement, the establishment of a U.N. peace observation corps for factfinding missions, and, by the end of the disarmament process, the build-up of a U.N. peace force with "sufficient armed forces and armaments so that no state could challenge it."

This recognition of the importance of developing the U.N.'s peacekeeping capacity to help us achieve world order is one of the major points separating the Western countries and the Communist bloc. For it is an unhappy fact of life that the Soviet Union has never accepted this concept of a disarmed world under law. The most highly publicized difference between the Western powers and the Soviet Union has been on the subject of inspection. But the difference on the peacekeeping role of the United Nations has been no less wide and no less fundamental.

During the summer of 1961, the United States engaged in lengthy negotiations with the Soviet Union—in Washington, Moscow, and New York—on a draft statement of principles governing general and complete disarmament. At the end of the negotiations, we did achieve an agreed statement, which noted, among other things, that the goal of negotiations is not only general and complete disarmament but also "the establishment of reliable procedures for the peaceful settlement of disputes and effective arrangements for the maintenance of peace in accordance with the principles of the United Nations Charter." As a matter of fact, the joint statement not only provided for the establishment of a United Nations peace force but specified that "arrangements for the use of this force should insure that the United Nations can effectively deter or suppress any threat or use of arms in violation of the purposes and principles of the United Nations."

As a result of this agreement, some people were encouraged to believe that the Soviet Union had at long last accepted the need for the building up of world-wide law and law enforcement as an accompaniment to general disarmament.

These hopes were quickly destroyed. In the negotiations that followed in Geneva, Soviet spokesmen attacked the emphasis placed by Western delegations on the relationship between disarmament and peacekeeping. Indeed, the Soviet delegate, Mr. Zorin, had this to say:

> In the statements of the Western representatives, a definite distortion of view is discernible. The fact that disarmament itself will be the surest and most certain means of securing peace and the security of the states is disregarded. When the means of waging war are destroyed, when states dispose of neither armies nor armaments, no one will be able to start a war and no one will be able to apply force or the threat of force in international relations.

This Soviet position is obviously untenable. One need only observe that under the Soviet disarmament plan, nations would be permitted to maintain—even at the end of the disarmament process—national forces for the "safe-guarding of frontiers." Without effective international measures for settling disputes and suppressing aggression, these forces—and even citizens armed with ordinary fire-arms—could be used to threaten the security of other nations. Moreover, Communist-bloc spokesmen in the disarmament negotiations have clearly reserved the right of Communist countries to continue to pursue their goals of world domination in a disarmed world through indirect aggression, subversion, and so-called "wars of national liberation."

To be sure, the Soviet Union pays lip service to the concept of peacekeeping, but it fails to support the concept when it comes to details. The disarmament plan it proposes would have a United Nations peace force operating under the Security Council (where it has a veto) and controlled by a military Troika (where it would have another veto).

The Soviet Union has sought a propaganda triumph with its four-year plan for general and complete disarmament, but it has steadfastly shut its eyes to the peacekeeping problem. Our response should be clear: No nation can claim sincerity about general and complete disarmament until it is prepared to face up to this issue. No one is entitled to a hearing on his brand of world order until he has a serious proposal on how to achieve it.

In the two decades of its existence, the United Nations has demonstrated a significant capacity for keeping the peace. Some aspects of this capacity have followed lines clearly anticipated at San Francisco. Others have taken directions that the framers of the Charter did not anticipate.

In the field of pacific settlement of international disputes, the statute of the International Court of Justice provided impressive machinery for judicial settlement. In addition, the Charter itself offered resources for pacific settlement through nonjudicial machinery—negotiation, enquiry, mediation, conciliation, arbitration, resort to regional arrangements, and consideration by the Security Council and General Assembly.

Looking back over the years since San Francisco, it must be admitted candidly that the original hopes for judicial settlement were somewhat exaggerated. The International Court has had comparatively little business, about two cases a year on the average. Few countries have been willing to accept the compulsory jurisdiction of the Court without reservations. And the adversary proceedings brought to the Court as a result of voluntary agreement between the parties have been relatively few.

The main reason for this has not been, as some people assert, that international law is too vague or ambiguous. It is rather that there are relatively few disputes that both parties are willing to have decided on the basis of the existing law. The major conflicts of our time are typically nonjusticiable, in the sense that at least one party is challenging the legal *status quo*. The disputes between the Soviet Union and the West over Berlin, between Red China and the Republic of China over Formosa, and between the Arab countries and Israel over Israel's very existence, are obvious examples. Clearly these are not disputes that are susceptible to solution by judicial settlement.

This is not to say that the role of the International Court has been insignificant. The Court has performed a useful function in a number of adversary proceedings. It could render further useful service if states could be persuaded to be more forthcoming in taking justiciable disputes to it. Moreover, in its advisory jurisdiction, the Court has acted with distinction as a kind of Constitutional Court for the United Nations system. In this latter function, its opinion affirming the binding character of peacekeeping assessments more than justified its existence.

Nevertheless, the primary means of pacific settlement in

the last two decades has been through nonjudicial machinery. The principal U.N. efforts in this area are well known:

—In 1947, a U.N. Commission for Indonesia helped to arrange a political settlement that gave independence to that country.

—In 1948, a U.N. Commission for India and Pakistan helped to achieve a cease-fire in Kashmir.

—In 1947–49, Count Bernadotte and Ralph Bunche served as U.N. mediators to help bring about an armistice between Israel and the Arab countries.

—In 1958, and subsequently, a U.N. "presence" in Jordan helped to ease tensions between Jordan and her neighbors.

—In 1962, a U.N. mediator played a central role in bringing about a settlement in West New Guinea.

—In 1963, U.N. intermediaries helped to ease relationships between the new Yemen Arab Republic and its neighbors.

—And since 1964, a U.N. mediator has worked to achieve a peaceful settlement on the troubled island of Cyprus.

Looking back across two decades of U.N. experience in pacific settlement, one major theme is unmistakable. This is the impressive development of the political role of the Secretary-General.

The Security Council and the General Assembly have, as the Charter anticipated, made important contributions in pacific settlement. What the drafters at San Francisco perhaps did not fully anticipate was the potential importance of Articles 98 and 99—the Secretary-General's progress, to use Michel Virally's apt description, from "moral authority to political authority." * For some of the U.N.'s major accomplishments in pacific settlement have resulted from political initiatives taken by the Secretary-General or his agents.

* "The Political Role of the Secretary-General of the United Nations," *L'Annuaire Français du Droit International,* IV, 1958.

With respect to its policing powers, the growth of the U.N. has been no less significant:

—In 1950, the Security Council, assisted by the voluntary absence of the Soviet Union, authorized the defense of South Korea against Communist aggression.

—In 1956, the General Assembly established the United Nations Emergency Force in the Middle East and made possible a resolution of the Suez crisis.

—In 1958, the Security Council dispatched a U.N. observer group to Lebanon to help prevent illegal infiltration of arms and personnel across that country's borders.

—In 1960, the Security Council established the United Nations operation in the Congo to protect the territorial integrity and political independence of that country.

—In 1964, the Security Council deployed a U.N. force to keep the peace in Cyprus.

—And in 1966, the Security Council authorized the sending of military observers to implement its demand for a cease-fire between India and Pakistan over Kashmir.

These U.N. policing actions have involved personnel from fifty-four countries. In the Congo alone, there were 20,000 troops from about thirty different members.

Just as in pacific settlement, the development of the U.N.'s policing powers has also taken a course not fully anticipated at San Francisco. The framers of the Charter placed primary emphasis on Article 43, under which all U.N. members were supposed to make agreements with the Security Council to make available to the Council, on its call, specified types of forces and facilities for use in peacekeeping operations. But Article 43 became a dead letter when it proved impossible to reach agreement with the Soviet Union on the type of forces to be supplied and on the procedures governing their use. In the absence of the armed forces that would have been available under Article 43, the U.N. has called on members to supply forces on an *ad hoc* basis, with much of the responsibility for directing them resting on the Secretary-General.

The framers of the Charter also placed primary emphasis on the Security Council for the initiation of peacekeeping operations. Contrary to a widely held view, the Council has by no means proved wholly impotent for this purpose. With the concurrence of the Soviet Union and the other permanent members, it launched the U.N. peace forces in Cyprus, the Congo, and the Indian subcontinent.

The speedy dissolution of the wartime alliance soon after the end of World War II, however, did point up the need for a supplementary procedure to facilitate U.N. peacekeeping action should the Security Council be paralyzed by great-power veto. This procedure took the form of the Uniting for Peace Resolution, passed in 1950, which provides for the calling of an emergency special session of the General Assembly at twenty-four hours' notice, upon the vote of any seven members of the Security Council or at the request of a majority of the members of the General Assembly, in the event that the Council has failed to exercise its primary responsibility for the maintenance of international peace and security due to lack of unanimity among the permanent members.

Under this resolution, the General Assembly can make recommendations to members for collective measures, including, if necessary, the use of armed forces. This was the instrument that established the United Nations Emergency Force in the Middle East in the midst of the Suez crisis in 1956.

The Soviet Union has challenged the legality of carrying out the U.N.'s policing responsibilities in these ways. It has cited the so-called "principle of unanimity," by which it means the U.N. can undertake and maintain policing action only with the agreement at every step of the way of all five permanent members of the Security Council.

Such an assertion, of course, is a perversion of the U.N.

Charter and of the veto provision. To be sure, it was originally hoped that there would be sufficient unanimity among the great powers to enable the organization to require the mandatory action of all the members to repel aggression. But in the absence of that unanimity, resort has been made to other provisions of the Charter enabling the United Nations to maintain security through the voluntary action of its members.

The United Nations Charter does provide that a major power can prevent its own forces from being used for policing actions with which it does not agree. It does not provide that a major power can prevent *other* powers from using *their* forces in a course of action to which *they* have agreed. To put the meaning the Soviets do on the "principle of unanimity" is justified neither by history nor reason. It would condemn the United Nations to impotence and frustration, to being a debating society devoid of executive capacity.

Moreover, it should be remembered that the only peacekeeping operation ever authorized by the General Assembly (the United Nations Emergency Force) was established with the consent of the country (Egypt) on whose territory the force was stationed. In affirming that UNEF was not an enforcement action and therefore not within the exclusive jurisdiction of the Security Council, the International Court of Justice placed special emphasis on this fact. There is very little by way of legal authority or political support for the Soviet Union's position that such peacekeeping operations—where forces are both contributed and received by states on the basis of consent—cannot be authorized by the General Assembly.

Some time ago Mr. Justice Stone noted in a Supreme Court opinion construing a provision of the U.S. Constitution, "If we remember that 'it is a Constitution we are expounding' we cannot rightly prefer, of the possible meaning of its words, that which will defeat rather than effectuate the Constitutional purpose." * The principal constitutional purpose of the United Nations is the maintenance of international peace and security. The accomplishments of the U.N. during the last two decades both in pacific settlement and in international policing have implemented that purpose through measures consistent with the Charter and have provided a good foundation for future efforts at building a stable world order.

Despite the considerable progress which has been made in the development of the U.N.'s peacekeeping capacity, we have no cause for complacency. Indeed, the accomplishments are still inadequate when weighed against the needs. This is true whether we measure those needs in terms of keeping the peace in the dangerous present or facilitating future progress toward general and complete disarmament.

There is no lack of proposals for strengthening the U.N.'s peacekeeping role. The problem is to select those that represent significant steps forward and that have some chance of political acceptance in the world in which we live. The following is a ten-point program that meets both tests:

1. *International Court of Justice.* The executive branch of the United States Government under both parties has supported repeal of the Connally Reservation to our acceptance of the compulsory jurisdiction of the International Court. This reservation provides that our acceptance of compulsory jurisdiction does not apply to matters within United States domestic jurisdiction as determined by the United States. It would be desirable to secure the unqualified acceptance by free-world nations of the compulsory jurisdiction of the Court at least with respect to the interpretation of international agreements—

* *United States v. Classic*, 313 U.S. 299, 316, 320(1941).

matters that clearly are not within a nation's domestic jurisdiction. This is a possibility that merits careful consideration.

2. *International Law Commission.* Consideration also should be given to accelerating the work of the International Law Commission. The Commission now meets for only about ten weeks each year. At its present rate of progress, it may well take ten years to complete the three subjects which the General Assembly has assigned to it on a priority basis—the Law of Treaties, State Responsibility, and the Succession of States and Governments—and at least twenty-five years to get through these and other important topics on the Commission's agenda. The codification and progressive development of international law is too important a matter to proceed at such a pace. It is for this reason that the United States has recently supported additional annual sessions for the Commission. The Department of State has also considered the possibility of putting the Commission on a full-time basis, but, so far, soundings with Commission members and governments have indicated substantial practical obstacles.

3. *The Political Role of the Secretary-General.* The continuing political role of the Secretary-General is a vital element in the U.N.'s effectiveness as a peacekeeping agency. To maintain this role, the Secretary-General should continue to use his senior aides and resident country representatives in missions of peaceful settlement—ranging from fact-finding and observation to mediation and conciliation. Continuing efforts will also be needed to maintain the efficiency and political independence of the international secretariat without which missions of this kind cannot take place.

4. *Rapporteurs.* The League of Nations made successful use of *rapporteurs* to report on the facts and recommend possible solutions in disputes between League members. The U.N. also has employed distinguished statesmen

of member countries to perform functions of fact-finding and conciliation, statesmen such as Ellsworth Bunker of the United States in the West New Guinea dispute and Sakari Tuomioja of Finland in Cyprus. This device merits more frequent application in disputes before the General Assembly and Security Council.

5. *United Nations Institute.* In 1963, the General Assembly, with strong support from the United States, established the U.N. Institute. The Institute will arrange programs to train personnel for political and economic service in the U.N. system or in U.N.-related assignments with their governments—particularly personnel from new U.N. member states that have a shortage of persons with the necessary training and experience. It will also serve as a center for operations research in major areas of U.N. activity. The Institute could also make available to the Secretary-General for important special missions the distinguished persons from member countries who may be associated with it as faculty members, research fellows, lecturers, or seminar participants.

6. *Analysis of Peacekeeping Experience.* The Congo presented the U.N. with peacekeeping problems of unprecedented difficulty. It raised questions about fundamental aspects of U.N. peacekeeping operations—training, supply, intelligence, public relations, military command, and political control. An intensive review and analysis of the Congo and other peacekeeping efforts would help the U.N. to do better in the future. This might well be one of the first tasks of operations research to be given to the U.N. Institute.

7. *U.N. Military Staff.* To promote the success of future peacekeeping operations, the Secretary-General needs an expanded military staff unit at U.N. Headquarters. The Secretary-General's appointment of Brigadier General Indar Jit Rikhye of India as his military adviser was a step in the right direction.

8. *Earmarking and Training National Forces for U.N. Use.* In future peacekeeping emergencies, it will be important to avoid the dangerous delays that have sometimes occurred in assembling U.N. forces. It will be important also to avoid the erosion of the U.N.'s authority that can result from thrusting into international peacekeeping actions national forces lacking the necessary training. U.N. members should therefore be encouraged to train and maintain in readiness special forces that could be employed by the U.N. in peacekeeping emergencies.

Some observers have gone beyond this proposal and called for the creation of a standing United Nations force. Such a force may eventually be required. But its creation at this time is neither practical nor necessary. The members of the United Nations are not now prepared to give the United Nations a blank check to use their armed forces in unspecified future operations. Nor are they prepared to give the U.N. funds to maintain such forces in continued readiness pending their use. Moreover—and this is frequently overlooked—a standing United Nations force would have to be extremely large and expensive to provide the flexibility needed to meet the different kinds of peacekeeping emergencies that might arise.

The experience of the United Nations has shown how different are the responses needed for different peacekeeping emergencies. In Korea, a nation had to be defended against outside Communist aggression. In the Congo, a police force was needed to preserve the unity of a country and protect it against the dangers of foreign intervention. In the Middle East and Kashmir, the need was for soldiers and observers to patrol armistice and cease-fire lines. In Cyprus, a force was required to prevent a civil war between two hostile communities. These different operations on different continents required soldiers with different weaponry, different political sponsorship, different racial composition, different language training, and other specifications tailored to the necessities of each case.

For all these reasons, there is a growing consensus that the next step for the United Nations should not be a standing army but a flexible call-up system. As Secretary-General U Thant told a meeting of Harvard College alumni in 1963, U.N. members should earmark military units that they might be prepared to make available on request by the United Nations. Earmarking would be voluntary, and, unlike a standing army, the earmarked units would be financed and controlled by the government concerned prior to their use, and would only be made available to the U.N. for a particular operation with the consent of that government. Denmark, Norway, Sweden, Finland, Canada, the Netherlands, Italy, New Zealand, and Iran have already offered to earmark units for U.N. use under such arrangements. Hopefully, other members from Asia, Africa, and Latin America, as well as Europe, will follow suit.

The earmarked units should be given the advance training necessary to prepare them for United Nations service. This would include not only training in languages but also political indoctrination in the special problems that military units have to face in the service of the U.N. Those who put on the blue helmet of the United Nations are soldiers without enemies—frequently under a mandate that calls more for the skills of the policeman or diplomat than for the skills of the traditional military officer.

The United Nations military staff can organize this earmarking and training of national military units, distill the lessons of peacekeeping experience, provide military advice to the Secretary-General, and prepare contingency plans and standard operating procedures for a variety of future military operations.

9. *Financing Peacekeeping Operations.* In some peacekeeping operations—as in West New Guinea and the Yemen—the parties to the dispute will share the costs them-

selves. In others—as in Cyprus—the costs will be met by countries supplying troops and by voluntary contributions. But the Cyprus experience, as U Thant has repeatedly emphasized, demonstrates the difficulties inherent in the voluntary approach: Contributions have lagged well behind requirements, and the financial burden has rested on a handful of members. Some other method is required—particularly for large operations—if adequate financing is to be assured and the financial burden equitably shared among the members. Moreover, members will be more likely to contribute military contingents if an operation has broad political support as reflected in widely shared financial participation.

The General Assembly is on record as favoring collective financial responsibility wherever possible, a principle the United States has strongly supported. The Article 19 crisis demonstrated, however, that the Assembly is not prepared to apply the loss-of-vote sanction to members who refuse to pay peacekeeping assessments. In the future, therefore, provision will have to be made for members who refuse to pay for peacekeeping operations on political grounds.

This can be done in one of three ways: assessment with an "opting" privilege for the Permanent Members of the Security Council; assessments with an "opting out" privilege for all; or non-mandatory apportionment. Under the last formula, the General Assembly would ask members to contribute specified percentages of the cost of peacekeeping operations, but the apportioned amounts would not be treaty obligations and failure to pay them would not result in loss of vote under Article 19. If certain members refused to pay the amounts apportioned to them, the shortfall would be filled by voluntary contributions from other members. It is this approach, according to the U.S. interpretation, which the 20th General Assembly chose for the financing of the U.N. Emergency Force in 1966, even though the U.N. Secretariat in its communications appears to treat it as a normal assessment.

Whichever method is used, there is a general consensus, supported by the United States, that peacekeeping operations should be subject to a special apportionment scale, under which the developed countries pay somewhat more and the less developed countries somewhat less than they do under the regular budget scale.

10. *Decision-Making Procedures.* Secretary of State Dean Rusk pointed out, in his Hammarskjöld Lecture at Columbia University early in 1964, that there are two extreme views of how decisions on peacekeeping should be taken in the United Nations: At one extreme is the Soviet view that nothing should be done without consent at every step of the way of all the permanent members of the Security Council. At the other extreme is the view of some countries that nothing should matter except the votes that can be mustered in the General Assembly—and that what a majority wants done must be done regardless of what states make up the majority.

Almost everyone agrees that acceptance of the first view would condemn the United Nations to frustration and paralysis. There is increasing agreement that the second view also violates common sense in a United Nations whose membership has more than doubled and may grow to 125 or 130 in the next decade before it levels off. The United States and other U.N. members have been seeking some middle ground that maintains the U.N.'s peacekeeping capacity while assuring that decisions on peacekeeping operations are supported by a sufficient number of the large and middle powers who bear the principal burden of implementing them.

One solution often proposed for this problem in public discussions is that of weighted voting. As indicated earlier, however, there is now no prospect of getting agreement on a weighted-voting formula that would satisfy all the major powers, nor is the necessary two-thirds majority for such a Charter amendment likely to be forthcoming.

Recent negotiations at the U.N. have focused instead on two measures that would rationalize the present decision-making process without requiring Charter amendment. The first would assure that the General Assembly would initiate a major peacekeeping operation involving military forces only after it had been discussed in the Security Council and the Council had been unable to take action upon it. The second would provide that financial arrangements for peacekeeping operations would have to be recommended to the Assembly by a committee in which the large and middle powers would have a greater proportionate representation than they have in the Assembly as a whole.

The program outlined above reflects the commitment of the United States to the progressive strengthening of the U.N.'s peacekeeping capacity. The United States has received a large measure of support on many of these proposals from other countries of the free world. Support has not been forthcoming, of course, from the Soviet Union.

Communist obstruction alone, however, will not destroy the U.N. as a peacekeeping agency. What could do so would be a failure of support within the free world.

The fact is that the Soviet leaders are not the only ones who oppose the build-up of the U.N.'s capacity to keep the peace. There are many people in the non-Communist world who proclaim that the development of the U.N.'s peace-keeping powers, and particularly the peacekeeping provisions of the U.S. outline disarmament treaty, are a threat to national security.

It is doubtful whether these critics have given adequate weight to the thoroughgoing transformation in international relations wrought by the advent of modern weap-

ons. In an age when the Soviet Union and the United
States possess nuclear warheads the largest of which can
cause more destruction than was wrought by all the wars in
recorded history; in an age when, no matter how many
weapons each side may build, neither can escape unim-
aginable destruction in a nuclear holocaust; in an age
when the danger of war by accident or miscalculation
grows with the increasing complexity of weapons systems
—in such an age there is no rational alternative but to develop a civilized system of collective security under the
aegis of the United Nations.

As Ambassador Arthur J. Goldberg put it in his statement on peacekeeping at the 20th General Assembly:

The stakes are so high that we should be willing to take
chances on the United Nations' capacity to act, and to back
it up even when some of its particular decisions go against
our immediate national desires. For the risks of a United
Nations without the capacity to act are far greater than the
risks of a United Nations with that capacity.

PART II

In Pursuit of
the General Welfare

Chapter **5**

The Decade of Development

FOREIGN POLICY is not only concerned with survival, or
with the maintenance of peace and security. It is also concerned with the promotion of welfare—both with material
well-being and with nonmaterial goals essential to the
fullest development of the human personality. The promotion of these economic and social objectives is not merely
desirable for its own sake; it is vitally related to the pursuit
of peace. The founders of the United Nations recognized
in the Charter that to "save succeeding generations from
the scourge of war" it is necessary to "promote social progress and better standards of life in larger freedom."

The promotion of the general welfare through economic
and social cooperation now occupies more than four-fifths
of the men and money in the United Nations system. It is
the concern not only of the General Assembly, the Economic and Social Council, and the U.N. Secretariat, but of
fourteen specialized and affiliated agencies, four regional
economic commissions, and four special programs. This
vast network of activity is supplemented by vital regional

economic institutions in the North Atlantic Community, in the inter-American system, and elsewhere, and even by some world-wide arrangements outside the U.N. system.

The large majority of the nearly 600 international conferences in which the United States participates each year are devoted to economic and social questions. These conferences seldom make the headlines; indeed, most of them are noticed only by a small fraternity of specialists. The average citizen would probably be surprised to hear that his life was directly affected by these conferences in any way; yet his well-being would be jeopardized without them. They cover a bewildering variety of subjects from atomic energy to zinc, from the conservation of Atlantic tuna to the control of desert locusts. The bread-and-butter character of the conference program is illustrated by the State Department's statistical breakdown for 1963. It showed that the largest number of conferences in that year were concerned with the pursuit of the general welfare in specialized technical fields—seventy-one with agriculture, fifty-six with economic development and resources, forty-five with trade, forty-two with science, twenty-seven with shipping, twenty-four with social development, twenty-four with fisheries, twenty-two with finance, twenty-two with fuel and power, twenty-one with industry, twenty-one with specific industrial products, seventeen with transportation, fifteen with aviation, fourteen with communications, and so on down the line through labor, housing, and health to tourism and travel, patents and royalties.

The extraordinary number and variety of these specialized meetings provide eloquent testimony to the fact of interdependence. For these meetings took place for one very simple reason: The participating countries could not promote the welfare of their citizens as well by acting alone. In many cases the specific subject could not be handled effectively at all except through multilateral diplomacy, usually diplomacy operating within the framework of a regional or world-wide organization.

The work of the world-wide functional organizations is important to the rich and large nations as well as to the poor and small. The United States itself is a major beneficiary of these activities. Here are some current examples:

The International Atomic Energy Agency (IAEA) promotes the security of the United States and other nations by administering safeguards against the diversion of nuclear fuel from peaceful reactors to military purposes.

The World Meteorological Organization (WMO) helps to bring better weather forecasts to the American people by assisting in the exchange of weather information from countries around the globe.

The International Monetary Fund (IMF) reinforces the dollar and the U.S. gold stock by dollar purchases and credit facilities.

The International Civil Aviation Organization (ICAO) assists American airlines and air passengers by specifying the world-wide application of minimum navigation aids and other safeguards essential to safe and efficient air transport.

The Intergovernmental Maritime Consultative Organization (IMCO) aids American shipping and American ocean passengers by administering rules for maritime safety.

The World Health Organization (WHO) helps to protect American citizens against the use of dangerous drugs, such as thalidomide, through a new world-wide warning system.

The International Telecommunication Union (ITU) is laying the basis for expanded overseas telephone and television services for Americans via communication satellites by its work in allocating essential radio frequencies and developing regulations for their use.

The Food and Agriculture Organization (FAO) promotes the safe and efficient marketing of foodstuffs by American agriculture and industry through the completion of a world-wide code of simplified food standards.

The Commission on Narcotic Drugs of the United Nations helps to safeguard the health of the American people through its work in limiting the production of and illicit traffic in narcotics.

The General Agreement on Tariffs and Trade (GATT) promotes the sale of American products in foreign markets through negotiations to reduce tariffs and other trade barriers.

These examples, which could be multiplied at length, emphasize that functional cooperation is not a one-way street. The United States benefits as well as other nations. The rich are beneficiaries as well as the poor. Yet international organizations, particularly those in the United Nations system, have increasingly focused on the special problems of the less developed countries. It is therefore necessary to take a closer look at these activities and to consider their contribution in promoting the general welfare and U.S. foreign-policy goals.

Let us begin with some facts about the present distribution of world income. The facts are well known, but they bear repeating. In the United States, the average annual income is about $3,000. In the other developed countries of the free world, it is about $1,200. In the less developed countries as a whole, it is about $150. In the vast majority of the less developed countries—a majority that includes two-thirds of humanity—it is less than $100.

There are many ways of dramatizing the meaning of these cold statistics. For example, U.S. Gross National Product in the three years 1961–63 increased by $100 billion—from $500 billion to $600 billion—an increase that is more than the combined national products of 84 members of the United Nations. Or perhaps this is best put in every-day terms: The average person in most less developed nations has to spend per day on all his needs—food, clothing, shelter, health, education—about what the average American spends when he goes to his corner drugstore to buy a pack of cigarettes.

Let us admit that such monetary comparisons of living standards around the world are subject to a margin of error. Economists have no way of taking precisely into account the differences in internal purchasing power of national currencies, or the fact that persons in rural and agricultural societies tend to consume a large part of their own production, which never receives a market valuation. Even allowing for a substantial margin of error, however, it remains clear that the conditions of life facing the mass of humanity are not compatible with minimum standards of human dignity.

Much is written these days about the importance of "closing the gap" between the rich and the poor countries of the world. If this is intended to mean a closing of the gap in absolute terms, it is almost certainly not a feasible objective. Growth rates are superimposed on huge existing absolute disparities. In the less-developed countries as a whole, national income has been growing at about 3 per cent a year, population at about 2 per cent a year, per capita income at about 1 per cent a year. For most of the less developed countries, therefore, the average annual increase in per capita income has been about $1. In the United States, per capita income has been increasing annually by close to $100. If present trends continue, average annual per capita income between now and the year 2000 will grow from $3,000 to about $6,000 in the United States, from $1,200 to about $2,400 in other developed countries of the free world, and from less than $100 to less than $150 in the majority of the less developed countries. Thus the absolute gap will more than double. Even if we could achieve a doubling of the present annual growth rate of per capita income in the less developed countries— a formidable assignment—the gap would still double in absolute terms.

A reduction of absolute differences in living standards between the developed and the less developed countries of the world could only be achieved by bringing to a virtual halt the increase in income in the developed countries. Such an objective, of course, is not only inconceivable on political grounds, it would not serve the interests of the less developed countries themselves. For the rapid growth of the developed countries provides a vital stimulus to the growth of the less developed countries through increased imports of their products and increased private investment and foreign aid. The discussion of development, therefore, should focus not on the reduction of income disparities, but on the achievement of a tolerable rate of improvement in the conditions of life of the people in the less developed areas.

The poverty of the less developed countries is an old story. What is new is their determination to do something about it. This determination—aptly termed "the revolution of rising expectations"—has brought to a large part of the world a turbulence and upheaval unique in history. Urgent demands for economic and social improvement are the dominant facts of life today in the poor countries of Asia, the Middle East, Africa, and Latin America. There is no longer any question of whether these countries will develop themselves—the only question is how.

The principal responsibility for the development of any country rests with the people of that country themselves. Paul Hoffman likes to say that in supervising preparation of the historic report that helped give birth to the Marshall Plan he wrote only the first sentence: "Only the Europeans can save Europe." This same truth applies to every part of the world. Most of the resources required for development must come from inside the developing country. Even more important, the policies and leadership and spirit to use these resources properly, whether they come from inside or outside, can only come from the governments and the people of the less developed countries. In the words of David Bell, U.S. AID Administrator:

> The commitment of energy and leadership—the will to achieve economic and social progress—is more important than any other single factor in accomplishing development. . . . Development must be achieved from within, by the people of the less-developed countries themselves. It cannot be imposed from without. This is a lesson we have had to learn over and over again. All of us know of excellent reports, impressive schemes, beautiful blueprints which have been drawn up by outsiders, showing convincingly how the . . . people of one country or another could overcome the obstacles that confront them. But in case after case nothing has happened. And the hard fact is that nothing will happen unless the local people are at the center of the process, unless they help plan and execute the projects, unless they understand how to maintain and carry on and use what has been built.*

All this is true. Yet as Bell himself has emphasized, it is also true that external assistance can provide the vital margin between failure and success. The rapid and phenomenal recovery of Europe would not have been possible without the efforts of the Europeans; but recovery under democratic institutions would not have been possible without the Marshall Plan.

If foreign aid can be a vital factor in reinforcing the efforts of less developed countries to help themselves, just what is the interest of developed countries in providing it? There is still great confusion on this subject. For some,

* Address before the International Rural Development Conference, Washington, D.C., July 27, 1964.

the principal purpose of foreign aid is humanitarian—it is an indispensable expression of the brotherhood of man. For others, the purpose of foreign aid is economic—it is to assure access to the raw materials and growing markets that are important to the growth and prosperity of the developed countries. For still others, the purpose of foreign aid is political—it is to influence the less developed countries in a favorable direction and prevent the spread of Communism. All of these viewpoints are wrong if they are designed to provide the sole explanation for a foreign-aid program. All of them are right if they are designed to express one of its purposes. For foreign aid has many purposes, just as has foreign policy.

Perhaps the best way to see the many purposes involved in foreign aid is to contemplate the central choice now facing the developed and less developed countries. For the less developed countries, there are three possible sources of the capital needed for their economic development: domestic, Communist, and free world. The relative emphasis they place on these three sources will profoundly affect their economic and political evolution, and hence the economic and political evolution of the whole world.

A good part of the capital needs of the underdeveloped countries can and must be supplied from domestic sources. But for most of these countries existing production is barely sufficient to cover current consumption needs. Only a small margin of production can be channeled into the formation of capital. If these countries despair of obtaining sufficient capital from abroad, they will be more likely to adopt totalitarian measures at home. They may seek development by ruthlessly suppressing consumption and by forcibly mobilizing capital and labor. They may succumb to a militant and embittered nationalism. For them, development will be likely to occur in a climate in which freedom cannot survive. For us, this could mean the loss of important raw materials and markets, a vast erosion of world power, and the end of an opportunity to further the cause of human freedom.

A second source of capital for the underdeveloped countries is the Communist world. We need not fear Communist aid to these countries as long as it is relatively small in comparison with the investment of the West. But when the Communist world—Soviet or Chinese—becomes the main source of trade or foreign capital for an underdeveloped country, it will use this leverage to try to bring it into the Communist orbit. Should this strategy prove successful in the case of some of the larger underdeveloped countries, the Communists would alter in their favor the balance of political and economic power. The free world cannot afford to let this happen.

The third and last source of capital is the industrialized North Atlantic Community and Japan. Aid from this source represents the only chance for many less developed countries to achieve a tolerable rate of economic development without sacrificing human values or becoming dependent on the Communist bloc. Moreover, this aid is one of the most effective ways to build a bridge between the developed and less developed countries and achieve a reciprocal influencing of values and institutions.

Thus foreign aid has a direct bearing on security and prosperity. But we should not restrict our calculations to material considerations alone. There is a very special respect in which foreign aid can promote nonmaterial ends. For the people of the United States, currently enjoying a power and prosperity unique in history, a foreign-aid program represents an opportunity to express their natural idealism, their concern for the brotherhood of man and the dignity of the individual. Together with associated undertakings like the Peace Corps, it offers something to work for above and beyond selfish interests—an antidote to self-indulgence and decadence. In this respect, our pursuit of human freedom abroad may be part and parcel of our quest for human freedom at home.

To say this does not mean that we must be crusaders for an ideology, that we should seek to impose our political, economic, and social institutions on other people. To the other people of the world we must never say "be like us," but "be what you want to be." Our purpose is to help men everywhere toward security, prosperity, and freedom, through institutions suited to their own traditions and environments.

In short, foreign aid is a matter of both politics and economics, of self-interest and ideals. It supports the enlightened national interest of countries of the North Atlantic Community in promoting free, strong, and independent nations in the Southern Hemisphere—the kind of world in which free institutions can survive and flourish. The Act for International Development—the new foreign-aid legislation adopted in the first year of the Kennedy Administration—put it well by declaring that it was a "primary necessity, opportunity, and responsibility of the United States, and consistent with its traditions and ideals . . . to help make a historic demonstration that economic growth and political democracy can go hand in hand to the end that an enlarged community of free, stable, and self-reliant countries can reduce world tensions and insecurity."

The multiple aspect of the United States interest in the economic development of the less developed countries was sharply underlined for the American people by President Lyndon B. Johnson on two successive days in the spring of 1964. On April 20, in New York City, the President defined the challenge as follows in a speech to the Associated Press:

Our mastery of technology has helped men to learn that poverty is not inevitable, that disease and hunger are not laws of nature. Having helped create hopes, we must help satisfy them, or witness a rising discontent which may ultimately menace our own welfare. What we desire for the developing nations is what we desire for ourselves—economic progress which will permit them to shape their own institutions, and the independence which will allow them to take a dignified place in the world community.

Let there be no mistake about our intention to win the war against poverty at home, and to help fight it around the world. This battle will not be easy or swift. It takes time to educate young minds, and shape the structure of a modern economy. But the world must not be divided into rich nations and poor nations, white nations and colored nations. In such division are the seeds of terrible discord and danger in decades to come.

The next day, the President took up the same theme in impromptu remarks before a group of editors and broadcasters in the Rose Garden of the White House:

Oh how I would like to feel that we could, here in the Rose Garden today, launch a new movement to develop a greater society, a better society in all the world, not only by driving poverty from our midst here at home . . . but . . . helping others help themselves, following the golden rule not only at home but abroad, saying to these 112 nations, "We are going to do unto you as we would have you do unto us if our positions were reversed."

We must help developing countries because our own welfare demands it. It takes no great gift of foresight to realize that unless there is progress and unless there is growing satisfaction of just desires, there will be discontent and there will be restlessness. The developing world would soon become a cauldron of violence, hatred, and revolution without some assistance. How would you feel if you were a member of a family whose total income was less than $80 per year? Yet a majority of the people of the world have incomes of less than $80 a year. Under such conditions, Communism, with its false and easy promises of a magic formula, might well be able to transform these popular desires into an instrument of revolution. That is why every American who is concerned about the future of his country must also be concerned about the future of Africa, Asia, and our old friends in Latin America.

If there are a number of aid purposes, it should come as no surprise that there are also a number of aid instruments. The counterparts of the fallacies that assistance must be given only for humanitarian, or economic, or political reasons are the fallacies that assistance should be given only through bilateral or only through multilateral channels. The United States and other free world industrial countries transfer skills and resources to the less developed countries in both ways. Both kinds of aid are needed—and will continue to be needed for the foreseeable future. The choice for the United States between giving aid bilaterally and giving aid through international organizations is a pragmatic one. The test is which route is more likely to achieve the purposes for which the particular kind of assistance is being granted.

The military assistance that the United States gives to less developed countries must normally be given bilaterally. The same is true of economic aid that closely supports security efforts. Bilateral aid also may be the only way to get adequate assistance to certain countries the U.S. wishes to help—the Republic of China, Korea, Viet Nam, and Turkey are obvious examples. In certain cases, bilateral aid may provide the U.S. with greater leverage to stimulate self-help in the receiving nation or otherwise to implement U.S. foreign-policy goals.

But multilateral aid may be superior to bilateral aid in other cases for a number of reasons:

First, some of the less developed countries—particularly those that are newly independent—are preoccupied with preserving their independence and maintaining neutrality in the Cold War. They are frequently reluctant to become too dependent for assistance on the United States or its NATO allies on the one side or on the Communist world on the other. They are also sensitive about accepting advice or conditions that affect the conduct of their internal affairs. This problem can be made more manageable when aid is furnished through international organizations in which these countries participate as full and equal members. The experience of the International Bank, the International Monetary Fund, and regional agencies shows that this is often true in the case of loans. The experience of the United Nations preinvestment programs shows that it is also often true in the case of technical assistance, especially in such delicate areas as development planning and the training of leaders in public administration.

Second, international agencies can help to increase the contributions from the larger developed countries that can and should be doing more, and from the smaller developed nations which would not undertake aid programs on their own. They can also encourage the nations receiving assistance to contribute substantially from their own resources.

Third, international institutions can draw on a worldwide pool of technical personnel which may not be available in the United States or any other single aid-giving country. In many cases, internationally recruited teams of experts are not only less expensive, they provide language skills and experience more relevant to the conditions existing in less developed countries than would be available in a team recruited in one aid-giving country alone.

Fourth, international organizations are frequently better able to encourage regional projects—such as that in the Mekong Basin—that overlap the boundaries of several nations.

Fifth, aid through international organizations can strengthen the international organizations themselves as instruments of peace and welfare. The increasing use of the United Nations system for technical and capital aid helps bind the members of the United Nations more closely to the organization through ties of economic interest. In some cases the deployment of economic resources by the United Nations can help achieve a political settlement: the role of the International Bank in the dispute between India and Pakistan over the Indus waters is an obvious example. Looking to the future, we may even envisage U.N. representatives who supervise assistance programs gradually evolving into a U.N. Diplomatic Corps available for political as well as economic assignments.

In considering these significant advantages of multilateral aid, we must also weigh the countervailing considerations on the other side. One obvious problem is the attitude of other aid-giving countries. The principal limiting factor in the channeling of United States assistance through international agencies in recent years has been the unwillingness of other developed countries to match U.S. contributions with appropriate contributions of their own. The history of recent pledging conferences for United Nations preinvestment programs and of recent negotiations for an increase in the capital of the International Development Association shows that more United States resources would have been made available had other countries been willing to raise their contributions. As a rule, the United States is not willing to assume more than a 40 per cent share in the technical assistance and lending programs of the United Nations system—a share roughly proportionate to its share of the national product of U.N. members and a level that does not compromise the international character of these programs.

The other obvious problem about multilateral aid is the problem of control. So long as the world is torn by political divisions—so long as assistance must serve political as well as economic and humanitarian aims—there will be a limit to which the United States and other nations will be willing to channel aid through international organizations.

A recent controversy over U.N. assistance illustrates this point. In May, 1961, just a few weeks after the abortive landing at the Bay of Pigs, the Governing Council of the U.N. Special Fund approved a grant of $1 million for the expansion of an agricultural experimental station in Cuba. The United States vigorously opposed this decision. Paul Hoffman, the Managing Director of the Special Fund, vigorously defended it, as did most of the countries represented on the Governing Council, on the grounds that the charter of the Special Fund, like the charters of other U.N. assistance agencies, prohibits the granting or withholding of assistance on the basis of political considerations. The U.S. representative in the Governing Council argued, however, that assistance to Cuba could not be justified under the economic and technical criteria laid down in the Special Fund's charter, in view of the chaos in Cuban agriculture that had resulted from the subordination of the economic and social welfare of the Cuban people to the narrow political aims of the Castro regime.

The failure of other United Nations members to support the United States in its opposition to the Cuban project was not caused in most cases by solicitude for Cuba, but by the fear that stopping the Cuban project would jeopardize other projects to which the Soviet Union and other countries had expressed objection. At the time of the Cuban project, the Special Fund had eleven projects, totaling $7.5 million, in Korea, Viet Nam, and the Republic of China that the Soviet Union did not like—and which have been carried out despite its misgivings.

Despite its opposition to the Cuban project, the United States has continued to support the Special Fund. The reason is clear enough: The price of participating in any political institution is that you cannot get your way all of the time. Neither the United States nor any other member of the United Nations can expect to get its way all of the time. There will be entries on the debit as well as on the credit side of the ledger. The central question is whether the credits exceed the debits, whether as a whole the institution is making a net contribution to the national interest. In the case of the Special Fund, the judgment of the United States is clearly in the affirmative.

Even in the narrowest sense, the free world has got more out of the Special Fund than it has put in, and the reverse has been true for the Communist world. At the time of the Cuban project, Communist bloc countries had contributed about $7 million dollars to the Special Fund; with the Cuban project, they had received $3 million in return. (If Yugoslavia is included, Communist contributions totaled $8 million, projects in Communist countries, $6 million.) Some 282 out of 288 Special Fund projects then authorized—involving about $248 million of a grand total of $254 million—went to the non-Communist world.

Of course, the United States could insure that 100 per cent of its assistance was spent where it wished if it relied exclusively on bilateral channels. But to do this would be to sacrifice the considerable advantages of multilateral aid. The problem with multilateral and bilateral aid is obviously to try to get the best of both worlds—to maximize their advantages and minimize their disadvantages.

The history of the Cuban project helps to explain why some limits must be placed on the use of multilateral aid. The United States opposed the creation of SUNFED, the proposed Special United Nations Fund for Economic Development, and currently opposes the creation of a capital development fund by the General Assembly, precisely because large amounts of capital aid would be disbursed under circumstances that would not assure the promotion of U.S. foreign-policy objectives. It is not merely that large amounts of aid might be given to Communist countries; it is also that the standards essential to the successful application of external aid would not be likely to be maintained.

Fortunately, the world has developed a variety of multilateral assistance institutions tailored for a variety of purposes. The Inter-American Development Bank and the Inter-American Committee on the Alliance for Progress now engaged in the multilateral examination of development efforts are working with growing effectiveness in the Western Hemisphere. The European Development Fund is transferring resources on a cooperative basis from members of the European Economic Community to their former African territories. The British Commonwealth has found a cooperative instrument for multilateral assistance in the Colombo Plan. The African Development Bank and the Asian Development Bank provide still other multilateral channels for development aid.

Beyond these essentially regional instruments, the United Nations system possesses two multilateral aid institutions of growing importance in the International Bank for Reconstruction and Development and the International Development Association. The United States and most other aid-giving countries of the free world have preferred to use the IDA for the transfer of public capital on liberal credit terms rather than a capital development fund, not merely because the weighted voting system of the International Bank applies, but also because the experienced management of the Bank is available to assure the efficient use of IDA resources. It is pragmatic considerations of this kind, rather than doctrinaire attitudes, that determine the policy of the United States and other countries—not only in the choice between bilateral and multilateral aid channels, but also in the choice between multilateral channels themselves.

The pattern of economic development assistance that has been emerging in recent years defies easy classification. It goes beyond bilateralism, but stops short of complete multilateralism, if that term is thought to mean the administration of all aid by international agencies. A large part of technical assistance and a smaller part of financial aid is now administered by the United Nations and other international organizations. For much of the rest, there is gradually emerging a kind of multilateral bilateralism, or multilateral coordination of bilateral programs, in which countries supply, on a voluntary basis, technical, financial, and commodity aid in support of projects and programs drawn up under international auspices. This pattern well serves the common interest of the United States and other countries by encouraging the maximum financial contribution from donor countries and the maximum cooperation in self-help and domestic reforms from the recipients themselves.

These pragmatic considerations of the common interest in promoting economic and social development through strengthened bilateral and multilateral cooperation were decisive in launching the United Nations Decade of Development. The initiative came from President Kennedy's address to the General Assembly on September 25, 1961:

Political sovereignty is but a mockery without the means of meeting poverty and illiteracy and disease. Self-determination is but a slogan if the future holds no hope.

That is why my nation—which has freely shared its capital and its technology to help others help themselves—now proposes officially designating this decade of the 1960's as the United Nations Decade of Development. Under the framework of that resolution the United Nations' existing efforts in promoting economic growth can be expanded and coordinated. Regional surveys and training institutes can now pool the talents of many. New research, technical assistance, and pilot projects can unlock the wealth of less developed lands and untapped waters. And development can become a cooperative and not a competitive enterprise—to enable all nations, however diverse in their systems and beliefs, to become in fact as well as in law both free and equal nations.

The sixteenth General Assembly responded swiftly to this appeal by designating the current decade as the United Nations Development Decade—a decade in which "Member States and their peoples will intensify their efforts to mobilize and sustain support for the measures required on the part of both developed and developing countries to accelerate progress towards self-sustaining growth." It further adopted as an official target for the end of the decade a minimum annual growth rate of 5 per cent in the national incomes of the less developed countries.

The launching of the U.N. Development Decade provides a symbolic framework to accelerate the economic and social progress of the less developed countries. The Development Decade is not intended to be a substitute for existing efforts in economic development—national and international, private and public. On the contrary, it is intended to provide new impetus to these efforts and to help fit them together more effectively in comprehensive programs in the less developed countries. One of the central tasks of the United Nations as it moves into the second half of the Development Decade, will be to take stock of the progress that has been made so far in this historic effort.

The work of the United Nations system in the Development Decade is so varied and complex, it has been the subject of so vast a torrent of documents and resolutions, that even the experts have difficulty in grasping the main threads. Indeed, there is some danger that the Development Decade may become all things to all men. To help prevent this, the United States has sought to emphasize several main themes. Some of these, concerning trade, finance, and population, will be discussed separately. Others require brief examination at this point.

1. *Preinvestment.* A major theme of the Development Decade is the expansion of the U.N.'s preinvestment programs. Recent experience has confirmed what should have been obvious all along—that capital investment does not yield instant development; it has to build upon an adequate foundation. The preinvestment work of the U.N. system is designed to help provide that foundation by the gathering of basic information about national resources, the drawing up of national development plans, the carrying out of research in products and techniques to reveal a nation's special potentialities, and, most important of all, the development of an adequate supply of trained manpower.

The principal bottleneck in the development process is people. Most of the resources of the U.N. preinvestment programs are used to supply the less developed countries with foreign experts and operational personnel and to train the nationals of those countries themselves. Adequate numbers of trained people—precisely what most less developed countries lack—are an obvious prerequisite to self-sustaining growth. Training is therefore a top-priority task of the Development Decade. In the words of B. R. Sen, Director General of FAO: "If you give a man a fish, you feed him for the day; if you teach him how to fish, you provide him with a livelihood."

The United Nations system now carries on its preinvestment work in four main ways:

First, the U.N. itself carries on a technical-assistance program funded from its regular budget. This comparatively modest program, which runs to approximately $6 million a year, is used mainly for assistance in formulating and carrying out development plans, for training in public administration, and for supplying operational and executive personnel (OPEX) from developed countries for senior positions in the national services of less developed countries.

Second, technical-assistance programs funded from the budgets of the Specialized Agencies help to train the nationals of less developed countries in the variety of specialized subjects with which these agencies are concerned: agriculture, health, education, labor, telecommunications, meteorology, civil aviation, and so forth. The International Bank finances a small technical-assistance program from its earnings on loans, and runs an Economic Development Institute in which leaders from less developed countries study practical problems of economic development. The General Agreement on Tariffs and Trade also conducts a small training program for officials of less developed countries concerned with the administration of customs laws and the development of trade policy.

Third, the Expanded Program of Technical Assistance (EPTA), launched at the initiative of the United States as the international counterpart to the Point Four program, is financed from a central fund of voluntary contributions that pays for projects executed by various participating Specialized Agencies. It now pays for nearly 2,000 experts in 100 countries and territories throughout the world, and for approximately 3,500 fellowships for nationals of these countries to study in educational and technical institutions.

Fourth, the United Nations Special Fund, established in 1958, concentrates on applied research, surveys, and feasibility studies, and the creation of institutions for manpower training. As of this writing, it has authorized a total of 522 projects costing $1.15 billion. Of this amount, $673 million, about 60 per cent, is being supplied by the recipient countries.

How this far-flung preinvestment program can lay the basis for the productive application of investment capital is illustrated by some projects of the Special Fund:

In Argentina, a $300,000 survey of electric power, financed by the Fund, helped to bring forth $300 million in investment from the International Bank, other international sources, and domestic investors.

In Nigeria, a Fund survey for the multipurpose development of the Niger River has resulted in an International Bank loan of $190 million.

In Thailand, a Fund-financed survey of a tributary of the Mekong has triggered construction of a $17 million dam for hydroelectric power, irrigation, and flood control.

At U.S. initiative, the General Assembly in 1961, as part of its program for the Development Decade, fixed $150 million a year as a target for contributions to the Expanded Program of Technical Assistance and the Special Fund. This target has now been passed, and the 20th General Assembly set a new target of $200 million for the two programs.

2. *Financial Aid.*   A second aim of the Development Decade is to increase the flow of financial aid. Since the end of World War II, the United States has supplied about $40 billion in foreign aid to less developed countries. It is currently providing approximately $3 billion a year in financial assistance for this purpose, mostly in the form of long-term, low-interest loans for key countries in Latin America, Africa, and Asia which have demonstrated the capacity to help themselves.* It is supplying about $1.5 billion a year in commodities through the Food for Freedom program. This annual U.S. bilateral effort of approximately $4.5 billion is now supplemented by $3 billion a year in bilateral assistance from other free world countries. Another $1 billion a year is being made available by the two capital-supplying agencies of the U.N. system, the International Bank and the International Development Association. About $.5 billion annually is flowing through regional development agencies in Latin America and Eu-

---

* This figure includes economic aid under the Foreign Assistance Act and loans made by the Export-Import Bank to less developed countries for terms of more than five years.

rope. A little under $1 billion in economic assistance is being supplied annually by the Communist world. In short, there is now close to $10 billion of public capital flowing each year to the less developed countries.

The steady progress that has been made in raising this figure is a major accomplishment of the Development Decade. A good part of the credit should be given to the Development Assistance Committee of the OECD. DAC consists of twelve countries supplying almost 95 per cent of all free world bilateral assistance. Each year the DAC countries engage in an intensive confrontation on their past aid activities and on their intentions for the future. Through this process, we are working to increase the flow of aid from free-world countries other than the United States, to ease their terms of lending toward lower interest rates and longer periods of repayment, to establish centralized foreign-aid administrations in other countries, to coordinate the bilateral aid programs of DAC members, and to broaden the geographic distribution of aid of European countries beyond their former overseas territories.

The capital-supplying agencies of the U.N. have also come a long way. When the Board of Governors of these agencies met in Tokyo in September, 1964, it could look back over an impressive record: nearly $8 billion in loans by the International Bank, more than $600 million in loans by the International Development Association. These two institutions are now committing about $1 billion a year. The decision to increase IDA resources from $1 billion to $1.75 billion, approved in 1964 by the U.S. Congress, will assure that International Bank loans on conservative credit terms (5–6 per cent, 15–25-year maturities) can be supplemented by substantial IDA lending at three-quarters of 1 per cent with 50-year maturities. Since IDA, unlike the Bank, does not depend on the private capital market, it can help to support projects in so-called social infrastructure which do not yield sufficient revenue to meet the tests of conventional financing.

One of the most impressive manifestations of cooperation in the capital-lending field during the Development Decade has been the establishment of so-called aid consortia. These consortia bring together donor countries and international financial institutions to assess development plans and aid needs and to work out measures of financing. The OECD has organized consortia for Greece and Turkey; the International Bank has done the same for India and Pakistan. In the three years 1961–63, these four consortia accounted for over $5 billion of free world aid— more than one-fifth of the total free world aid flow.

3. *Private Investment.* Another objective of the Development Decade is to promote private investment. In emphasizing the contribution of private capital to development, the United States does not seek to impose its economic system on other nations. But it does emphasize the fact that in the non-Communist world development has been fastest where the private sector has been encouraged. Moreover, in the United States and other industrial nations of the free world, the bulk of capital and skills is in private hands. The potentiality of private resources is far from being realized at the present time, when gross capital flow to the less developed countries averages no more than $2–3 billion a year.

Much can be done to stimulate the flow of private capital to less developed countries by the capital-exporting countries themselves. In recent years, the United States has greatly expanded its investment guarantee program; financed development banks to lend to private investors in less developed countries; made local currency loans to American firms abroad; supported investment surveys to determine the feasibility of overseas investments; financed pilot projects to stimulate the interest of American and foreign investors; and created an International Executive

Service Corps to encourage U.S. business executives with managerial and technical know-how to serve in developing countries. In 1964, President Johnson also proposed far-reaching tax incentives for American investment in less developed countries.

Less developed countries have also taken steps to encourage private investment. They have passed special investment laws guaranteeing foreign investors against expropriation and assuring the remittance of investment earnings; established national development banks to encourage domestic investment by their own nationals; and adopted economic policies designed to produce an attractive climate for private investment.

It is frequently forgotten that the flow of foreign aid through multilateral and bilateral channels also encourages private investment by developing port facilities, roads, power, communications, and the other ingredients of a modern economy. Bilateral and multilateral preinvestment programs serve the same purpose by training people, encouraging research, and surveying resources. International organizations are also contributing to the flow of private investment in other ways:

The International Bank and the International Finance Corporation are tapping increasing amounts of private capital for investment in less developed countries. Most of the money for Bank loans is raised by the issuance of bonds in the private capital market, not only in the United States, but increasingly in other free world industrial countries. The International Finance Corporation, with its $100 million of government contributions, assists private enterprises in less developed countries by investing in shares or making loans without government guarantee of repayment.

The United Nations carries out research on the role of private investment in economic development. Hopefully, this research will promote a wider understanding of the contribution private capital can make to development. Many leaders of less developed countries tend to be suspicious of private enterprise: some see in particular an inevitable conflict between the profit-making interest of a foreign corporation and the interest of the country in which it does business. The periodic reports of the U.N. Secretariat on the flow of private capital and the country surveys of the International Bank help to dispel these misconceptions by showing the specific ways in which foreign as well as domestic capital can contribute to economic development.

Debates in United Nations forums can also help the flow of private capital. For some years, U.N. members were engaged in drafting a Declaration on Permanent Sovereignty Over Natural Resources. The United States and other industrial countries were understandably concerned that the elaboration of this theme, unexceptionable in itself, would be exploited by Communist countries and others to justify violations of private property rights. But when the Declaration was finally adopted by the General Assembly, in December, 1962, it had become, on the whole, a responsible document. Extreme Communist amendments were defeated; the Declaration not only affirmed the sovereignty of nations over their natural wealth and resources, but also recognized the obligation to pay compensation where domestic and foreign property is taken, to observe agreements between less developed countries and foreign investors (including agreements to arbitrate), and to abide by other requirements of international law.

The United Nations system also provides resources for the protection of the rights of foreign investors. The International Court of Justice is available to states that wish to bring claims on behalf of their nationals against other states for the seizure of property in violation of international law. Although few such cases have actually been brought, the potentiality of the Court for adjudication of this kind has encouraged the settlement of claims through quiet diplomacy. Moreover, the International Bank is now engaged in the creation of a new facility in the form of a center for the conciliation or arbitration of investment disputes. The draft convention on this subject that has been prepared under the Bank's auspices would provide facilities (conciliation commissions and arbitration tribunals) to which investors as well as governments could have access on a voluntary basis. Agreements between foreign investors and host governments could provide in advance for resort to such facilities in the event of disputes. The establishment of these new facilities would be a major step in the encouragement of private foreign investment.

Perhaps most important of all, the United Nations system works generally to create an adequate "investment climate"—that constellation of government policies and conditions which determines the security of investment and profit opportunities. The work of the General Agreement on Tariffs and Trade in removing trade barriers, the work of the International Monetary Fund in encouraging responsible fiscal policies and foreign exchange practices, the work of the International Bank and other agencies in drawing rational development plans—these and other efforts are all important in creating conditions necessary for private investment.

4. *World Food Program.* Another aim of the Development Decade is to increase food supplies in less developed countries and to use the food abundance of the developed countries to promote economic development. According to the FAO, 300–450 million people actually go hungry each day; three times as many—one-third to one-half of the world's population—suffer from undernutrition or malnutrition. FAO further estimates that world food supplies will have to be trebled by the turn of the century to provide an adequate level of nutrition for the world's growing population. Obviously a major effort is needed to stimu-

late agricultural productivity in the less developed countries. And while this effort is going on, food transfers will be needed in large quantities.

Food aid is not a substitute for financial aid, but it can stretch the limited amount of finance that is available. As economies develop, demands for food tend to grow faster than the growth in agricultural production, and the resulting food deficiency cannot always be filled through commercial imports, since most less developed countries are short of foreign exchange. Food aid can fill this deficiency without draining scarce foreign exchange resources, can forestall an inflation in agricultural prices, and can help to sustain a faster pace of development with less suffering.

The United States is making major efforts in support of development through its Food for Freedom program, which is now transferring about $1.5 billion dollars worth of food each year to more than 90 million people. Surplus food that would otherwise lie in storage at a cost to American taxpayers is being used in less developed countries as partial wage payment in programs of reforestation and of school, hospital, and house construction. It is providing ingredients for hot lunches for approximately one-third of the school children of Latin America—for most of them the only hot meal they have each day.

One of the first innovations of the Development Decade was the establishment of a multilateral food program as a counterpart to the U.S. bilateral effort. Inaugurated in 1962, the World Food Program is an experimental program to determine how multilateral food transfers can contribute to economic and social development.

The World Food Program started modestly—$100 million in foodstuffs and cash. But it was founded on the recognition that advances in farm technology will put more and more countries in a position to distribute food on special terms as the Development Decade proceeds. While the U.S. Food for Freedom program can and must continue, a multilateral effort can serve to discourage a number of competitive food distribution programs working at cross-purposes. It can also encourage countries with food surpluses to make contributions to economic development and stimulate less developed countries to explore new ways of using food aid from abroad.

The World Food Program is concentrating its efforts on emergency food needs, preschool and school feeding, and pilot projects in the use of food for economic and social development—for example, direct food payments to workers in labor-intensive projects. In 1965, the FAO and the General Assembly decided to continue the World Food Program for three more years at an expanded level of activity.

5. *Social Development.* The fifth objective of the Development Decade is to achieve balanced economic and social growth. In U.N. usage, social development means progress in health, education, housing, and social welfare. The United States has sought to emphasize the central importance of these activities in the implementation of the Development Decade. If they are overlooked because of a preoccupation with increases in Gross National Product, economic development will fail in its primary purpose—the achievement of at least minimum levels of human dignity.

Public opinion is now being alerted to the dangers of the "population explosion." But there is also what the World Health Organization has called the "population implosion"—the massive and unprecedented migration of people from the countryside to the cities. The manifestations of this world-wide phenomenon can be seen in New York, London, and Tokyo, as well as in Istanbul, Calcutta, and Rio de Janeiro. But its consequences can be catastrophic in the less developed countries, which are much less able to cope with them. If present trends continue, for example, it is estimated that by the year 2000, the urban population of the world will greatly exceed the total world population at the present time. In the next 40 years, more houses will have to be built than heretofore in the entire history of man.

If violent upheavals are to be avoided, we must have a strategy of social development to deal with these massive population transfers. Such a strategy must be two-sided. It must deal with the problems of housing, health, education, and social welfare arising in the swelling metropolitan areas. It must also devise ways of improving conditions of rural life that will reduce to tolerable levels the move to the cities.

The United Nations system is helping in many ways to alert its members to these social problems and to give them some means of coping with them:

Several Specialized Agencies—the World Health Organization, the International Labor Organization, and UNESCO—are engaged in research and technical assistance directly related to social development.

The United Nations Children's Fund (UNICEF) is devoting increasing resources to special programs in the health, education, welfare, and feeding of children, including those who suffer most from the disruptions and deprivations of the drift to the cities.

The United Nations Secretariat, under the guidance of the Social Commission, is strengthening the research and advisory social-welfare services that have been offered to members through its Bureau of Social Affairs.

A Committee on Housing, Building, and Planning is considering ways in which the United Nations system can help to solve the housing crisis in less developed countries, stimulated by U.N. estimates that more than 1 billion people in Africa, Asia, and Latin America—one-half of the total population of these continents—are "homeless or living in housing which is a health hazard and an affront to human dignity."

6. *Science and Technology.* The United Nations Con-

ference on the Application of Science and Technology for
the Benefit of Less Developed Areas (UNCSAT), held in
Geneva in February, 1963, was another major event in the
Development Decade. The 1,665 scientists and administrators who attended this conference did not come to deal
with theoretical questions. They came to tackle the practical problems of how to apply the world's fund of scientific knowledge and of how to bring it to bear on the
special problems of less developed countries.

As a result of UNCSAT, a major review is now under
way of the ways and means of improving the scientific and
technological work of the United Nations system. The
eighteen-nation Advisory Committee appointed to deal
with science and technology is particularly concerned
with the urgent need of the less developed countries to
establish planning machinery, to develop adequate institutions in science and technology, and to increase investment in these areas.

The Advisory Committee is also drawing up a list of
problems in science and technology that should receive
priority attention—problems whose solution would bring
unusually great benefits to the developing countries and
where a breakthrough appears possible if a massive world-
wide effort is made. Among the subjects being considered
for the list are: an economic desalinization plant for areas
short of fresh water; a small energy unit for village use;
new telecommunications procedures for education and
training; improved farm implements suited to local conditions; new forms of acceptable protein food that could be
made available on a massive scale to combat malnutrition.

7. *Coordination of Effort.* The Development Decade
should not simply be an instrument for expanding the size
of United Nations operations, nor should it be the occasion for galloping off in all directions at once. If everything
is given priority, nothing has priority. The greatest challenge to the United Nations system in implementing the

Development Decade is to achieve organizational reforms that will help it to focus on priority problems.

We have probably reached the outer limits in the proliferation of specialized functions in the U.N. system of agencies. Specialists play an indispensable role in turning the wheels of our highly complex international society, but they have this great defect: Each of them believes that his particular specialty is the key to everything else. Such a case can and has been made for population control, education, agriculture, industry, health, housing, science, transport, communications, and labor. There may even be a meteorologist somewhere who believes that weather control will eventually provide the ultimate answer! Given an independent base of operations and an independent budget, the specialists in any of these fields, unless their enthusiasm is appropriately restrained through coordination with other specialists, will tend to spend limited resources in ways that cannot be justified on the basis of over-all priorities.

To put it bluntly, there is a real danger of the economic and social work of the U.N. coming apart at the seams. The urgent need is not to fragment it further but to bind it together more effectively.

The case for an integrated effort is as obvious in economic development as in any other area of human activity. When a man builds a house, he does not commission plumbers, electricians, carpenters, and so on, to go forward independently to produce what they think he should have in their respective lines. He asks that a blueprint be produced of the total structure, a blueprint drawn up in the light of his total needs and the total funds he has available to meet those needs. The various specialists then proceed to perform their work within the guidelines of the basic blueprint with full authority to perform their specialized tasks so long as the results fit together as integral parts of the total structure.

One of the central tasks of the less developed countries during the Development Decade is to formulate and carry out comprehensive and realistic development plans that establish clear priorities permitting the most effective use of available resources, including assistance from abroad. Precisely because they are underdeveloped, many of these countries have encountered serious difficulties in coordinating their own activities and in implementing such plans. Their problems must not be compounded by the presence of a score of United Nations agencies—not to mention foreign official and private representatives—each offering contradictory advice and pushing projects in different fields.

In the past two decades, the work of the U.N. system in the economic and social field has been radically transformed. The Specialized Agencies, once devoted almost entirely to research and standard-setting, are now mainly engaged in the transfer of skills and resources to less developed countries. Organizational arrangements adequate to the former era of U.N. activity are no longer adequate today. The activities of the Specialized Agencies, the regional economic commissions, and the special programs must be related more successfully.

The United States has pressed for two basic reforms in United Nations machinery to achieve the integrated effort essential to the success of the Development Decade:

The first measure is to merge and strengthen the two large preinvestment programs at U.N. Headquarters, the Expanded Program of Technical Assistance and the U.N. Special Fund. In August, 1964, the Economic and Social Council recommended a merger of the two into a U.N. Development Program with a single governing body of government representatives, a single interagency advisory committee, and a single administration. This merger, approved by the Assembly in 1965, will make for greater administrative efficiency and fewer meetings. It will reduce the tendency to allocate funds among the Specialized Agencies according to historic shares. It will also mean a better focusing of those funds on the priority needs of the developing countries.

The second measure is the strengthening of the role of the United Nations Resident Representatives in the less developed countries. Thanks in part to the urging of the United States and other U.N. members, these officials now serve simultaneously as representatives for the Special Fund, EPTA, and the World Food Program. As the quality of these representatives improves, and as they are assured of adequate staff resources and administrative support, they will be increasingly valuable to host governments in the preparation of development plans, the establishment of priorities, and the formulation of requests for assistance to the major U.N. programs. They will also play an important coordinating role with respect to the activities of the various Specialized Agencies that are financed from regular agency budgets.

The time has come for a serious assessment of the progress made so far in realizing the aims of the Development Decade. If this assessment is to be useful, it must concentrate less on self-congratulation and more on what still needs to be done.

Despite the extraordinary variety of United Nations activities already underway, the institutions for economic and social cooperation have not yet pulled abreast of the requirements of interdependence. This is true in development of the less developed countries; it is true in other tasks as well. A little-noted paragraph in President Kennedy's speech to the General Assembly in September, 1963, hinted at a vast challenge still unmet. In this paragraph President Kennedy called upon the members of the United Nations to recognize their common interest in husbanding the resources of their common planet: to unite in an effort to "protect the forest and wild game preserves now in danger of extinction—to improve the marine harvests of food from our oceans—and prevent the contamination of air and water by industrial as well as nuclear pollution."

President Johnson developed this theme on June 10, 1964, when he proposed to dedicate International Cooperation Year to a new struggle "not of man against man, but of man against nature." He promised "to call upon all the resources of this great nation—both public and private —to work with other nations to find new methods of improving the life of man."

Urgent problems in the management of natural resources now demand immediate attention. The contamination of streams with industrial wastes; the pollution of air above major cities; the destruction of wildlife and natural areas; the need to increase the marine harvest to feed growing populations; the dangers to human and animal life from drugs and pesticides; the dramatic possibilities of desalting water by means of nuclear power—these are challenges that call for international as well as national action.

Some effective measures to husband resources can be taken by individual nations alone. But there are resources that belong to no nation—the air, the sea, migratory animals, international rivers—whose effective management requires international cooperation. And even the management of resources within the confines of a single nation may benefit from the sharing of national experience.

The uncontrolled exploitation of science and technology could spell disaster for mankind, not only in the service of military ambitions, but in the service of economic ends. To maintain the balance of nature, to exploit nature's abundance without destroying it, and to preserve and extend the dignity of life require cooperative action by men and nations. The words of Dr. Luther Terry, Surgeon

General of the Public Health Service, could well serve as a call to arms for International Cooperation Year:

> All are inspired by the longing of the human spirit to free and ennoble itself so that man may live in harmony with the very forces of Creation with which he is seemingly at war. We are in danger, on the one hand, of creating an incredible disharmony in nature which will ultimately degrade and enslave us. Or we can create an environment which can enrich our lives, our society, and our individual well-being. It is for our generation to decide. We must make that critical decision now! *

* "Environmental Health: The Time Is Now," Address delivered on the occasion of the dedication of the Kettering Laboratory, Cincinnati, Ohio, April 1, 1964.

Chapter 6

Turning Point in World Trade

THE EFFECTIVE TRANSFER of skills and resources to less developed countries through multilateral as well as bilateral channels is a central element in the Decade of Development. But the utility of international institutions in the economic field does not stop there. They are also proving to be indispensable in coping with the related challenges that face the United States in its trade relations with other nations—challenges posed by a rapidly changing world economy. The first challenge is to reduce the trade barriers that presently impair the economic efficiency and political unity of the free world—particularly of the North Atlantic Community and Japan. The second challenge is to find additional ways to deal with the special problems that affect the trade of less developed countries. International organizations are now the focus of efforts to cope with both of these challenges.

The opening of the Kennedy Round of tariff negotiations in 1964 marked the beginning of the most ambitious effort at the reduction of trade barriers the world has ever seen. This effort was stimulated by the conviction in the U.S. and other countries that giant strides should now be taken toward an open and nondiscriminatory trading system. Such progress, as recent events have made abundantly clear, may be impeded by serious obstacles. But the effort must continue—for both economic and political reasons.

The central economic purpose of the Kennedy Round is clear enough. It is designed to provide a stimulus to prosperity and growth by moving the world substantially closer to an international division of labor based on comparative efficiencies of production. A consideration of the national interest of the United States, as well as of other countries, demonstrates the close connection between this effort of trade liberalization and the achievement of higher living standards.

Although imports account for only 3 per cent of its Gross National Product, the United States is becoming increasingly dependent on them to maintain a prosperous economy. Some 10 per cent of the raw materials that feed our industrial plant come from other countries, a figure expected to grow to 20 per cent by 1975. We import almost all of our natural rubber, chromium, tin, and manganese (which is essential to the manufacture of steel). We also import a large proportion of our consumption of zinc, copper, and raw wool. Quite apart from essential raw materials, imports bring us many nonessentials that are "the spice of life" and that cannot be produced here—for example, coffee, tea, cocoa, and other tropical agricultural products. Imports also include products like bicycles, wines and spirits, and handmade glass, which we can produce only at greater cost. The reduction of import restrictions here and abroad helps the American consumer, like his counterpart in other countries, to get more for his money in terms of a greater variety of products at lower prices. It also **helps** the American manufacturer who needs materials from abroad.

Expanding trade is also necessary to maintain and expand domestic employment. American exports provide some 3 million jobs for American workers. Another 1 million jobs are accounted for by those engaged in handling, processing, and distributing imported materials. Thus some 4 million American jobs depend on foreign trade. While such matters are difficult to measure, the employment consequences of the successful conclusion of the Kennedy Round have been estimated. The estimates indicate that the U.S. could gain several billion dollars in new exports over the next five years—each $1 billion in exports creating approximately 100,000 jobs. The resulting increase of imports will displace workers, of course. According to these same estimates, special assistance would be required to help the approximately 18,000 workers a year who would not quickly find alternative employment. Granting that these estimates are subject to a substantial margin of error and that they may posit greater reductions in trade barriers (and hence greater employment effects) than will in fact occur, they nevertheless appear to show that the net impact of the Kennedy Round on employment will almost certainly be favorable, providing many more new jobs and preserving existing jobs that would otherwise be lost through reduced exports.

These figures may surprise those obsessed by the bugaboo of an inundation of imports made by "cheap foreign labor." It is true that wage rates abroad are often a good deal lower than those in the United States—sometimes as little as one-third or one-quarter of ours. But indirect wage payments to foreign labor are frequently much greater than our own. Moreover, because of more advanced machinery, the productivity of the American worker is usually several times that of his foreign counterpart. Thus, despite our higher wage rates, the wage cost per unit of output in the United States is often lower than it is abroad. Another point is that nonlabor costs in the United States—the cost of power, capital, merchandising, and so on—are lower than they are abroad. And, obviously, American enterprises do not have to bear the transport cost that foreign ones do in order to reach the American market. The fact that U.S. merchandise exports exceed merchandise imports by an average of $5 billion a year—$3 billion if the aid component is excluded—is proof of our ability to compete in world markets.

In the preoccupation with the employment consequences of trade expansion it is often forgotten that the rational end of economic policy is not just full employment, but full *and productive* employment. If we seek to protect the present occupation of every worker who might be displaced by foreign competition we may achieve full employment, but it will be full employment of large numbers of people producing inferior products at ridiculous costs. This *reductio ad absurdum* of the protectionist philosophy was effectively satirized in the following petition drafted a century ago by the Frenchman Frédéric Bastiat:

> To the Chamber of Deputies:
> We are subjected to the intolerable competition of a foreign rival, who enjoys such superior facilities for the production of light that he can inundate our national market at reduced price. This rival is no other than the sun. Our petition is to pass a law shutting up all windows, openings, and fissures through which the light of the sun is used to penetrate our dwellings, to the prejudice of the profitable produce we have been enabled to bestow on the country.
>
> (*Signed*) Candlestick Makers

One of the most significant consequences of expanding imports through trade liberalization is that it lets in the sun—by checking domestic inflation, stimulating productivity, and accelerating economic growth. American industries troubled by increasing competition from products imported from abroad are typically low-wage industries ($1.87 an hour on the average) which suffer from a multitude of ills, many of them having nothing to do with imports. Export industries, on the other hand, are typically those that pay the highest wage rates in the United States ($2.47 an hour on the average) and make the greatest use of our rapidly progressing technology. The road to prosperity for the United States—as for other countries—is clearly through adjustment of domestic resources into lines of production in which we enjoy a comparative advantage.

Yet another way in which the Kennedy Round can serve free world economic interests is in helping to deal constructively with the U.S. balance-of-payments problem. The U.S. payments deficit results from the fact that our total outpayments for free world defense, economic aid, and private foreign investment have overbalanced our healthy surplus of goods and services. We could, of course, try to balance our international accounts by drastically cutting our payments for defense, aid, and foreign investment. But this would have dangerous consequences for the security of the United States and of the entire free world. The only rational alternative is to increase our surplus of goods and services, in particular to induce our European partners to buy goods that increase the real consumption of their people rather than to add further to their gold and dollar reserves.

At this point the special importance of the European Common Market becomes apparent. The United States exports approximately $4 billion in goods to the six nations of the Common Market and imports about $2.5 billion in return. This surplus of $1.5 billion in our merchandise trade cannot be maintained and expanded without substantial progress in the Kennedy Round. The Common Market is now moving swiftly toward the elimination of its internal tariffs and to the creation of a new common tariff against outside countries. In the years ahead, therefore, producers in the Common Market will have a growing advantage in that market over American competitors. At the same time, the European countries will be making strides toward the achievement of the high consumption standards that now characterize the United States. If these countries were to have the same standards we now have, they would buy an additional 50 million cars, 50 million television sets, and 135 million radios. Western Europe is one of the fastest growing parts of the world economy. Consumption will be increasing particularly in the products in which the United States has demonstrated its comparative advantage. A bold policy of trade liberalization is our entrance ticket into this expanding market.

Of course, we cannot appreciate the importance of trade policy in promoting our economic objectives by considering the trade of the United States alone. We must also consider the dependence on international trade of other countries in whose welfare we have an important stake. The ratio of international trade to total production in the United Kingdom is three to four times as great as in the United States. For smaller nations, such as Belgium, the Netherlands, Sweden, and Switzerland, it is five to nine times as great. Our main industrial allies are even more dependent than we are on foreign supplies of raw materials. For some of these industrial countries international trade is not simply an important aid to the economy, it is the very means of survival. Dependence on international trade is no less striking in the case of most of the underdeveloped countries. All of them must go abroad for capital and technical assistance vital to their economic development. Their capacity to import is highly dependent on their capacity to export one or two primary commodities. The loss of foreign markets for these products or a collapse in commodity prices can plunge these countries into a serious crisis. The failure to enlarge the markets for the exports of these countries will frustrate our common aspirations for their economic development.

These considerations serve to underline the fact that a substantial reduction of trade barriers in the Kennedy Round serves political as well as economic objectives. The collective security of the industrial countries of the North Atlantic Community and Japan and the defense of freedom in the less developed countries will be importantly influenced by the extent to which the free world can provide satisfactory alternatives to trade with the Communist bloc. Moreover, substantial reductions in the external trade barriers of the Common Market and other regional trading groups are necessary to avoid widening political divisions that further complicate efforts toward Western unity.

The natural forces of interdependence have bound the United States, the industrial countries, and the underdeveloped countries of the non-Communist world into an intimate relationship. The weakness of that relationship is our weakness; its strength, our strength. The health of the other free world economies affects the health of our foreign markets and sources of supply, and therefore our prosperity. It affects the capacity of our allies to defend themselves and the political stability of the new independent nations, and therefore our security. It affects the material basis for the development of freedom abroad, and therefore our own freedom.

The case for freeing international trade is not new. Neither is the decision to act upon it. The passage of the Trade Agreements Act of 1934 laid the basis for nearly thirty years of progress under American leadership in negotiating reductions in tariffs and other trade barriers. What is new is that the United States now possesses a much more potent instrument for the accomplishment of this objective. The Trade Expansion Act of 1962 represents a breakthrough toward trade expansion in several respects:

1. It authorizes the President to reduce all but a few U.S. tariffs by 50 per cent and to eliminate low tariffs of 5 per cent or less.

2. It permits the President to negotiate reciprocal reductions in trade barriers now maintained by industrial countries on tropical product exports of less developed countries that are produced in the United States in negligible amounts.

3. It allows the President to negotiate for the reduction of tariffs on an across-the-board basis (a flat percentage reduction applying automatically) rather than on a product-by-product basis.

4. It helps those affected by tariff reductions to adjust to more economic lines of production through retraining and moving allowances for workers, and loans, tax benefits, and technical aid for firms.

5. It permits the termination of trade concessions through the "escape clause" only when it is required to avert genuine hardship.

These powers to reduce U.S. import barriers are not, of course, to be employed unilaterally. They are to be employed to strike a bargain in which other countries reduce their restrictions on a basis of mutual advantage. It is no surprise, therefore, that the effort to strike such a bargain —the Kennedy Round—should require the services of a multilateral institution.

The chosen instrument for the Kennedy Round, the General Agreement on Tariffs and Trade, is regarded by some as a subject suitable only for experts schooled in the mysteries of trade negotiations. These people believe that any attempt to understand GATT by the ordinary citizen concerned with foreign policy is as futile as an attempt to master Einstein's theory. It has, indeed, been said of

GATT that "only ten people in the world understand it, and they are not telling anybody."

But the ways of GATT are not forbidding or mysterious. Basically, GATT is a multilateral agreement embodying reciprocal rights and obligations of countries in the field of trade policy. Sixty-eight countries (as of mid-1966) were full contracting parties, and twelve others had acceded provisionally or were otherwise participating in some of GATT's activities. In other words, eighty countries, responsible for more than 80 per cent of total world trade, are now employing GATT as an instrument for their international trade relations.

The checkered history of GATT provides a striking illustration of the famous French axiom *"C'est le provisoire qui dure."* GATT was conceived in 1947 as a stopgap arrangement for multilateral efforts at trade liberalization pending establishment of the International Trade Organization. The ITO, whose charter was negotiated in a series of United Nations conferences in 1946–48, was to take its place alongside the International Bank, International Monetary Fund, and other U.N. Specialized Agencies. It was to deal not only with the questions of commercial policy covered by GATT, but also with policies on full employment, foreign investment, restrictive business practices, and commodity agreements. The nature of these provisions and the ebbing of wartime enthusiasm for international economic organization made it impossible, however, to secure the necessary approval of the U.S. Congress. This left GATT as the only general multilateral instrument for trade cooperation.

Despite this uncertain beginning, GATT gradually gained the strength necessary to meet the world's needs. Even the collapse of the second attempt to give it a formal organizational basis—the abortive agreement for an Organization for Trade Cooperation drafted in 1954–55—failed to impair its creative evolution. GATT strengthened its secretariat, established a council to meet between periodic meetings of the Contracting Parties, and developed effective working relations with the United Nations and other multilateral organizations.

GATT now serves the free world in four principal ways: as a forum for negotiations on the reduction of tariffs and other trade barriers; as a set of trade rules governing the conduct of trade policy; as an instrument for the interpretation of these rules and the adjustment of differences; and as a vehicle for developing and articulating new trade policy. Each of these functions is important in the current effort to clear the channels of world trade.

As a negotiating forum, GATT is the indispensable focus for the Kennedy Round. Our experience with bilateral trade agreements in the pre-GATT era illustrates why. In the interwar period, it was found necessary to include in bilateral trade agreements not only tariff concessions but also other provisions to protect the integrity of the tariff concessions by restricting the use of alternative forms of protection. Bilateral agreements also included the unconditional most-favored-nation clause, a commitment to extend immediately and unconditionally to the other party the benefits of the tariff and other commitments granted to third countries. Without this rule of equal treatment (subject to some carefully defined exceptions), a country's tariff and other trade restrictions applicable to a particular product might vary widely according to the country of origin— an undesirable state of affairs on both administrative and political grounds. But countries were reluctant to make bilateral agreements that incorporated substantial tariff cuts and other concessions which would be automatically available to third countries because of most-favored-nation commitments, without knowing what those third countries would give in return. Only by bringing the third countries into the bargaining process through GATT has it been

possible to induce countries to make far-reaching concessions in the trade field.

The fact that the Kennedy Round is based on an across-
the-board approach to tariff reduction, as opposed to the
product-by-product approach used in GATT's five previous rounds of negotiations, has given GATT an assignment of unprecedented complexity. The first task of
GATT was to reach an agreement on a set of rules for the
conduct of the negotiations. The work on these rules had
proceeded far enough by November, 1964, to permit actual
negotiations to begin through the exchange of "exceptions
lists"—lists of products countries were unwilling to subject
to the negotiating formula.

Although the agreed-on rules did not cover all outstanding issues of principle, they did embody agreements on industrial tariffs essential to the success of the Kennedy
Round. The members of GATT have agreed to a "working
hypothesis" of an across-the-board tariff cut of 50 per cent,
the same figure used in the Trade Expansion Act. They have
agreed that exceptions should be permitted to this cut
only when required by overriding national interests and
that such exceptions should be held to a minimum and be
subject to confrontation, justification, and negotiation.
They have agreed to make special efforts to reduce tariffs
on items of interest to less developed countries and not to
ask full reciprocity from these countries in return. And
they have agreed that the negotiations must cover nontariff barriers as well as tariffs, and that to be satisfactory
the final agreement must contain adequate commitments
on agricultural as well as industrial products.

The phase of actual tariff bargaining through the exchange of exceptions lists has now gotten under way despite
previous differences on the issue of tariff "disparities." Although the average height of the Common Market's external tariff and that of the United States are both in the
10–12 per cent range, the United States tends to have more

very high and very low rates. The Common Market countries have argued that the rigid application of a 50 per cent reduction in cases where the U.S. tariff is now substantially higher might leave the U.S. with an effective degree of protection while permitting a significant increase of imports in the Common Market from the United States. No rule has been agreed on to cover tariff disparities, and the possibility exists that the Common Market countries will seek to make lesser tariff cuts than the United States on items where they believe disparities exist.

The main problem facing the negotiators, of course, concerns agricultural products. The revolution in farm technology has brought to Europe some of the same problems that have long beset the United States. To deal with farm surpluses and to assure acceptable levels of farm income, the members of the Common Market have been developing a common agricultural policy. Its basic elements are domestic price supports for farm commodities, and variable levies on the imports of these same commodities from outside the Common Market—levies designed to make up the difference between the world market price and the domestic support price. In the face of this development, the United States and other countries have insisted on assurances that they not only will be able to maintain past levels of farm exports to Common Market countries, but will share fairly in the growth of Common Market farm consumption. United States negotiators have said that the conclusion of any bargain on industrial items is contingent on the successful resolution of the agricultural question. Since their authority to negotiate under the Trade Expansion Act runs out in the summer of 1967, it is clear that the Kennedy Round has reached a decisive phase. The U.S. and the Common Market thus face some difficult decisions that could affect world trade for years to come.

The outcome of these issues is still uncertain as of this writing. But one thing is perfectly plain: There would be no hope of resolving them if GATT were not available as a multilateral negotiating forum to bring together the interested parties and to put pressure on countries to find a solution consistent with the interests of all involved.

As a set of rules governing the conduct of commercial policy, GATT is no less important in the current efforts of trade expansion. These trade rules are highly complex, covering no less than seventy closely printed pages of the General Agreement. They are concerned mainly with giving effect to two principles: that trade should be conducted on the basis of nondiscrimination, and that such protection as might be needed for domestic industries should be afforded exclusively through tariffs and not through other restrictive devices. To implement these principles, GATT provides that tariffs and other import restrictions shall be applied equally (subject to certain limited exceptions) to all other contracting parties on a most-favored-nation basis; that internal taxes shall not be applied in place of tariffs to protect domestic industry; and that quantitative restrictions shall be prohibited except where essential to safeguard the balance of payments, domestic programs of agricultural price support, or development programs of less developed countries—and even then shall be applied so far as possible on a limited and nondiscriminatory basis. Other articles deal with transit trade, antidumping duties, customs valuation, customs formalities, marks of origin, subsidies, state trading, customs unions and free trade areas, and the special problems of less developed countries.

The provisions on quantitative restrictions are especially important in the present effort at trade expansion. Quantitative restrictions are a particularly obnoxious form of protection; unlike tariffs, they place an absolute ceiling on the quantity of imports. During the early postwar years, the majority of GATT members were obliged to apply quantitative restrictions for balance-of-payments reasons, thus frustrating in large measure the effect of their tariff concessions. With the success of the Marshall Plan and postwar recovery efforts, these restrictions were gradually removed, leaving the hard core "residual" restrictions serving protectionist purposes. To meet this problem, the members of GATT adopted in 1960 a set of general procedures requiring countries to report such restrictions to GATT and to consult upon the request of any country that considers its interests affected. Where consultations fail to give satisfaction to the complaining country, the Contracting Parties to GATT can be called on to investigate the matter and make recommendations or rulings. In appropriate circumstances they can even authorize the complaining country to suspend tariff or other concessions made to the offending country. Through use of this consultation procedure, the United States has secured removal of quantitative restrictions by France and Italy that impaired market access for U.S. products.

The GATT provisions on regional arrangements have also assumed a special importance. Customs unions, in which participating states entirely eliminate their internal barriers and adopt a common trade policy toward the outside world, have long been acknowledged as an exception to the principle of nondiscrimination contained in the most-favored-nation clause. GATT also recognizes the desirability of these regional arrangements as an exception to nondiscrimination—as it does with free trade areas in which the participating countries remove restrictions among themselves but follow independent policies toward outsiders—provided that the participating countries eliminate restrictions on substantially all trade among themselves, and that their external tariffs and other trade restrictions are not on the whole higher or more restrictive than the general incidence of those that previously applied. In accordance with these and other GATT requirements, the European Economic Community, the European Free Trade Association, the Latin American Free

Trade Association, and other regional arrangements have been subjected to close and continuing scrutiny by the Contracting Parties. This scrutiny has not succeeded in giving full satisfaction to nonparticipating countries, but GATT has provided an opportunity for consistent pressure by the United States and other countries to influence the Common Market and other regional arrangements in an outward-looking direction.

As an instrument for interpreting the trade rules and adjusting trade differences, GATT has developed a competence vital to the stability of trade relations. Under the administrative provisions of GATT, any contracting party may bring a complaint when it considers that a benefit to which it is entitled is being nullified or impaired, or that the attainment of any objective of the General Agreement is being impeded. If consultations with the interested parties yield no satisfactory result, the Contracting Parties as a group can be asked to carry out an investigation and make a recommendation or ruling. For this purpose, GATT usually employs conciliation panels of experts from member countries with no direct interest in the matter. Over the years, the decisions of the Contracting Parties about the consistency of national policies with GATT provisions have built up an impressive body of case law in the field of commercial policy.

These procedures have given additional precision to the trade rules embodied in GATT and have clarified the border line between permissible and impermissible trade practices. They have made trade policy more stable and predictable. They have provided means of recourse to countries adversely affected by illegal trade practices. Under a bilateral trade agreement, a party with a valid grievance is left to the tender mercies of the other interested party; failing an adjustment of differences, it can retaliate only at the risk of provoking retaliation in return. Under GATT, a party with a valid grievance can have its case confirmed by a disinterested conciliation panel and a ruling made in its favor by the Contracting Parties as a whole. The offending party would then be asked by the Contracting Parties to withdraw the measure in question or to compensate the aggrieved party by providing some other concession of equivalent value in trade terms. If the aggrieved party does not receive this satisfaction, the Contracting Parties may authorize it to withdraw concessions deemed appropriate in the circumstances.

One of the most publicized uses of GATT's administrative provisions occurred during the famous "chicken war" between the United States and the Common Market, arising out of actions by the Federal Republic of Germany. With the application of the new variable levy system of the Common Market on certain farm products in July, 1962, the Federal Republic increased its duties on U.S. poultry exports from 4.9 to 13.4 cents per pound. This action impaired previous rights that had been granted to the United States in GATT negotiations. U.S. representations to the European Economic Community and the German Government produced only an insignificant reduction in the new levy. In November, 1963, the U.S. and the EEC jointly submitted the dispute to a GATT panel for an advisory opinion. The panel decided that $26 million worth of U.S. exports of poultry to West Germany were involved. On the basis of this valuation, the United States then proceeded to withdraw an equivalent amount of concessions from the Common Market as of January, 1964, on potato starch, brandy, dextrine and other starches, and small trucks.

The use of GATT in the "chicken war" did not produce the primary objective sought by the United States—the removal of the offending restrictions. Its contribution to the cause of trade promotion was indirect: The authorization to the U.S. to withdraw an equivalent amount of concessions served notice on the Common Market of the consequences of protectionist action. It thus had a deterrent value.

On other occasions, GATT's administrative procedures have served their primary purpose in removing restrictions. Many of these cases resulted in the removal of barriers to American exports. In recent years, for example:

Austria removed import controls in 1963–64 on a number of items of interest to the United States, including purified and cottonseed oil; certain prepared vegetables and fruits; macaroni, spaghetti, and similar products; coin-operated phonographs; and paper stationery and other paperboard products.

Great Britain removed restrictions in March, 1964, against U.S. citrus, specifically frozen orange concentrate.

France agreed to enlarge its quotas on U.S. fruits and vegetables in the spring of 1964 after a GATT conciliation panel found that these restrictions were no longer justified for balance-of-payments reasons.

The Federal Republic of Germany agreed in 1963–64 to reduce restrictions on U.S. leather and remove restrictions on canned apricots, asparagus, and beans.

Canada, in compliance with a 1962 GATT decision, eliminated import surcharges it had imposed earlier for balance-of-payments reasons, which had affected $1.8 billion of U.S. exports to Canada.

Italy removed most of its remaining restrictions after December, 1962, on products of trade interest to the United States in response to a formal complaint by the U.S.

GATT's administrative provisions, of course, do not work in just one direction. They have been invoked against the United States when it has strayed from the path of trade expansion. In 1952, for instance, the Netherlands was authorized to withdraw concessions from us on exports of wheat flour in return for our imposition of quotas on dairy products. GATT serves as a continuing reminder to the United States that, despite the Trade Expansion Act, its generally liberal trade philosophy is not consistently applied in practice.

GATT's procedures for the settlement of trade disputes provide additional assurance that the commitments resulting from the Kennedy Round will not be lightly frustrated by participating countries. The process of controlled reprisal embodied in these procedures serves as an important discipline on protectionist tendencies and reinforces the trend toward liberal trade. It strengthens the hand of leaders in every country who wish to contain protectionist demands from import-competing industries, for these leaders can now point with certainty to the adverse consequences for export industries that would inevitably result from acceptance of such demands. This process of neutralizing protectionist pressures with countervailing export pressures forces leaders to take account of interests other than those of particularly vocal groups.

But the countervailing interests of import-competing and export industries are not all that have to be considered in the fashioning of trade policies. As emphasized earlier, every citizen has interests in the economic gains from international trade and the political gains from closer economic cooperation. Unfortunately, these interests do not always have a forceful constituency. GATT helps to substitute for that constituency. It permits leaders of nations to oppose restrictive practices on the grounds that they violate a multilateral agreement.

Eric Wyndham White, GATT's Director General, likes to tell of a visit with the foreign trade minister of a leading GATT member. In the presence of numerous trade officials, the minister criticized GATT at length for preventing him from taking various actions ardently advocated by important domestic groups. The minister seemed somewhat shaken when Wyndham White assured him that none of the actions he proposed was actually a violation of the GATT rules. After the meeting had concluded, he took Wyndham White aside and whispered: "Why on earth did you have to say that? I don't really want to do those things anyway!" GATT's administrative procedures are no proof against protection, but they do provide a handle to government leaders who "really don't want to do" things that would impede pursuit of the general welfare.

As a vehicle for developing and articulating new trade policy, GATT has only recently come into its own. Perhaps the best example of this is in the special measures it has encouraged dealing with trade problems of the developing countries. As already indicated, the Contracting Parties have agreed to give the less developed countries special consideration in the Kennedy Round negotiations. Beyond this, they have adopted a new GATT Chapter codifying the various forms of special treatment which are to be accorded to the less developed countries. They have established a center to provide these countries with trade information and trade promotion services. They have initiated studies of the trade aspects of specific national development plans.

Perhaps the most significant single step which GATT has taken to help the developing countries was the adoption of the Program of Action, in May, 1963. With some qualifications, this program was supported by the United States and most other industrial countries in GATT, with the notable exception of the members of the Common Market. It calls for: (1) a freeze on new tariff or nontariff barriers applicable to products of particular interest to less developed countries; (2) elimination of quantitative restrictions that are inconsistent with GATT provisions on imports from these countries; (3) duty-free entry on tropical products; (4) elimination of tariffs on primary products important to the trade of less developed countries; (5) reduction and even elimination of tariffs on semiprocessed and processed products from less developed countries; (6) elimination of internal charges and revenue duties on products wholly or mainly produced in less developed countries.

Under the Action Program, all the industrialized countries maintaining these barriers make annual reports to the GATT secretariat on what they have done to implement these decisions and what additional measures they propose in the future. And the GATT members as a whole continue to give urgent consideration to the adoption of other appropriate measures to facilitate the efforts of less developed countries to diversify their economies, strengthen their export capacity, and increase their earnings from overseas sales.

GATT has sometimes been described as a "rich man's club." This description never fit particularly well, since several important less developed countries were members from the beginning. It certainly does not fit at all today. In recent years, the newly independent nations have entered GATT in force. As a result, they now outnumber the developed countries in GATT by more than two to one. Their nationals play an increasingly important role in GATT meetings and in the secretariat. They will almost certainly have an important influence on GATT's future, pushing it toward further actions designed to deal with their special trade problems.

For most of the twenty years since the founding of the United Nations, GATT has been the focus of multilateral cooperation in the field of trade. But when GATT inaugurated the Kennedy Round in May, 1964, it had to share the spotlight with another meeting on world trade, the United Nations Conference on Trade and Development. The simultaneous occurrence of these two meetings in Geneva was a sign that the special trading needs of the developing countries would henceforth receive equal attention with the general assault on trade barriers.

UNCTAD, as it came to be known by trade officials around the world, was called by the Economic and Social Council at the initiative of the less developed countries, which had prepared for it diligently in meetings of U.N. regional commissions and special caucuses in Latin America, Africa, and Asia. They described the meeting as the most important international conference since the San Francisco Conference that produced the United Nations Charter, and as "a significant step towards creating a new and just world economic order." * Whether it lived up to that billing will be long debated, but by any measure it was certainly the biggest international conference ever held, involving 2,000 delegates from 119 countries and lasting nearly three months.

The central purpose of UNCTAD, as defined by the developing countries and articulated by its Secretary General, Raul Prebisch, was to consider ways of bridging the gap between what the developing countries will need in foreign exchange to finance their import requirements for development and what they are likely to earn in foreign exchange from exports of goods and services. Prebisch estimated in his report to UNCTAD that by 1970 this gap would reach $20 billion a year, assuming imports sufficient to support the 5 per cent annual growth target for national income laid down by the United Nations for the Decade of Development. Even if half of this gap could be filled by foreign aid, he estimated, it would still leave about $10 billion that would have to be financed through increased exports by the less developed countries. He drew up the following balance sheet for these countries in 1970:

* Joint Declaration of the Seventy-Seven Developing Countries Made at the Conclusion of the United Nations Conference on Trade and Development, *UNCTAD Final Act,* E/Conf.46/L.28, Annex B, p. 2 (June 16, 1964).

Imports (Costs)	$41 billion
Plus Debt Service (Costs)	8 billion
Less Exports (Revenue)	29 billion
Equals Gap	20 billion
Less Foreign Aid	10 billion
Remaining Gap	10 billion

The accuracy of these calculations can be—and has been —challenged. Even assuming a substantial margin of error, however, they have a rhetorical value in calling attention to ominous trends in world trade which must be reversed if satisfactory rates of growth are to be achieved in the world's Southern Hemisphere. From 1950 to 1960, the less developed countries' share of world trade dropped from 30 per cent to 20 per cent; their exports lagged further and further behind their imports. Some of the reasons for these trends are evident. About 90 per cent of the exports of the less developed countries still consists of foodstuffs and raw materials. World demand for these is growing rather slowly due to the switch to synthetics, their low "income elasticity of demand" (demand not very responsive to rising income), protectionist measures in many developed countries, and the developed countries' expanded output of the same products. At the same time, the production of many primary products by less developed countries has risen rapidly. As a result, prices of these products have tended to decline both in absolute terms and in relation to prices of the manufactured goods imported by less developed countries for their economic growth.

The future implications of these facts are clear enough. The exports of less developed countries account for three times the foreign exchange that is provided to them through foreign aid and private investment. The eventual substitution of trade for aid—and the realization of development goals—will require urgent efforts to expand the less developed countries' export earnings.

But UNCTAD was more than an exercise for trade experts; it had a political significance as well. The leaders of the less developed countries are beginning to see that their prospects for increased foreign aid and private investment are limited; they are losing confidence in the possibility of achieving development objectives through existing trade arrangements. Many argue as a consequence that the existing trade rules are rigged against them; that they must be changed to give the less developed countries a larger share of world income as a matter of right. UNCTAD was the great opportunity to press this claim. Indeed, it is perhaps not too much to say that, for the leaders of some of the less developed countries, UNCTAD was the answer to a political gap no less ominous than the trade gap; the gap between the rising demands of their growing populations at home and their ability to meet these demands through existing development efforts. Some sought to transfer responsibility for this gap from the home front to the international trading system—from themselves to the industrial countries. As one delegate put it:

> In this conference, we all should seek to advance the attainment of collective economic security under which developing countries can fully exercise their rights to develop. If, to this day, these rights have in fact been denied us, it is due, to a large extent, to the actions and omissions of the developed countries.

A frequent refrain at UNCTAD was that the less developed countries are being "exploited" in the world economy today much as the working classes were "exploited" under nineteenth-century capitalism. The less developed countries did more than draw this analogy; they acted upon it. They formed a "trade union" to assert their claims and enhance their bargaining power. The seventy-five (later seventy-seven) less developed countries caucused together, negotiated through common spokesmen, and voted as a bloc. They themselves rightly described this unity as "the outstanding feature of the entire conference and an event of historic significance." * It made UNCTAD the first major international conference in recent history in which the East-West confrontation was submerged by the North-South confrontation.

This new alignment of forces posed special problems not only for the industrial countries of the free world but also for the Soviet Union. One shrewd observer aptly summarized the Soviet dilemma: "The Soviet Union qualifies as rich in the eyes of the poor, but not rich enough to have been interesting in this conference." And so it was: The Soviet Union suffered the double discomfort at UNCTAD of being on the receiving end of the less developed countries' demands and of having so little to offer that it was largely ignored. Soviet generalities and propaganda claims failed repeatedly to make an impression. For example, when the Soviet delegate offered to eliminate all Soviet tariffs on imports from the developing countries, the gesture was quickly recognized as having only limited meaning, since tariffs do not significantly affect the planned imports of the Soviet foreign trade monopoly. The Soviet Union was willing to make few commitments of practical interest to the less developed countries. For example, it was not prepared to commit itself to reduce the large margins between the prices at which tropical products are imported into the Soviet Union and the prices at which they are sold to the Soviet people, or to free less developed countries from its rigid bilateralism in foreign trade by paying for imports in convertible currencies.

The less developed countries recognized that the Soviet Union was not prepared to offer trade commitments comparable to those in the GATT Action Program. They acted on that recognition—and on the realization that their exports to the free-world industrial countries are

* *Ibid.*

more than twelve times their exports to the Communist bloc. They concentrated their attention on the West. This was true to such an extent that the Soviet Union was left out of the negotiations that produced the basic resolutions embodied in the Final Act. When these resolutions emerged from the negotiations between the less developed countries and the Western countries in the closing days, the Soviet delegation called a hasty press conference to warn the less developed countries not to let the Conference "stick in the mud of an unscrupulous compromise." But in the end there was no alternative for the Soviet Union but to swallow its pride and vote for the resolutions. It was an ironic turn of events for a country that had pressed eagerly for the Conference in the hope of reaping political dividends.

Thus the confrontation at UNCTAD was really not North-South, but West-South. It centered on four areas of controversy. The first was access to markets. Here the less developed countries demanded speedy implementation of the GATT Program of Action. Indeed, they wanted to go beyond it: They asked for the elimination of all forms of protection by the industrial countries on farm products and raw materials that constitute an actual or potential barrier to their exports. And they called for the granting of tariff preferences by the industrial countries for their exports of manufactures and semimanufactures.

This preference issue was one of the most divisive at UNCTAD. It split the industrial countries into different camps. The Common Market countries expressed a willingness to grant on a selective and temporary basis preferences similar to those now granted to the Associated Overseas Territories—which consist mainly of the former French colonies in Africa. The United Kingdom said it was prepared—if other developed countries were willing to do likewise and less developed Commonwealth member states agreed—to extend to all less developed countries alike preferential duty-free or low duty entry into the U.K. market. And the United States declined to support preferences at all, on the grounds that they would not significantly expand developing countries' export earnings; that they would introduce a new element of economic discrimination; that they would tend to foster uneconomic, noncompetitive production; and that they could inhibit the general reduction of trade barriers on a most-favored-nation basis. Under Secretary of State George Ball also pointed out that a series of closed trading arrangements between selected industrial countries and selected less developed countries, of the kind that had emerged with the Common Market, might lead to undesirable political consequences:

> Struggling new nations now enjoying positions of preference and discrimination in metropolitan markets may find it hard to give them up. Yet, most of these nations are aware that special trading relations are likely to carry with them special political, financial and economic relations that will impair their freedom of choice or action. Given the brooding fear of what is loosely called "neo-colonialism," special ties of this kind may be too suggestive of "spheres of influence" to be wholly comfortable.

The second area of controversy at UNCTAD was on commodity policy and how to deal with deterioration in the terms of trade of the developing countries. As expected, the developing countries wanted it agreed that there should be more commodity agreements and that such agreements should be designed not merely to stabilize the prices of their primary product exports, but to raise them in relation to those of their manufactured imports. At the same time, however, they generally recognized the validity of the argument made by the industrial countries that in many cases direct action on prices is not desirable, since it may encourage shifts to synthetics and substitutes, stimulate overproduction, and slow the process of diversification. They therefore endorsed the Prebisch thesis that commodity agreements can contribute in only a limited way to stabilizing and expanding their export earnings, and that the real answer to their commodity problems lies in compensatory financing. They pressed the argument that, even if everything possible is done by way of improved access to markets and price stabilization arrangements in the field of commodity trade, there will still remain a problem of export "losses" due to fluctuations in terms of trade, for which they should be entitled to receive automatic compensatory payments. The industrial countries could not accept the concept of automatic compensation, but they were willing to consider a different measure, discussed below, for dealing with commodity problems in the context of development lending.

The third area of UNCTAD discussion centered on invisibles and finance. Here the less developed countries pressed for ways to reduce their payments for shipping, insurance, and the servicing of foreign debts. They urged new measures to stimulate the flow of private capital, technical assistance, and foreign aid. There were few significant new proposals on these questions that commanded general agreement. But a significant consensus did emerge on supplementary financial measures to help less developed countries faced with falling commodity prices. It was generally agreed that the measures undertaken by the International Monetary Fund to increase its short-term lending to help less developed countries cope with the consequences of commodity price fluctuations should, if feasible, now be supplemented by new measures of long-term financing—measures that would enable countries to prevent adverse movements of export proceeds from disrupting sound development programs.

The Final Act of UNCTAD embodied agreement on many questions. In some important areas, however, a broad consensus was not achieved. This lent particular significance to the fourth subject of UNCTAD debate—the institutional arrangements through which future work on these questions could be carried on. The proposal pressed by many less developed countries, with the support of the Soviet bloc, was for an International Trade Organization that would eventually absorb GATT and that would drastically revise the present arrangements for the conduct of world trade. This proposal met with the determined opposition of the U.S. and the other industrial countries of the free world. In the end the less developed countries and the Soviet bloc accepted a compromise that placed the new machinery firmly within the existing United Nations structure: a U.N. Conference on Trade and Development, to meet at least once every three years; a fifty-five-nation Trade and Development Board, to meet between sessions of the Conference; and a secretariat within the United Nations Secretariat, to service the new institutions. This machinery, subsequently established by the 19th General Assembly, will focus on the trade and related development problems facing the less developed countries.

The negotiations for these new institutions raised one issue of particular difficulty—the procedures by which the new machinery would operate. In the closing days of UNCTAD there was an encouraging disposition on all sides to reach a consensus on some subjects. But there were also occasions when the voting bloc of seventy-five less developed countries passed resolutions over the opposition of a minority of industrial countries on matters affecting vital economic interests. It was true that these were recommendations only and that any decisions taken by the new machinery would be recommendations only. But the currency of such recommendations would be hopelessly debased if they failed to reflect a substantial consensus among all countries, including the countries that would bear the principal responsibility for implementing them. The anxiety many delegates felt on this score found expression in a joke that made the rounds of UNCTAD in the closing weeks. At the Swiss National Exposition, which had just opened in Lausanne, there was a large and prominent piece of machinery whose parts moved a lot and made a lot of noise, but served no purpose. It soon came to be known at UNCTAD as "the continuing machinery."

This comparison may prove all too accurate unless the new trade machinery operates under ground rules that take adequate account of political realities. The purpose of the new machinery is to influence government policies through persuasion. The process of persuasion is assisted when delegates seek a consensus through conciliation and express that consensus in resolutions. It is not assisted—it may even be set back—by the passage of self-serving resolutions by automatic majorities. Public opinion in the industrial countries cannot fail to react adversely to recommendations that are passed over the opposition of the industrial countries but call for action by them. It is therefore in the interest of all nations—less developed as well as developed —to substitute conciliation for voting on the difficult issues that divide the two groups.

The United States, supported by other developed countries, pressed successfully at UNCTAD for recognition that the new machinery contain procedures "designed to establish a process of conciliation to take place before voting and to provide an adequate basis for the adoption of recommendations with regard to proposals of a specific nature for action substantially affecting the economic or financial interests of particular countries." These procedures were successfully worked out after the UNCTAD Conference by a special committee appointed by the United Nations' Secretary-General.*

The success of the new machinery will be determined not merely by the adequacy of its procedures, but also by

* For a description of these procedures, see the Appendix.

the spirit in which both less developed and developed countries operate within it. Secretary-General U Thant, in a significant statement to the Economic and Social Council shortly after the close of UNCTAD, called on members to think of the United Nations "as an instrument for reconciling differences of opinion and not only as a framework in which they can manifest themselves." If this advice is heeded, the members of the United Nations will see the new trade machinery not as a means for ringing up automatic majorities but as a forum for persuasion and conciliation of differences. As the delegate from the Philippines observed at UNCTAD: "It is an obvious fact that on the basis of simple majority the developing nations can outvote the developed nations at any time. Yet what will it avail . . . to reach decisions by simple majority if the defeated minority includes the very countries from whom concessions are expected?"

Any realistic approach to the trade problems of the less developed countries must recognize the two-sided character of the problem. Undoubtedly the developed countries need to do more to assure that less developed nations can earn increasing amounts of foreign exchange to finance their development. But UNCTAD was a warning that one must not expect too much from this line of action. The problem of exports cannot be divorced from the problem of production. Development can make at least as much of a contribution to trade as trade can to development. A central issue, therefore, is what the less developed countries can and will do for themselves.

The leaders of the less developed countries at UNCTAD had much to say about the gap in living standards between the rich and poor countries, but they will also have to deal with the gap between rich and poor in their own countries if they are to create domestic markets large enough to sustain efficient production. They talked much about restructuring world trade in their favor, but they will also have to face the task of restructuring their domestic economies. This means hard and politically unpalatable decisions on such matters as monetary and fiscal policy, land reform, population growth, the efficient development of human resources, more encouragement of private enterprise, and the elimination of inefficiency and corruption in public administration.

UNCTAD heralds a new era in international organization in the field of trade. Important new institutions will now deal with the trade problems of the developing countries. The United States recognizes its special responsibility to make these institutions live up to the high aspirations that gave them birth. But the responsibility does not rest on any one country alone. The new institutions will be successful only if there is a general recognition of the shared responsibility for making them work. As Harlan Cleveland told the Economic and Social Council in the wake of UNCTAD:

> International cooperation for development will not work if it is conceived as a battleground and set up as an adversary proceeding, a game of "I win—you lose" between haves and have-nots. . . . It would be bad for the developing countries, and bad for international cooperation, if the peoples and parliaments of the developed nations came to believe that recommendations on trade and development matters bearing the U.N. trademark had been produced by an automatic majority of the seventy-five. It would be far better if people in both developed and developing countries came to believe that the U.N. stands for procedures that force both groups to study their common problems in depth, and open their minds to the processes of mutual persuasion. . . .
> Debates in which the industrialized countries attribute the lack of economic growth to internal obstacles in the developing countries, and the developing countries in turn attribute their troubles to commercial restrictions in the industrialized countries, will be worse than useless. But some-

thing useful can and will happen in the new machinery if —so to speak—we all leave the rostrum and move together to the workbench—that is, if we jointly address ourselves to the problem rather than merely addressing ourselves to each other.

Chapter **7**

Solving the Monetary Dilemma

THE GREAT EFFORTS under way to clear the channels of world trade and deal with the special trade problems of the less developed countries cannot succeed if a weak international monetary system forces countries to restrict their foreign trade or painfully deflate their domestic economies. The effective transfer of assistance to developing countries must also be based on a solid foundation of financial cooperation. The pursuit of an expanding world economy demands action in aid, trade, and monetary arrangements. Progress in any one area ultimately depends on progress in the other two.

The central purpose of international financial cooperation is to reconcile international and domestic economic objectives—to reap the gains from free multilateral trade abroad while maintaining full employment, a satisfactory rate of growth, and reasonable price stability at home. The gold standard subordinated the pursuit of domestic expansion to the achievement of multilateral trade. Some modern systems of planned economy sacrifice the achievement of multilateral trade to the pursuit of domestic expansion. Both extremes result in national policies that are not merely self-destructive, but harmful to the welfare of others. To solve the monetary dilemma and promote the achievement of international and domestic objectives in a manner that takes account of the interests of all nations is the central purpose of financial cooperation.

The balance-of-payments problem of the United States has stimulated new concern with the monetary dilemma. Only a few years ago, many people saw an irreversible tendency for the United States to run persistent surpluses in its accounts with the rest of the world. As late as 1957, Sir Geoffrey Crowther, former editor of *The Economist,* proudly reminded a Harvard audience that for twenty years he had preached the doctrine of "a permanent and organic shortage of dollars . . . The more time passes the more convinced do I become that I am right. . . . It is difficult to believe that there can ever have been another case of a country where the demand of the rest of the world for its products was so urgent and its demand for the products of the rest of the world so indifferent." * Suddenly, in the late 1950's, people stopped worrying about a persistent U.S. surplus and started worrying about a persistent U.S. deficit. What had happened?

To some extent, a deterioration had occurred in the U.S. payments situation—there was a sharp increase in gold outflow and foreign dollar holdings. But this could not entirely explain the change in attitude, for the U.S. had been running deficits and losing reserves even during the period of the so-called dollar shortage. In those years, U.S. foreign aid and overseas military spending were regarded as items that balanced what otherwise would have been a substantial surplus of U.S. exports over U.S. imports. They

* *Balance and Imbalance of Payments* (Boston, 1957), pp. 34, 48.

were considered valuable in redistributing the gold and foreign-exchange reserves that had become heavily concentrated in the United States in the war and early postwar years.

By the late 1950's, this view of the U.S. balance of payments had changed. Foreign aid and military spending were now regarded as relatively permanent items necessary to finance the growth and defense of the free world; the redistribution of reserves to the rest of the world had taken place; and the United States faced a resurgent Europe and formidable competition in the world market. At this point the problem changed from how the rest of the world could finance the troublesome U.S. commercial surplus to how the United States could generate a sufficient one to finance payments for free-world growth and defense.

The orderly reduction and elimination of the payments deficit has for some years been a major objective of the United States. The reasons are obvious. During the eight-year period 1958–65, the cumulative U.S. deficit was approximately $23 billion. Part of this deficit was met by running down the U.S. stock of gold from $22 billion to $14 billion; the rest was financed by increases in foreign holdings of dollars and other forms of international lending. Obviously there is a limit to the willingness of foreign countries to increase their dollar holdings and extend credit. There is also a limit on the extent to which the U.S. gold stock can be further depleted—particularly since part of it is required by law as backing for the dollar.* A solution to the payments problem is therefore urgently required to assure the defense of the dollar. This is a matter of concern not only to the United States, but to the entire free world, which looks to the dollar as one of its principal means of international payment and as its most important

*The gold cover requirement was reduced by the Congress in 1964, and it can be suspended in accordance with the Federal Reserve Act, but there would be substantial political difficulties in eliminating it entirely.

reserve currency. Trouble for the banker means trouble for his depositor. This is true in any community, and it is true for the free world.

There is no question, of course, about the ability of the United States to close the deficit in its balance of payments. It could strike a balance by drastically curtailing foreign military spending and economic aid, restricting imports and private foreign investment, or painfully deflating its domestic economy. But these measures would solve the U.S. balance-of-payments problem by sacrificing security and prosperity both in the United States and in the entire free world. They would stifle completely the new efforts being made to clear the channels of world trade and accelerate the development of less developed countries. The real question—the most serious current instance of the monetary dilemma—is not whether the U.S. deficit can be eliminated, but how this can be done without sacrificing policies vital to the achievement of our national and international aims.

A large measure of the responsibility for solving its payments problem lies with the United States itself. In recent years, the U.S. Government has attacked the payments drain through a wide variety of national actions: (1) by controlling inflation and stimulating productivity to make U.S. goods more competitive in world markets; (2) by programs to increase exports and foreign tourism in the United States; (3) by reducing military spending abroad and transferring military procurement to the U.S.; (4) by tying aid wherever possible to U.S. products; (5) by an interest equalization tax to discourage the purchase of securities in other industrial countries; and (6) by a voluntary program in which U.S. banks and business firms are asked to limit foreign loans and investments.

These and other essentially national actions have made increasing inroads on the payments deficit. But they cannot solve the problem alone; the cooperation of other countries is also required. This assistance is being provided: (1) by the prepayment of foreign debts owed the United States; (2) by encouraging the use of European capital markets to meet European capital needs and stimulating European investment in the United States; (3) by harmonizing the movement of European interest rates with those in the United States; (4) by eliminating foreign restrictions on U.S. exports; (5) by greater sharing by the industrial countries of the burden of free world aid and military defense; and (6) by developing a new system of monetary arrangements to defend the dollar in all foreign exchange markets.

These measures have been pursued through various forms of cooperation—through actions of the private financial community as well as of governments and central bankers, through bilateral as well as multilateral diplomacy.

Regional action by the North Atlantic countries and Japan has played a special role in building this essential cooperation. The North Atlantic Community accounts for the bulk of the world's trade, aid, and finance; it contains the world's key currencies and the world's principal sources of international credit. Because of these facts the United States has placed particular emphasis on economic and monetary cooperation through key organs of the Organization for Economic Cooperation and Development. The Development Assistance Committee has made important progress in inducing other countries to bear a greater share of the burden of aid to less-developed areas. The Trade Committee has sought to eliminate conflicts in the trade policies of the North Atlantic countries. Perhaps most relevant of all for the U.S. payments problem, the Economic Policy Committee has organized working parties on economic growth and on international payments. Working Party 3, concerned with the latter subject, brings together senior officials from treasuries and central banks every six to eight weeks to consult on national and international monetary policies. Like most other organs of the OECD, Working Party 3 receives little publicity, but it enables national policy-makers to achieve a better appreciation of trends and attitudes in other key countries and thus a better understanding of the likely consequences of future policies. In essence, its purpose is to inform and influence national policy-makers while their ideas are still in the formative stage. In this way, in its work in aid and trade, and in economic policy and finance, OECD has encouraged national policies that contribute to a reduction in the U.S. payments deficit.

At the center of the structure of international financial cooperation, and supplementing national and regional efforts at financial stability, is the International Monetary Fund. The product primarily of Anglo-American negotiations, later mainly a vehicle for a score of developed countries, it now has more than 100 members, including not only every economically advanced country in the free world except Switzerland, but also nearly all of the less-developed countries.

The men who signed the Fund's charter at Bretton Woods more than twenty years ago revolutionized the management of international finance. They had been deeply impressed with the facts of economic interdependence. Hence they were willing to accept unprecedented restraints upon the freedom of action of their own nations and to offer unprecedented facilities to other nations—all, of course, as part of a general financial arrangement whereby others did the same. The Fund's charter reflected their conviction that only by establishing a code of conduct for international monetary affairs, by providing the machinery for continuing consultation and cooperation on financial matters, and by assuring reasonable access to financial resources to meet national foreign-exchange difficulties, would it be possible for nations of the world to avoid the disastrous financial crises of the interwar years and put an end to aggressive, self-centered, and internationally irresponsible financial policies.

In the years since Bretton Woods, the Fund has with growing success discharged four main functions.

First, the Fund is an instrument for the elimination of exchange restrictions and exchange discrimination. As such, it is an indispensable counterpart to the activities of GATT, since the elimination of tariffs and other restrictions on the flow of goods can easily be frustrated by restrictions with equivalent effect upon the flow of payments. When the Fund began operations at the end of World War II, the United States was the only major country not employing exchange restrictions. In succeeding years the Fund presided over gradual steps toward the freeing of exchange restrictions, culminating in the return to convertibility of the principal European currencies in December, 1958. Today, twenty-five countries, which finance the bulk of world trade, have eliminated restrictions on current payments in accordance with the Fund's articles. Other Fund members who are maintaining restrictions—mainly less-developed countries—are obliged to consult regularly with the Fund on steps that can be taken for their gradual elimination. Through its work in eliminating exchange restrictions, the Fund has materially aided the exports of the United States as well as of other countries, and enabled its members to share more fully in the gains from multilateral trade.

Second, the Fund is an instrument for the maintenance of exchange-rate stability. According to the Fund charter, the currencies of members are fixed in terms of gold and in relation to one another. They can only be altered to correct a "fundamental disequilibrium"—a persistent imbalance in international payments resulting from fundamental changes in conditions of supply or demand. Thanks to this aspect of the Fund's activities, substantial changes in exchange rates of major currencies have been comparatively infrequent in recent years; the world has avoided the competitive exchange-rate depreciation that complicated the quest for stability during the interwar period. The resulting regime of fixed exchanges has lent confidence to international trade and investment and contributed to orderly economic growth.

Third, the Fund is an instrument for the provision of international liquidity. It provides a pool of currencies to supplement the individual currency reserves of member nations. A country in temporary exchange difficulty can sell its own currency to the Fund in exchange for another currency that it needs to purchase goods. One of the Fund's great advantages over previous bilateral stabilization loans is that its resources are always available to plug any financial holes that may emerge in the world economy. The Fund has provided its members with over $7 billion of short- and medium-term credits, funds that have given countries time to correct their balance-of-payments deficits without drastic measures of internal deflation or external restriction. Even more important than the actual use of these resources has been the fact that the resources were there. They have served as a contingent stand-by facility, a second line of defense behind national currencies, and a reassuring element in the world economy. Through them, the Fund has made a major contribution to solving the monetary dilemma and has thus implemented one of its primary purposes: "To give confidence to members by making the Fund's resources available to them under adequate safeguards, thus providing them with opportunity to correct maladjustments in their balance of payments without resorting to measures destructive of national or international prosperity."

For many years, the United States looked upon this function of the Fund as a means of transferring to countries needing them the dollars paid in by the United States under its quota. The possibility that the United States itself might find the Fund an important source of assistance in its balance-of-payments problems was scarcely anticipated. But the emergence of the U.S. payments deficit altered the picture significantly. The United States' strong creditor position in the Fund gradually diminished as other countries repaid their dollar drawings of the postwar years. Between 1959 and 1962, the Fund increased its holdings of dollars by about $1 billion, thus absorbing a substantial portion of the U.S. reserve drain and reducing pressure on the dollar. The Fund also sold over $1.5 billion in gold to the United States in order to replenish its dollar holdings and invest in U.S. Treasury bills, thus adding substantially to the U.S. gold stock. And in 1963, the United States requested and received approval for a $500 million stand-by credit—an arrangement that was renewed in 1964. Although the principal purpose of this stand-by arrangement was a technical one—to facilitate repayments to the Fund out of the accumulated reserves of Fund debtors—it demonstrated that the United States is prepared and able to call upon the Fund's resources in appropriate circumstances.

Fourth, the Fund is an instrument for encouraging the domestic adjustments in the economies of member nations that are needed to maintain equilibrium in their international accounts. The Fund's resources for this purpose are limited and available only in the form of three- to five-year loans. This means that a borrowing country must set about to reduce its balance-of-payments deficit by adjusting its domestic economy and its external policies so as to curtail imports, promote exports, and attract capital from abroad. Essentially, the Fund seeks to provide the kind of internal monetary discipline once provided by the gold standard, but in a much more flexible way. Failing such discipline, the Fund's resources would be quickly exhausted, and its essential purposes frustrated. In the words of U.S. Under Secretary of the Treasury Robert Roosa:

> We need liquidity so that economic ills can be cured without the use of shock treatment. We do not need, and cannot successfully use, liquidity to avoid the necessity of a cure. . . . Any consideration of liquidity must proceed hand-in-hand with consideration of ways and means of improving the balance-of-payments adjustment process and making it more efficient.*

To understand just how the Fund encourages the process of adjustment, it is necessary to recall briefly its basic ground rules. The Fund's present total of about $21 billion in resources represents national subscriptions (quotas) of which 25 per cent is normally received in gold and 75 per cent in a member's currency. The Fund Articles provide that a member may not, without a waiver from the Fund, draw more than the equivalent of 25 per cent of its quota in a period of twelve months, or draw beyond the point at which the Fund's holdings of its currency equals 200 per cent of its quota. The 25 per cent limitation has frequently been waived by the Fund, but the 200 per cent limitation has been waived only rarely. Thus the United States could normally draw no more than $1.25 billion a year of its $5 billion quota. Its total borrowings could not, save under most exceptional circumstances, exceed the difference between the amount of dollars in its subscription ($3.75 billion) and 200 per cent of its quota ($10 billion)—in other words, $6.25 billion.

The Fund's policies in dealing with requests to draw put increasing pressure on a member to take corrective measures as it moves away from equilibrium:

1. For a drawing that does not raise the Fund's holdings of a member's currency above 100 per cent of its quota (e.g., a drawing that makes a member a net debtor in the

* Address to the American Bankers Association, Vienna, May 21, 1964.

Fund only in an amount equal to its gold subscription), a member has virtually automatic access to Fund assistance. This drawing right is known as the "gold tranche."

2. For a drawing that does not raise the Fund's holdings of a member's currency above 125 per cent of quota, the Fund will approve if the member shows that it is making reasonable efforts to deal with its financial problems.

3. For a drawing beyond this point, the Fund requires a substantial justification: evidence that the member has set up a sound program aimed at establishing or maintaining the enduring stability of its currency at a realistic rate of exchange. Such programs of currency stabilization are often worked out by members in consultation with the Fund, and the main commitments to a stabilization program may be formally embodied in the terms on which the Fund approves the member's request to draw.

Through these negotiations with borrowers the Fund has exerted powerful leverage in the direction of sound domestic policies. Its influence has been particularly useful in the case of developing countries that approach the Fund for loans or consult with it periodically about their exchange restrictions. Indeed, its lending function has made a contribution to sound policies in a manner that was not originally foreseen: Fund loans have tended to certify the credit of the borrowing country and have thus made it easier to obtain credit from other sources. In this way, the Fund has become an international arbiter of appropriate domestic policies that qualify a country for external assistance—lending the "Good Housekeeping Seal of Approval" necessary to reassure creditor countries.

Through its technical missions and its periodic consultations with members, the Fund has provided guidance on financial policy and training in financial techniques that have supported the formulation and maintenance of responsible fiscal programs and monetary standards. The existence of a disinterested body like the Fund, willing to assume the responsibility for giving difficult advice, has been of crucial importance to the officials of many countries in overcoming the political and administrative barriers that stand in the way of maintaining moderate financial policies. Moreover, the Fund's assistance to the less developed countries in balance-of-payments difficulties has helped avoid interruptions in their economic development programs and thus reinforced the programs of economic assistance financed by the United States and other industrialized nations.

Substantial as all these accomplishments have been, new challenges lie ahead for the Fund and its members in developing an adequate framework of monetary cooperation. Serious questions have been raised about the adequacy of international liquidity. The persistent U.S. payments deficit, for all its drawbacks, has been a means of pumping additional liquidity into the world's monetary system. As that deficit is eliminated, this source of liquidity will vanish. Will the world then have an adequate supply of cash and credit on which to base new efforts in international trade and development?

Those who see an impending shortage of international liquidity point to the inadequacy of the world's gold supply as a source of future reserves. The ratio of free world gold to annual free world imports was approximately 100 per cent in 1938; it was down to 60 per cent in 1950; it was further reduced to 40 per cent in 1960. With the free world's gold mines adding less than $1 billion a year to the free world's monetary gold stock, compared with annual increases of imports of $7–8 billion, gold as a ratio of annual imports will be about 25 per cent in 1970.

Of course, gold alone is not an adequate measure of international liquidity. Reserves in foreign exchange amounted to 17.5 per cent of world imports in 1960. In addition, bilateral and multilateral credit facilities provide considerable flexibility in financing imbalances. For this and other reasons, there is no particular fixed ratio of reserves to import trade, or any other simple ratio, that provides a definitive guide to the optimum level of reserves. The amplitude and duration of imbalances, for example, is one of the main determinants, and no one can now be sure how these imbalances would develop if the continuing U.S. payments deficit were eliminated.

There does remain, however, the central question as to how to supplement the relative shrinkage of gold and dollar reserves that seems likely in the years ahead. The United States and the other principal financial countries of the free world have ruled out any increase in the price of gold or any abandonment of fixed exchange rates, both of which would break faith with the world's dollar holders and undermine confidence in the dollar as a reserve currency. This means that some source of liquidity other than the use of reserve currencies may need to be found to supplement gold.

So far the free world has supplemented gold in a number of ways. It has increasingly used national currencies as reserves, mainly the dollar and sterling. But as suggested earlier, the piling up of liquid claims against the two key currency countries cannot go on indefinitely.

The free world has also resorted increasingly to the International Monetary Fund, whose quotas were increased in 1959–60 and 1964–65 to reach the present $22 billion total. This $22 billion includes not only $4.6 billion in gold assets, but $11 billion in dollars, sterling, and other convertible currencies which can be used to bolster international liquidity. Moreover, its resources were significantly strengthened in 1962 when the Fund entered into an arrangement with ten major industrial countries, the so-called Group of Ten, by which a further $6 billion of convertible currencies has been made available to it. The Fund has also adopted more flexible procedures about access to its resources—such as the compensatory finance arrangements designed to help countries in temporary difficulty due to fluctuations in commodity prices.

These multilateral facilities have been further supplemented by a network of bilateral credit arrangements. The United States has negotiated bilateral swap facilities between the Federal Reserve and other central banks and arranged for the issuance by the U.S. Treasury of foreign currency bonds. These arrangements have provided the U.S. and the other participants with a substantial amount of additional liquidity.

There are two extreme views about what is to be done next. At one extreme are those who oppose any further measures to increase liquidity. They believe existing arrangements have already increased liquidity too much and have dangerously weakened the discipline that should be operating on the United States and other countries to take the measures necessary to balance their international accounts.

At the other extreme are those who believe that revolutionary measures must be taken soon to avoid a grave liquidity shortage which could destroy the liberal policies on trade, aid, and finance vital to the success of the Development Decade. The most ambitious proposal advanced by the protagonists of this viewpoint is for the transformation of the International Monetary Fund into a world central bank. Under this proposal, countries would no longer hold reserves in dollars or sterling but would deposit their holdings of these currencies in the bank, together with a portion of their gold reserves. The bank would give its members credit facilities in return for their deposits, and would be empowered to create additional credit in amounts to be determined in advance by international agreement to meet the needs of an expanding world economy.

Two studies of liquidity completed in 1964—one by the staff of the International Monetary Fund, the other by the

Group of Ten—take a middle position between these extremes. They suggest that existing liquidity is about right to maintain an adequate amount of economic expansion and an adequate degree of financial discipline. They suggest that gradual increases in liquidity should be sought through an evolution of existing institutions rather than through a decisive reshaping of the entire system. One of the consequences of these studies was the negotiation launched at the Fund's annual meeting in Tokyo in September, 1964, on a further increase in Fund quotas.

The controversy over liquidity is not merely technical, it is also political. This is not only because those who favor more or less liquidity are making important judgments about the degree to which the world should pursue different objectives of economic policy. The difference is also over how liquidity is to be managed—the degree of emphasis on bilateral and multilateral credit arrangements and the degree of discretion to vest in international authorities. The transformation of the Fund into an international central bank with substantial powers of credit-creation would mean giving an international agency considerable influence over the level of economic activity in member countries and the distribution of world resources. Such a development would imply a degree of integration in the spheres of aid, trade, politics, and defense which the Fund members have not yet demonstrated the willingness to undertake. Pierre-Paul Schweitzer, Managing Director of the International Monetary Fund, may have had these considerations in mind when he remarked:

> I would look forward not to drastic change but rather to continued innovations along the lines presently followed. . . . The implications of greater reliance on international agreements for the creation of liquidity are considerable. It is my belief that such an evolution can best take place through the gradual creation of precedent in a continuing

agency so that adequate assurance is given of the way in which the international authority will be used.*

It is probably too early to say whether the world will be able to meet its requirements for liquidity through a gradual evolution of present institutions or whether a drastic reshaping of the system will eventually be required. But one thing is already clear: Both the industrialized and the less developed countries will require more rather than less monetary cooperation in the future than in the past, and will need increasing access to a centralized source of international liquidity. This means a growing role in the years ahead for the International Monetary Fund as a central element in our strategy for a rapidly expanding world economy.

* Address to the New York Chamber of Commerce, May 5, 1964.

Chapter **8**

The Population Explosion

UNTIL VERY RECENTLY, Western thought has been characterized by an optimistic faith in the inevitability of progress. Despite two terrible wars, the Great Depression, and the revolutionary ferment that is currently shaking our civilization, many of us still cling to the assumption that the human condition is destined to improve as time goes on.

This confident assumption is somewhat undermined by the realization that, despite all the progress of science and technology in recent years, there are more people living in misery and deprivation today than there were at the turn of the century. Of course, there are also more people enjoying adequate living standards. But the increase in the number of people living in poverty has exceeded the increase of everyone else. Whether such a development can be considered progress is, to say the least, an open question.

To be sure, some people cite as evidence of progress the upward trend of aggregate statistics. But progress cannot be measured merely by increases in Gross National Product. The object of economic development is the welfare and dignity of the individual human being. We must concern ourselves not with aggregate statistics but with the progress made in assuring each person a full and satisfactory life: adequate levels of personal consumption, including food and housing, health and education, and satisfaction of those political, cultural, and spiritual needs that are fundamental to all men.

If the condition of the individual, not gross statistics, is to be the measure of our progress, it is absolutely essential that we be concerned with population trends. *So long as we are concerned with the quality of life, we have no choice but to be concerned with the quantity of life.*

There are today some 3 billion people in the world. It required hundreds of thousands of years, from the beginning of life on earth to the beginning of this century, to reach 1.5 billion. Within the last sixty years, we have doubled that number. According to United Nations estimates, we shall double that number again to more than 6 billion by the end of this century.

It is obvious from these statistics that the world's population is not growing merely in absolute numbers. The rate of population growth has increased at an extraordinary pace. The annual growth rate has doubled from 1 per cent in 1945—itself an unprecedented high in history—to almost 2 per cent today. It is expected to go even higher. But even if the present growth rate of world population is maintained, the numbers we have to contemplate are staggering.

Whether the growth of world population continues at its present rate, whether a reduction in that rate is brought about by increases in the death rate or decreases in the birth rate, and whether, to reduce the birth rate, measures are found that are consistent with the economic, cultural, and religious circumstances of individual countries—these are all questions of paramount importance.

These questions have particular urgency for the less developed countries. For reasons that are well known, the rate of population growth tends to be higher in these countries than in the developed countries—about 70 per cent higher on the average. About 80 per cent of the one-half billion growth in world population in the last decade took place in the less developed areas. In the years ahead, the highest rates of growth are likely to continue to be in these areas. It is estimated, for example, that, if present rates of growth continue until the year 2000, the population of North America will increase from 200 to 300 million, while the population of South and Central America would grow from some 200 to 600 million.

It is bad enough that less developed countries tend to have a higher rate of population growth than developed countries. But the problem is compounded further by the fact that the less developed countries are less able to cope with the consequences of rapid population growth. The problem for developed countries is to increase already high per-capita income levels and to devote increasing portions of already large national savings to services such as medical care, education, and housing. But less developed countries whose people live at subsistence level may be able to save little or nothing for improvements in their social infrastructure.

It is all that many of the developing countries can do to enlarge the total economic product as fast as the added people. Yet they must provide not merely additional facilities for the increased population, they must create new and adequate facilities for the existing population as well.

For newly developing countries, the problem of population growth is not, as some people think, the problem of avoiding starvation or finding standing room. It is the problem of finding sufficient savings after current consumption needs are met to assure a tolerable rate of progress toward modernization and higher standards of living based on self-sustaining economic growth.

The General Assembly, as noted earlier, has set as its goal for the United Nations Development Decade the achievement by 1970 of an annual growth rate of 5 per cent a year in aggregate national income in the developing countries. The achievement of this goal will require enormous effort. It has been estimated that, in the 1950's, the developing countries over-all had an annual growth rate of 3 per cent and an annual population increase of 2 per cent, with annual per-capita increases in income of 1 per cent. Making the generally accepted assumption of a capital-output ratio of three to one, these countries will have to increase their savings and investment from 9 to 15 per cent of their Gross National Product to achieve the goals of the Development Decade. This is obviously a formidable task at present levels of population growth.

Assuming that the goals of the Development Decade are achieved, prospective increases in population will greatly dilute the impact of over-all increases in income on individual levels of welfare. For example, gradual progress toward the 5 per cent annual growth goal during the Development Decade would by the end of this decade increase a $100 per capita income to $123 in a country with a 2 per cent rate of population growth and $111 in a country with a 3 per cent rate of population growth.

Obviously, there is much that we do not know about the relationship of population growth to economic and social development. But from an examination of these and other facts, one conclusion seems inescapable: Existing rates of population growth in certain less developed countries make it virtually impossible at the present time, even with maximum external assistance and maximum self-help, to bring about a rate of economic growth that will provide the rate of improvement in individual living standards that these countries seek to attain and that, more fundamentally, is essential to the proper exercise of the individual's human faculties.

Unfortunately, population growth in the future is predetermined to a large extent by the population growth of the past. Thanks to the rapid increase of recent years, children under fifteen years of age account for about 40 per cent of total population in less developed countries. When this group passes through the child-bearing years, population increase will be substantial, even if family size falls. Moreover, further reductions in mortality rates can be expected, as the benefits of modern science and technology are brought increasingly to the developing nations. For these reasons, and because appropriate measures to reduce the birth rate in different countries may take time to discover and carry out, it may be some years before significant reductions take place in rates of population growth. And even if growth rates fall, we shall have to learn to live, during this century at least, with continuous large increases in world population.

Thus, measures to deal with the population problem can be no substitute for economic assistance and other measures to accelerate the economic development of less developed countries. Nor will they alter the demographic facts of life easily or speedily. But what is done in the next few years about the population problem can make the difference between rates of population growth that are compatible with substantial material progress and those that spell certain misery for the majority of the world's people.

December 18, 1962, marked a turning point in the recognition by the international community of the world population problem. On that day, the United Nations General Assembly concluded the first debate in its history devoted entirely to the subject of population. It adopted, with sixty-nine affirmative votes (including that of the

United States), twenty-seven abstentions, and not a single negative vote, a major resolution calling for an intensified program of international cooperation in the field of population.

Except for the members of the Soviet bloc, all of whom abstained, countries of every major political, economic, cultural, religious, and geographic identification were among those voting in the affirmative. In the presence of an issue of such incalculable importance to the future of mankind, the divisions that characterize so many debates on international problems dissolved, giving way to a broad consensus on the importance of the population problem.

While the Resolution on Population Growth and Economic Development was the first of its kind ever passed by the General Assembly, the United Nations had not previously been inactive in the population field. It already had:

—established a population unit in the Secretariat (now the Population Branch of the Bureau of Social Affairs).

—created the Population Commission, a group of government representatives meeting once every two years.

—held a World Population Conference under U.N. auspices in 1954.

—encouraged Regional Economic Commissions located in the less developed areas—the Economic Commission for Asia and the Far East, the Economic Commission for Latin America, and the Economic Commission for Africa—to become more active in the population field.

—and organized Regional Demographic Research and Training Centers in Bombay, Santiago, and Cairo, to provide advisory services to countries of the Asian, Latin American, and African regions.

Through activities such as these, the United Nations has been making a major contribution to an understanding of the population problem. It has encouraged and assisted member governments to obtain factual information on the size, composition, and trends of their populations and the interrelation between population growth and economic and social development. It has helped develop a whole range of skills in the demographic field—in census-taking, population projections, and economic analysis. And it has promoted a full and responsible exchange of ideas on all aspects of the population problem.

These United Nations contributions should not be underestimated. When the Population Commission met for the first time in 1947, demographic statistics, including census and vital statistics, were so incomplete that it was scarcely possible to speak knowledgeably of *world* population trends or *world* population problems. It is easy to overlook the fact that if it were not for the devoted labors of the population and statistical sections of the U.N. Secretariat, both operating under the guidance of the Population and Statistical Commissions, we should not be able even now to discern the outlines of the *world* population problem or the problems of most major regions.

Many years of slow and careful accumulation of basic factual information helped to lay the groundwork for enlightened consideration of the economic and social implications of population trends. Building on this solid record of achievement, the General Assembly Resolution on Population Growth and Economic Development was designed to increase the level of U.N. involvement in the population field. The resolution called for action under five main heads:

First, the Secretary-General was requested to conduct an "inquiry" among member states "concerning the particular problems confronting them as a result of the reciprocal action of economic development and population changes." This inquiry has helped to focus the attention of responsible officials in all countries on the implications of population trends for economic and social planning, to open up channels of communication between policy makers and local demographic experts, and to encourage governments without competent experts of their own to seek outside assistance. Such assistance is available not only from the United Nations but from various foreign governments and private institutions—in the case of the U.S., from the Agency for International Development, the U.S. Census Bureau, the Ford Foundation, and the Population Council.

Second, the Economic and Social Council of the United Nations was asked, in cooperation with the Specialized Agencies, Regional Economic Commissions, and the Population Commission to "intensify its studies and research on the interrelationship of population growth and economic and social development with particular reference to the needs of the developing countries for investment in health and educational facilities." This directive requires not only a substantial increase in the work program of the population section at U.N. headquarters, the demographic staffs of the Regional Economic Commissions, and the Regional Demographic Research and Training Centers, but also correlative studies of problems in education and public health conducted in cooperation with UNESCO and the World Health Organization.

Third, the Economic and Social Council was directed to report its findings with respect to all of the foregoing to the General Assembly, not later than at the Assembly's 19th session in 1964.

Fourth, United Nations agencies were asked to encourage and assist governments, especially of the less developed countries, "in obtaining basic data and carrying out essential studies of the demographic aspects as well as other aspects of their economic and social development problems."

Fifth, the World Population Conference scheduled for 1965 was requested to "pay special attention to the interrelationships of population growth with economic and social development particularly in countries that are less developed."

Although this Resolution was approved with no negative votes, a good deal of controversy developed over another section, not included in the Resolution as finally adopted, which read: "that the United Nations give technical assistance as requested by governments for national projects and programs dealing with the problems of population." This section was widely interpreted as calling for United Nations technical assistance in the actual implementation of family-planning programs. It was approved by a narrow margin in Committee but in the Plenary, where a two-thirds majority is required on important questions, it failed of adoption by a vote of thirty-four in favor, thirty-four against, with thirty-two abstentions. As a practical matter, however, the defeat of this paragraph did not alter the authority the United Nations already possessed as a result of previous resolutions of the General Assembly and of the Economic and Social Council to grant technical assistance upon request to member nations.

The momentum generated by the General Assembly Resolution was maintained at subsequent meetings of the United Nations. A Resolution on Intensification of Demographic Studies, Research, and Training—introduced by the United States in association with Japan and the United Arab Republic—was unanimously adopted by the Population Commission in February, 1963, and by the Economic and Social Council in April, 1963. This Resolution spelled out some of the practical implications of the General Assembly Resolution and contained other important provisions as well. Among other things, it invited the Regional Economic Commissions to intensify their demographic work; urged the U.N. to accelerate preparation of technical manuals for use in demographic work, hasten revision of certain basic demographic publications, and study the use of electronic computers in the analysis of demographic data; and requested adequate budgetary provision for this and other work. It also urged the developed countries to "consider the value to the developing countries" of initiating or expanding research on the interrelationship between population trends and economic and social development; of training experts in the less developed countries in demography and statistics; and of providing technical assistance to the developing countries in census-taking, the compilation of vital statistics, and the utilization of demographic data in social and economic planning.

Following the passage of the General Assembly Resolution, the U.N. Secretariat also began work on the inquiry to member governments. This inquiry took the form of a questionnaire that was sent to each member of the United Nations or of the Specialized Agencies. When the answers were compiled, analyzed, and laid before the Economic and Social Council and the General Assembly in 1964, the United Nations had before it the most complete information ever assembled on the attitudes and policies of governments on the population problem. The United States reply to the U.N. inquiry, prepared under the direction of the President's Council of Economic Advisers, was the first comprehensive look at the nature and implications of U.S. population trends in more than twenty-five years.

The debate in the General Assembly that preceded the passage of the Resolution on Population Growth and Economic Development provided a striking illustration of the unique value of the United Nations as an international forum. Four principal viewpoints emerged:

The first viewpoint was represented by the Government of Sweden and the other sponsors of the resolution—Ceylon, Denmark, Ghana, Greece, Nepal, Norway, Pakistan, Tunisia, Turkey, Uganda, and the United Arab Republic. These twelve nations argued that population growth posed grave problems for economic and social development and that urgent action was required to deal with it. They advocated a major increase in United Nations activity in the population field—including technical assistance in the field of family planning. Support for this viewpoint was expressed by most Moslem countries (e.g., United Arab Republic, Tunisia, Turkey, and Pakistan), some countries of Asia (e.g., India, Nepal, Thailand, Malaya, and Japan) and some countries of Africa (e.g., Ghana, Guinea, and Uganda). This viewpoint found only scattered support in Latin America.

A second viewpoint was advanced by Argentina and Ireland, with support from a few other countries, principally in Latin America. These countries questioned the existence of a population problem, challenged the right of the United Nations to discuss it, and were particularly outspoken in opposing a U.N. program in family planning financed from technical-assistance funds to which they were contributing.

A third viewpoint—expressed by a substantial number of member states including France and other countries of continental Europe, some French African countries, and some Latin American countries—conceded the existence of population problems in some areas but argued that action by the United Nations should be deferred pending further study. They opposed the controversial technical-assistance section and took the initiative in introducing the proposal for an inquiry on member countries' population problems.

A fourth viewpoint was expressed by the members of the Soviet bloc. During the General Assembly debate, the Soviet Union and some of the Eastern European countries expounded the traditional Communist position that Western discussions of the population problem were based on "neo-Malthusian fallacies" and that population problems ceased to exist under Communism. This Communist line was poorly received by the Assembly. At least one representative of a less developed country chided the Soviets for favoring planning in all sectors of economic life except the human sector—the one most important in its implications for economic and social growth.

The negative Soviet statement in the population debate was followed by a significant shift in the Communist line. When it came time to vote, the Soviet bloc did not oppose, but merely abstained on, the General Assembly Resolution. What is even more surprising, the Soviet representative at the subsequent meeting of the Economic and Social Council commended the United Nations for its population work, agreed that population growth is an urgent problem for less developed countries, and announced the willingness of the Soviet Union to provide technical assistance in the population field.

This change in the Soviet position in the United Nations on the population problem followed reports of the increasing resort within the Soviet Union and some other bloc countries in recent years to birth control and abortion and of Khrushchev's personal interest in a U.S. publication stressing the economic dangers of overpopulation.

The recent discussions at the United Nations may signal a new Soviet line on the subject of population. Whether because of internal problems, or a desire to cultivate the favor of less developed countries, or both, the Soviet Union may now be ready to exercise leadership in action programs concerned with the population problem.

What role did the United States play in the United Nations debate? It made a strong statement underlining the importance of the population problem, the need for more knowledge about it, the necessity for each country to determine its own population policy in accordance with its economic, social, cultural, and religious circumstances, and the willingness of the United States to "help other countries, upon request, to find potential sources of information and assistance on ways and means of dealing with population problems." It expressed support for the Resolution on Population Growth and Economic Development in its original form, which included the controversial section on technical assistance. It abstained, however, in the separate vote on this section, first, because it was superfluous, neither adding to nor subtracting from the authority already possessed by the United Nations to grant technical assistance upon request to member nations; second, because it was not clear from the debate whether technical assistance would involve the actual supply of contraceptive devices, which the United States, for reasons explained below, would not have supported and did not support; and third, because in the light of the differences of opinion among member states expressed during the debate, it seemed best, for the immediate future, to emphasize the three areas in which there appeared to be broad agreement among them—namely, information, training, and discussion on population problems.

The focusing of world opinion on the population problem in the United Nations coincided with a rising tide of public attention on this subject in the United States. Indeed, in the months following the U.N. debate, American public attitudes and American official policy concentrated to an unprecedented degree on the world population problem and on ways and means of dealing with it:

—President Kennedy, in response to a press-conference question, declared that we need to "know more about the whole reproductive cycle" and that this knowledge should then "be made more available to the world."

—The Department of State and the Agency for International Development distributed to embassies and missions overseas the official U.S. policy statement made in the United Nations debate expressing concern about the population problem and the willingness of the United States to provide assistance to other countries upon request.

—The National Institutes of Health issued a report showing 758 projects costing $8.2 million under way in the United States in research relating to fertility control, of which NIH itself was supporting $3.4 million.

—At the World Health Organization Assembly in Geneva, the United States called for more WHO-sponsored research in the medical aspects of human reproduction, and pledged $500,000 to support such a program.

—The Congress adopted an amendment to the foreign-aid bill introduced by Senator J. W. Fulbright of Arkansas authorizing use of AID development research funds "to conduct research into the problems of population growth."

—Two other Senators, Joseph S. Clark of Pennsylvania and Ernest Gruening of Alaska, introduced a Joint Resolution requesting the President "speedily to implement the policies of the United States regarding population growth as declared before the United Nations by inaugurating substantially increased programs of research within the National Institutes of Health and by taking steps to make the results of such research freely available to countries requesting such assistance."

—The House Judiciary Committee's Subcommittee on Immigration and Population held extensive hearings on population trends in the United States and overseas.

—Former Vice President Richard M. Nixon called on the U.S. Government to "take the leadership in cooperation with recipient governments to develop, in conjunction with our foreign aid programs, population control programs which are consistent, to the extent possible, with the religious traditions of the nation involved."

—Former President Dwight D. Eisenhower, who had stated as President in 1959 that "I cannot imagine anything more emphatically a subject that is not proper political or governmental activity or function or responsibility" declared: "As I now look back, it may be that I was carrying that conviction too far. . . . We should tell receiving nations how population growth threatens them and what can be done about it."

—The National Academy of Sciences' Committee on Science and Public Policy, headed by Dr. George Kistiakowsky of Harvard University, former Science Advisor to President Eisenhower, issued a report stating that "international cooperation in studies concerned with voluntary fertility regulation and family planning is highly desirable, and the United States Government should actively participate in fostering such cooperation."

—Dr. John Rock attracted national attention with his book *The Time Has Come,* in which he called for an end to doctrinal controversy and for further research to find family-planning techniques acceptable to all religious groups.

—Georgetown University established a new Center for Population Studies under the direction of Dr. Benedict J. Duffy, and the Harvard University School of Public Health established a Population Institute to encourage an interdisciplinary attack on the population problem.

—The Ford and Rockefeller foundations both significantly expanded their support of research and assistance to other countries in the field of population.

—And the American Assembly of Columbia University held its first session on the population problem, followed by regional Assemblies in other parts of the country.

This list of events, far from exhaustive, adds up to a major break-through in U.S. opinion and policy on the world population problem.

What conclusions can be drawn from the debates on the population problem in the United Nations and the United States? What forms of international cooperation should we be seeking on this subject in the years ahead?

A significant consensus seems to be emerging on the subject of population. This review of the first U.N. debate on the population problem has emphasized the differences between the member countries. Yet, just as recent discussions within the United States have done, this debate also revealed a large measure of common ground.

To begin with, the desire for increased knowledge about population trends—and particularly their relation to economic and social development—is now nearly universal. We have passed, almost without noticing it, from a period in which the great uncertainty concerned the existence of the world population problem, to a period in which the great uncertainty is what can and should be done about it.

Moreover, even in the matter of what should be done about the population problem, there is no significant body of responsible opinion among people of any major religious, ethical, or ideological persuasion that advocates totally unplanned or unregulated fertility, although there are sincere differences of opinion about the means that are morally permissible and the effectiveness of the means that are available. There is also virtually universal agreement, on both ethical and practical grounds, that decisions about responsible parenthood can be made only by individual parents themselves in the light of their responsibilities to their children and their society, and to the moral values that govern alike parents, children, and societies.

The time has come to develop out of this consensus a blueprint for international cooperation that takes account of the politics as well as the economics of the population problem. The fundamental concept in such a blueprint should be the principle of free choice. Despite the growing consensus on the matters already mentioned, differences continue to exist between religious groups on specific methods of family planning. When it comes to the implementation of population policy, the views of all groups should be respected. Obviously, programs of family planning carried out in a particular country require the agreement and support of the government concerned. Fortunately, there are natural and artificial methods for the regulation of pregnancy that are acceptable and appropriate in every culture, creed, and economic level, whether in the developed or the developing countries.

In the pluralistic society of the free world, there is a wide variety of sources of assistance—governments, international organizations, foundations, universities, and even private business firms. All of these have something to contribute to the solution of the population problem. All can make more substantial contributions in the future than they have in the past. What we need is an international division of labor, taking account of the comparative advantage—from the political as well as the economic and technical points of view—of the different sources of potential assistance.

The following is a rough blueprint of a program of international cooperation that the United States has been supporting with respect to the key elements of the population problem:

1. *Information and Analysis.* There is, as noted earlier, a need for more demographic information and analysis, particularly on the interrelation between population growth and economic and social development. Since there is universal agreement that this need exists, all governments and international organizations, as well as private institutions, can help significantly to fill it.

The United States will continue to support the expansion of United Nations activities in the demographic field. The United Nations should be able to help member countries to learn more about their own population trends, particularly in relation to the implications for economic and social development, and to learn more about the attitudes of their people toward marriage, child-rearing, and family size. The United States continues to believe that the U.N.

and its Specialized Agencies such as WHO and UNESCO should be prepared to advise countries upon request on how to transmit information on family planning that is consistent with the cultural and religious values of their people.

Moreover, the Agency for International Development will respond to requests from developing countries for assistance in preparing, executing, and analyzing population censuses, utilizing demographic data and analyses in social and economic planning, and communicating family-planning information to their people. It will do this both by making United States advisers available and by training experts from the developing countries themselves.

2. *Medical Research.* There seems to be widespread agreement on the need for more knowledge about the basic life processes that govern child-bearing. As President Kennedy pointed out, we need to know more about the whole reproductive cycle, and this information should be made more available to the world, so that everyone can make his own judgment.

Paradoxical as it may seem, we need more knowledge on how to overcome both involuntary childlessness and involuntary parenthood through measures that are consistent with different religious, cultural, and economic circumstances. We need particularly a great deal more study of human fertility and reproduction. The United States supports studies to this end through its own National Institutes of Health. Moreover, it supports the conduct of such studies through the United Nations, specifically through the medical research program of the World Health Organization. With the encouragement of the United States, the WHO has made the study of human reproduction a priority item in the program. The U.S. pledge of $500,000 will help the WHO to support national research efforts in the medical aspects of human reproduction where such efforts are currently inadequate and thus to promote the search for family-planning techniques that are acceptable in different national environments.

3. *Health and Social Services.* The major obstacle to the implementation of family-planning policies in the less developed countries is the lack of a network of health and social services at the village level. The development of institutions and personnel in health and social welfare is desirable for its own sake as well as for the implementation of family-planning policies. It commands widespread endorsement and should be the object of intensified efforts by governments and private institutions as well as by United Nations agencies. The Agency for International Development is devoting increasing attention to the training of doctors and auxiliary personnel of developing countries for work in maternal and child health in rural areas.

4. *The Implementation of Family-Planning Programs.* This is the area in which little has been done until recently—and where dramatic changes are now under way.

In the United States, the Federal Government, with what appears to be overwhelming public support, has begun to cooperate with state and local governments and private organizations to make family-planning services and information available to all Americans who wish to have them. This is significant not only for the achievement of the Great Society at home; it is important for American leadership abroad. The United States should not be in a position of asking other countries to do things to limit population growth which it is not prepared to do itself.

In his 1965 State of the Union message, President Johnson gave new impetus to the policy inaugurated by President Kennedy when he pledged to "seek new ways to use our knowledge to help deal with the explosion of world population." With the encouragement of the White House, the Agency for International Development, in March of that year, issued a historic instruction to its overseas missions. The instruction stated that AID would entertain requests for direct U.S. assistance in support of family-planning programs, including technical aid and aid in the form of commodities and U.S.-owned local currencies. It emphasized that freedom of choice should be available in any U.S.-supported program. It indicated that AID would not consider requests for contraceptive devices or equipment for their manufacture, since experience had made clear that the cost of these latter items was not prohibitive for countries developing effective programs.

In November, 1965, President Johnson's International Cooperation Year Committee on Population recommended that the United States be prepared to make available up to $100 million a year to help other countries implement family-planning programs. Shortly thereafter, AID set side $10 millon for this purpose in its program for Fiscal Year 1967 and gave indications that this sum would be doubled the following year and could increase still further in response to foreign requests for assistance. As activity on the world population problem moved from the discussion to the operational phase, it became clear that the principal question was not the availability of U.S. assistance, but, rather, whether all the governments of the developing countries faced with population problems were convinced of the need to deal with them, and whether they could find the administrators, doctors, and health workers to implement family-planning programs on the necessary scale. Fortunately, a growing determination to deal with population problems was clearly evident in countries such as India, Pakistan, Turkey, the United Arab Republic, Tunisia, and Chile.

These developments have had their effect on United Nations agencies. The World Health Assembly has asked its Director-General to provide advisory services to members in support of family-planning programs. The Economic and Social Council has formally requested the Secretary-General to offer "advisory services and training on action programs in population." Even before that request, the U.N. sent an expert mission to India to advise on that country's family-planning program.

In the nuclear age, no race or nation achieves wealth or power through unregulated fertility. This message can best be transmitted by a world organization where responsibility for action is widely shared. In an area of such sensitivity and such significance to the human race as a whole, multilateral cooperation has particular value.

After years of neglect, the nations of the world are moving to cope with the population explosion. The question is whether they will move fast enough. As President Johnson's ICY Population Committee has warned: "Time is of the essence. The rate of growth of world population is so great —its consequences are so grave—that this may be the last generation which has the opportunity to cope with the problem on the basis of free choice."

Chapter **9**

Outer Space:
New Frontier for Cooperation

THE EXPLORATION OF THE WEST has faded from our national consciousness. The exploration of space has replaced it as a challenge for our time. But the assault on this last of mankind's physical frontiers recalls the sense of opportunity, mystery, and adventure that drove men westward across a continent 100 years ago. And like the western frontier, the realm of outer space engenders among its pioneers a spirit of cooperation not found as readily within conventional boundaries.

There are ways, however, in which the twentieth-century venture into outer space differs radically from the eighteenth- and nineteenth-century push westward. Today, the most advanced science and technology have supplanted the covered wagon, the rifle, and the six gun, and complex forms of statecraft have replaced the diplomacy of that earlier time. Most important, the exploration of outer space has widened our frontiers far beyond the boundaries of one continent or one nation. Outer space is not a national experience, but an international, a global one. It is the proper concern of all mankind and thus, inevitably, of the United Nations.

It was President Johnson himself who, as a member of the U.S. Senate, came before the United Nations General Assembly one year after the dawn of the Space Age—on November 17, 1958—to propose the creation of a United Nations *Ad Hoc* Committee on the Peaceful Uses of Outer Space. President Johnson said:

> To keep space as man has found it and to harvest the yield of peace which it promises, we of the United States see one course—and only one—which the nations of earth may intelligently pursue. That is the course of full and complete and immediate cooperation to make the exploration of outer space a joint adventure.

The *Ad Hoc* Committee established at this session of the Assembly prepared a valuable report on the needs and opportunities for cooperation in space exploration and the resources for such cooperation available in the U.N. system. But the desire for cooperation was not yet strong enough to overcome political barriers. A permanent U.N. Committee on Outer Space established in 1959 failed to get off its launching pad and bogged down in arguments with the Soviet Union over composition and procedures. Not until the Space Age was four years old did a United Nations program of cooperation in space get off the ground.

The thrust that finally put the program in orbit was supplied by President Kennedy in his speech at the United Nations on September 25, 1961, when he laid before the 16th General Assembly a four-point program of space cooperation under United Nations auspices. The program called for a regime of law and order in outer space; the promotion of scientific cooperation and the exchange of information; a world-wide undertaking in weather forecasting and weather research; and international cooperation in the establishment of a global system of communication satellites. This program commanded such widespread endorsement that the Soviet Union, after some initial hesitation, decided to co-sponsor the resolution incorporating it, which was adopted unanimously by the General Assembly on December 20, 1961. The United Nations Committee on the Peaceful Uses of Outer Space finally began its work—with the Soviet Union on board.

The U.N. effort thus begun was aided by the network of bilateral arrangements already developed between the United States and other free-world countries. It gained momentum from the exchange of letters between President Kennedy and Premier Khrushchev early in 1962 following the successful orbital flight of Lieutenant Colonel John H. Glenn, Jr. In accordance with this exchange, bilateral conversations began between Dr. Hugh Dryden, Deputy Director of the National Aeronautics and Space Administration, and A. A. Blagonravov of the Soviet Academy of Sciences, culminating in the first agreement on space cooperation between the two countries.

Just what has been accomplished so far in outer-space cooperation through international organizations? How far is cooperation likely to go in the future? To answer these questions, we must take a closer look at the four parts of the program approved by the General Assembly.

The first part of the Resolution adopted at the 1961 Assembly looks to a regime of law and order in outer space on the basis of two fundamental principles:

1. International law, including the United Nations Charter, applies to outer space and celestial bodies.
2. Outer space and celestial bodies are free for exploration and use by all states in conformity with international law and are not subject to national appropriation.

The General Assembly quite rightly did not seek to

define just where air space leaves off and outer space begins. It has been the general view, not challenged by any nation, that satellites so far placed in orbit have been operating in outer space. There are, in addition, powerful practical reasons why the ceiling on sovereign air space within the exclusive unilateral control of underlying states should be a good deal lower than the lowest point reached by orbiting satellites. In both ascent and re-entry, space vehicles follow relatively "flat" flight paths. Unless there is a realistic boundary to the upward limit of national sovereignty, it will be impossible for some nations to get in and out of space without violating the territorial air space of other nations. It is of little value to speak of the freedom of outer space if men cannot travel freely to that realm and back again to earth. But the drawing of a precise boundary at a suitably low level is not a practical proposition at the present time. This task must await further experience and a consensus among nations. To undertake it now might extend the limit of national sovereignty too far upward to the highest common denominator of national altitudes.

The General Assembly Resolution of 1961 takes international law and the U.N. Charter as the standard for space activities. Mankind is thus free to use space on the same basis as it uses the high seas—free of any restraints save those on exclusive use and illegal activity such as aggression. This formula is calculated to promote the maximum exploitation of space technology in the service of human needs. It is designed to prevent space and celestial bodies from being subjected to competing national claims.

The 1961 Resolution, besides laying down two basic legal principles, called upon the Committee on the Peaceful Uses of Outer Space "to study and report on the legal problems which may arise from the exploration and use of outer space." By the time the Legal Subcommittee established for this purpose met in Geneva in May, 1962, three principal subjects had emerged for its future con-

sideration: liability for space vehicle accidents; assistance
to and return of space vehicles and astronauts; and legal
principles to govern the activities of states in the exploration and use of outer space.

The third of these subjects yielded concrete results with
the Declaration of Legal Principles adopted unanimously
by the General Assembly on December 13, 1963. This
Declaration defines the mutual restraints and reciprocal
undertakings that the members of the United Nations are
presently prepared to accept in outer space.

The road toward agreement on this Declaration was not
easy. Throughout 1962 and early 1963, the Soviet Union
had refused to agree on a document containing principles
that all sides could accept, but rather had insisted on a comprehensive legal code along the lines of an earlier Soviet
"Declaration of Basic Principles" that contained a number
of provisions which were totally unacceptable to most
other countries, including the United States. On October
17, 1963, however, the Assembly passed a resolution by ac-
clamation solemnly calling upon all states to refrain from
"placing in orbit around the earth any objects carrying
nuclear weapons or any other kinds of weapons of mass
destruction" and from "installing such weapons on celestial
bodies." This resolution and the limited test ban concluded in August, 1963, served to prohibit an extension of
the nuclear arms race into outer space. Together, they reflected a change in the previous policy of the Soviet Union
to insist on comprehensive agreements on its own terms,
and heralded the agreement on limited common positions
included in the Declaration of Legal Principles.

The Declaration is a significant step in the development
of law for outer space. Drawing upon themes included in
the 1961 Resolution, its first four paragraphs declare:

—that the exploration and use of outer space shall be carried
on for the benefit and in the interests of all mankind.

—that outer space and celestial bodies are free for exploration and use by all states on a basis of equality and in accordance with international law.

—that outer space and celestial bodies are not subject to national appropriation, by claim of sovereignty, by means of use or occupation, or by any other means, and

—that activities of states in the exploration and use of outer space shall be carried on in accordance with international law, including the Charter of the United Nations, in the interest of maintaining international peace and security and promoting international cooperation and understanding.

The Declaration's fifth principle is new. It declares that a state bears international responsibility for its activities and for the activities of its nationals in space, and that space activities carried on by private parties require government authorization and continuing supervision. In the case of an international organization carrying on activities in space, it declares that responsibility for compliance with the principles in the Declaration shall be borne by the international organization and the states participating in it.

The Soviet Union had originally insisted on the principle that space activities be carried out "wholly and exclusively by states." This provision, which would bar private enterprise from space activities, was an attempt to impose socialist principles on an important sector of human activity and was an obvious attack on the corporation called for in the U.S. communication-satellite legislation. The United States saw no reason why private enterprise should be prevented from operating in space any more than it is from sailing on international waters. The fifth principle upheld this view while at the same time assuring the Soviets that states would assume their appropriate responsibilities.

The sixth principle provides that, if a state has reason to believe that an outer-space activity or experiment planned by it or its nationals would cause potentially harmful interference with activities of other states in their peaceful pursuits in space, it shall hold appropriate international consultations before going ahead. It also upholds the right of another state to request consultations if it believes that the launching state's activities will interfere with its own.

The Soviet Union had insisted that prior discussion and agreement must take place on any measures to be undertaken by a state that "might in any way hinder the exploration or use of outer space for peaceful purposes by other countries." This principle would have effectively extended the veto into space. One can imagine the difficulties that would result from a multilateral clearance system. Space exploration could be slowed down or halted entirely by red tape or political obstructionism.

The principle finally agreed on is fully in accord with existing United States practice as reflected in the handling of our West Ford experiment. Project West Ford placed a large number of tiny filaments in a short-lived orbital belt around the earth. The purpose was to determine the feasibility of using filaments as passive reflectors to relay communications. Project West Ford was carefully considered in advance by both the President's Science Advisory Committee and the Space Science Board of the National Academy of Sciences. The full details of the experiment were made known well in advance to interested scientists both here and abroad. A report by the Space Science Board based on an exhaustive study following the experiment showed there was no interference with radio or optical astronomy.

The United States is prepared to undertake similar consultation for other scientific experiments. With the conclusion of the partial nuclear test ban, nuclear testing in outer space has, of course, been eliminated from the list of possible experiments that might cause potentially harmful interference.

The seventh principle of the Declaration deals with the status of objects launched into outer space. It provides that a state on whose registry an object launched into outer space is carried shall retain jurisdiction and control over the spacecraft and its personnel while in outer space. Ownership is not affected by passage of the spacecraft through space or by its return to earth. Finally, objects shall be returned to the state of registry, which shall furnish identifying data upon request prior to their return. These provisions are in large measure extensions of principles found in the law of the sea and in aviation law.

The eighth principle deals with the thorny problem of liability for space-vehicle accidents. It declares that each state that launches or procures the launching of an object into outer space, and each state from whose territory or facility an object is launched, is jointly and severally liable. The principle is broadly framed and covers personal injury, loss of life, and property damage. It embraces accidents occurring on the earth, in air space, or in outer space.

The last principle covers return of astronauts, as the seventh deals with return of objects, launched into space. It declares that states shall regard astronauts as envoys of mankind, and shall render them all possible assistance in the event they have an accident, suffer distress, or make an emergency landing. It provides for their return to the launching state if they make such a landing.

In agreeing to the Declaration, the Soviet Union had to forego its earlier insistence on other principles that were widely considered objectionable. It had sought, for example, a sweeping prohibition on the use of outer space for "propagating war, national or racial hatred, or enmity between nations." The previous use of these phrases by the Soviet Union indicated that they could embrace virtually any criticism of Soviet policy or even advocacy of increased military preparedness. This issue was resolved by inserting into the preamble a reference to a General Assembly Resolution of 1947 that condemned in precise terms "propaganda designed or likely to provoke or encourage any threat to the peace, breach of the peace, or act of aggression." The 1947 Resolution contains a provision, important for democratic countries, that requests action by the government of each member "within its constitutional limits."

The most objectionable principle that the Soviet Union was obliged to set aside declared that the collection of intelligence from space is "incompatible with the objectives of mankind in the conquest of outer space." The United States made it clear from the outset that it would accept no proposition along these lines. Observation and photography from outer space are clearly consistent with international law and the United Nations Charter, as are observation and photography from the high seas. Moreover, space observation can help to reduce the risk of war by accident or miscalculation inherent in dealings with a closed society. Observation from space may help the U.N. to monitor an armistice or patrol a border. It may be used in the verification of a disarmament agreement. Premier Khrushchev was reported to have said in private conversations that the Soviet Union itself carries on space observation and photography and even suggested that satellites could be used for disarmament inspection.

In the end, no provision on intelligence from space was inserted in the Declaration. But discussion of this problem suggests another larger question. Should there be a principle that prohibits military activity of any kind in space? On close analysis, the answer is no.

The attempt to build peaceful space cooperation and a regime of law for outer space does not eliminate the need for military programs in outer space to maintain the security of the United States and the free world. There is no inconsistency in moving simultaneously on both fronts. For the foreseeable future, we shall need military space

programs to help keep the peace, and civilian space programs to help us live better in peace. In outer space, as on
earth, the achievement of law and order depends ultimately on the power of free nations.

The test of the legitimacy of a particular use of outer
space is not whether it is military or nonmilitary, but
whether it is peaceful or aggressive. Russian cosmonauts
are members of the Soviet Air Force, but this is no reason
to challenge their activities. There is, in any event, no
workable dividing line between military and nonmilitary
uses of space. A navigational satellite in outer space can
guide a submarine as well as a merchant ship. The United
States has military space programs, but all of its space
activities will continue to be for peaceful—i.e., nonaggres-
sive and beneficial—purposes.

In the interest of the security of the free world, the
United States cannot refrain unilaterally from the development of the military uses of outer space until more
progress has been made in regulating armaments generally. For the military uses of space and the military uses of
earth are part of the same problem. The Soviet Union,
interestingly enough, has taken the same position in recent
discussions before the United Nations. President Kennedy
put the matter clearly shortly before his death:

> If cooperation is possible, we mean to cooperate, and we
> shall do so from a position made strong and solid by our na-
> tional effort in space. If cooperation is not possible—and as
> realists we must plan for this contingency too—then the same
> strong national effort will serve all free men's interests in
> space, and protect us also against possible hazards to our
> national security.*

The Declaration of Legal Principles quite properly,
therefore, does not ban military activities from outer space.

* Letter to Congressman Albert Thomas (D., Tex.), September 23, 1963.

But this subject can and should be dealt with in our negotiations for general and complete disarmament.

With the approval of the Declaration, the Outer Space Committee turned to the other subjects put before it in the legal field. On December 13, 1963, the General Assembly approved a resolution calling for the prompt preparation of international agreements on liability for space vehicle accidents and assistance to and return of astronauts and space vehicles.

In May, 1966, still other possibilities were opened up for the development of space law. With the landing of a man on the moon only a few short years away, President Johnson called on the U.N. to proceed as quickly as possible with the negotiation of a treaty governing celestial bodies. According to the U.S. proposal, the treaty should provide, among other things, that the moon and other celestial bodies be free for exploration by all, in accordance with international law; that they not be subject to any claim of sovereignty; that there be scientific cooperation and freedom of scientific investigation; that states report on their exploration and that open access to all areas on celestial bodies be assured; that the stationing of weapons of mass destruction be forbidden, as well as military fortifications, weapons tests, and military maneuvers; that astronauts of one nation render assistance to other astronauts; and that states study and take appropriate steps to avoid harmful contamination of celestial bodies from earth and of the earth from celestial bodies.

The second part of the U.N. outer-space program concerns cooperation in technical and scientific work. The Outer Space Committee, together with a small expert unit in the U.N. Secretariat, serves as a focal point for the exchange of information and the initiation of cooperative projects.

One measure of information exchange is well under way. Pursuant to the Resolution of December, 1961, a comprehensive public registry of all objects launched into orbit or beyond is being maintained by the United Nations. The United Nations registry is of interest to all nations that wish to identify space vehicles. It may be helpful in fixing responsibility for any damage caused by a space vehicle on its return to earth. It may also help to develop procedures that would be useful for the advance registration and inspection of space launches called for in the Western draft treaty for general and complete disarmament.

The United States makes regular filings in the U.N. registry listing the international designation of its space objects, their launch vehicles, launch dates, general purpose, and orbital characteristics. The initial report, submitting information as of February 15, 1962, included all U.S. objects in orbit as of that date. Since then, the U.S. has registered all its launchings—successes and failures, orbiting parts or boosters as well as payloads, launchings under the supervision of the National Aeronautics and Space Administration and those under the Department of Defense.

The Soviet Union also registers its space launchings with the United Nations. However, it only registers payloads, and not parts or boosters; it only records successes, and not failures; it fails to report, as the U.S. does, when objects are no longer in orbit. At the time of this writing, it had still failed to record the launchings of the six objects that went into earth orbit whose omission from the registry was called to the U.N.'s attention in a note from the U.S. of June 6, 1963.

Beyond this registry, the following projects have been undertaken by the Outer Space Committee in cooperation with the Secretariat and pursuant to recommendations of the General Assembly:

—A report on the activities and resources of the United Nations, the Specialized Agencies, and other international bodies relating to outer space. This may encourage multilateral cooperation by acquainting nations with the capabilities of multilateral institutions.

—A summary of national and cooperative international space activities. The dissemination of this information will be of particular value to less developed countries, for it will acquaint them with the programs of countries active in space, ways in which they can participate in these programs, activities they might undertake on their own, and potential sources of advice and assistance.

—A compilation of bibliographic and abstracting services. This will help make information readily available to scientists and officials, particularly to U.N. delegates who are called upon to make decisions concerning outer-space matters.

—A review of facilities for education and training in universities and other places of learning. A report of this kind will be useful to less developed countries seeking to play a part in space activity.

In 1965, the General Assembly approved a further proposal that the United Nations serve as a clearing house for information on opportunities for education and training. By periodically informing members of offers and requests in this field, the Secretariat can help to stimulate international cooperation and broaden the geographic base for space exploration.

In June, 1962, the United States proposed that the U.N. endorse an international sounding-rocket facility located near the geomagnetic equator to be available for use by member nations. A sounding rocket, as the name suggests, is designed to take soundings of the upper atmosphere, including measurements of atmospheric density, wind, cloud formations, and radiation. It is used principally for meteorological experiments above the effective level of operation of weather balloons and, in general, below the level at which artificial satellites orbit. Its launching apparatus, guidance system, and instrumentation are considerably less expensive than those of orbiting satellites, which makes sounding-rocket experiments accessible to countries that cannot mount large-scale space programs.

The Government of India has now established a sounding-rocket facility at Thumba, near the geomagnetic equator. At the September meeting of the Outer Space Committee in 1963, India requested that a group of six scientists be sent to visit the facility and advise the Committee on its eligibility for United Nations sponsorship in accordance with basic principles endorsed by the General Assembly in 1962. This group, in which both an American and a Soviet scientist participated, visited Thumba in January, 1964, and recommended to the Committee that United Nations sponsorship be granted. Thus the Indian facility will be available to all members of the organization for scientific research.

The Outer Space Committee has also encouraged participation in other bilateral and multilateral projects now in operation. It has stimulated contributions to the World Magnetic Survey and the International Year of the Quiet Sun, two world-wide scientific programs under the auspices of the International Council of Scientific Unions. It has also provided a convenient meeting ground for discussions on bilateral cooperation, including talks between the United States and the Soviet Union, which may provide a further impetus to multilateral cooperation. Such talks have already produced the Dryden-Blagonravov agreements calling for the coordinated launching of weather satellites and exchange of weather data, exchange of data from satellites mapping the earth's magnetic field, and cooperative experiments in space communications using U.S. passive reflector satellites. These agreements were supplemented in 1964 by an agreement to work on a joint publication on the biological and medical aspects of outer space and space travel.

The third part of the U.N. space program looks toward a world-wide program of weather forecasting and research.

The space age has brought revolutionary advances in meteorology. When Tiros I was launched by the U.S. on April 1, 1960, we acquired a space platform to observe weather phenomena on an unprecedented scale. The orbiting of weather satellites—supplementing other advances in meteorological technology such as sounding rockets, radar, and electronic computers—will make it possible for the first time to keep the entire atmosphere of the earth under constant observation.

The U.N. program calls upon the World Meteorological Organization (WMO)—in collaboration with the scientific community—to develop two kinds of proposals: an international service program for weather observation and forecasting; and an international research program to yield greater knowledge of the atmosphere, needed for improved weather prediction and perhaps eventually weather control.

The United Nations has made a good beginning on this part of its space program. Following the passage of the General Assembly Resolution of 1961, the WMO invited the United States and the Soviet Union to send experts to Geneva to help develop proposals for a cooperative weather program. In response to this invitation, the late Dr. Harry Wexler, then Director of Meteorological Research of the U.S. Weather Bureau, and Dr. V. A. Bugaev, Director of the Soviet Central Weather Forecasting Institute, produced a draft which, with some modifications, was subsequently approved by the WMO's Executive Committee.

The WMO program received further impetus from the Dryden-Blagonravov agreement of late 1962. This agreement called for the coordinated launching of U.S. and Soviet weather satellites and for the exchange of weather photographs and other data. It also called for an exchange of techniques of interpretation and analysis, and for a communications link between Moscow and Washington to transmit both satellite and conventional weather information. All exchanges of data will be on a reciprocal basis, and the United States will not transmit satellite meteorological data until the Soviet Union has orbited a weather satellite and is prepared to furnish data in return. The communications link will permit the United States to collect complete weather data for the entire Eastern Hemisphere four hours earlier than is now possible. It will also serve other nations, which can have access to the link once it is operating satisfactorily.

Building on this bilateral agreement, the WMO system envisages the establishment of world weather centers —in Washington, Moscow, and a city in the Southern Hemisphere—for the collection, interpretation, and dissemination of data gained from satellites and ground-based instruments. Communication satellites would be used for the transmission of weather information. Existing gaps in the network of ground and ship observatories would be filled in order to assure global weather coverage. Manned meteorological stations might be replaced in large part by automatic equipment.

At its Fourth Congress in 1963, the WMO laid the financial and organizational basis for this ambitious program. A new Development Fund was voted to accelerate research in instrumentation, train qualified personnel, and fill the most serious gaps in the world's network of weather stations. In cooperation with the International Council of Scientific Unions, an Advisory Committee was established to draw up more detailed proposals for the weather service and research programs. A complete design for a world weather watch—including global observation, communications, and data processing systems—will be presented to the Fifth WMO Congress in 1967 for consideration and action.

It is important not to promise too much from any new scientific development—and this one is no exception. But it is no exaggeration to say that the weather satellite portends a revolution in meteorology, a peaceful revolution that can benefit all peoples on the earth, particularly in the less developed regions that presently lack adequate weather information.

The benefit from weather satellites that has made perhaps the greatest impact on the popular mind is the saving in lives and property resulting from storm warnings. In 1961, Tiros III photographed twenty tropical storms and gave the first warning of Hurricane Esther sighted in the south Atlantic. But this is only one of many applications. Satellites will increase our knowledge of the forces that shape the weather and will help us to forecast storms, floods, rainfall, drought, and climate with greater accuracy. This will make possible increases in agricultural yields and the more efficient use of fuels, water resources, and raw materials. Moreover, increased knowledge of the atmosphere may lead to new solutions to air pollution above our cities. Eventually, it may help us break up dangerous storms and achieve some control over climate and rainfall. In the words of the first WMO report, "It is not unrealistic to expect that mankind will eventually have the power to influence weather and even climate on a large scale."

These benefits from weather satellites are of value to all nations. Moreover, they will be hastened and enhanced through cooperation by all nations. No country, including the United States, can achieve the full benefits of weather prediction and weather research by acting alone. Each country needs to know the weather that is coming at it, so to speak, from the territory of other countries and from the three-quarters of the earth covered by the seas.

Every country can surely benefit by sharing the cost of weather stations with other countries. The two great space powers can both benefit by coordinating their efforts in the orbiting of weather satellites. With weather there is not, and should not be, an iron curtain separating East and West. And given the long-term possibility of weather control, the development now of international cooperation may reduce the risk that some day one nation might use this power to achieve military or economic advantage at the expense of another.

The improved weather services resulting from worldwide cooperation could lead to the saving of billions of dollars in the United States alone. They hold special promise for countries in the tropics and in the Southern Hemisphere, where vast uninhabited and ocean areas are not covered by conventional techniques. One recent breakthrough in technology promises special benefits to less developed countries. This is the Automatic Picture Transmission System, first carried by Tiros VIII, which transmits automatically to ground receiver stations, without command from the ground, photographs of cloud cover over an area of more than 1,000 miles square around the ground station. The receiving equipment can be procured for about $50,000.

To assure continued U.S. leadership in this important international effort, a bold national program in meteorology was proposed in 1963 by an interagency committee chaired by Assistant Secretary of Commerce Herbert Holloman. This committee had the benefit of a report on the atmospheric sciences and hydrology prepared by an expert group of the National Academy of Sciences. The Holloman Committee report, which is now being implemented, calls for a major increase in the U.S. national meteorological effort, including a global system analysis supplementing the WMO study, the development of instrumentation, accelerated research, and the stimulation of education and training in other countries.

The cost of these national and international efforts now under way will be small compared to their potential benefits. The challenge to the United Nations in the years ahead is to find ways to encourage the necessary cooperation among nations in weather research, in training weather experts, in financing weather stations, in orbiting weather satellites, and in exchanging weather information.

The fourth part of the U.N. program of space cooperation looks toward the establishment of a global system of communication satellites.

The dramatic success of Telstar, Relay, and Syncom have focused public attention on the vast possibilities that space technology holds for world communications. Within the next few years, we have within our reach a global system for communication by telephone, telegraph, television, radio, facsimile and high-speed data transmission.

The communication satellite will have a profound impact on the future of mankind. Before 1965, telephone communication between continents took place either by bouncing radio signals off the ionosphere, which frequently resulted in poor-quality communication, or by means of cables whose capacity has not kept pace with rapidly growing demand. With the launching of the Early Bird communication satellite in March, 1965, transcontinental telephone communication became immeasurably easier. One satellite over the North Atlantic will soon offer more telephone channels than are available in all existing transatlantic cables.

The simultaneous transmission of television between continents opens up no less far-reaching possibilities. According to the U.S. Information Agency, there are now some 100 million television receivers in use in 75 countries

of the world. By the end of this decade, when a communication-satellite network could be operating, there will be
double that number. Television programs will have a potential world audience of nearly 1 billion people.

This dramatic advance in communications technology
could affect the lives of people everywhere. It could enable
people to see and hear news events taking place in other
parts of the world at the very moment of their occurrence
—or at least on the same day, something that is not regularly accomplished now, when television tapes are carried
by jet aircraft. It could provide a new means to increase
literacy and help education in remote areas where TV communication over land lines may be prohibitively expensive.
It could enable leaders of nations to talk on a convenient
and reliable basis.

Some time in the future—probably in the 1970's—lies the
prospect of direct broadcast by radio and television. When
this day comes, it will be possible to beam programs from
communication satellites directly into people's homes. The
satellite system likely to be in use within this decade, however, will be for point-to-point relay between central installations in different countries. This means that the benefits
of space communications can be made available to all peoples only through political as well as technical cooperation.

The United Nations program is designed to be a contribution to such cooperation. It starts from the first of
three principles included in the 1961 U.N. Resolution—
"that communication by satellite should be available to
the nations of the world as soon as practicable on a global
and non-discriminatory basis."

A second principle underlying the program is that the
United Nations and its related agencies should be able to
use the satellites both in communicating with their representatives around the world and in transmitting programs
of information and education. Early Bird and other satellites have been used for live TV transmission across the

North Atlantic of events at the United Nations. From this beginning, it may be possible to encourage a practice by which all members of the United Nations will permit their people to see and hear U.N. proceedings.

A third principle is the importance of expanding technical assistance and economic aid to develop the internal communication systems of less developed countries. A country with an inadequate telephone and radio system and no television at all cannot participate in a global communications network.

Like the WMO in the weather field, the International Telecommunication Union was asked by the General Assembly to promote cooperation in space communications. The prerequisite for cooperation in this field is agreement on the allocation of radio frequencies to assure that nations do not interfere with one another's communications. In October–November, 1963, an Extraordinary Administrative Radio Conference of the ITU allocated frequency bands for satellite communications sufficient to accommodate anticipated traffic growth until the period 1975–80. It also allocated frequencies for meteorological and navigational satellites, space research, radio astronomy, amateur space activities, and aeronautical space services. And it approved procedures governing the use of these frequencies that will, among other things, facilitate the sharing of frequencies between terrestrial and space services. The successful conclusion of this conference helped to clear the way for the establishment of an efficient global communication system.

The chosen instrument for U.S. participation in this global system is a private corporation under federal regulation—the Communication Satellite Corporation authorized by Congressional legislation in 1962. Half of its stock is held by U.S. common carriers—such as the American Telephone and Telegraph Company—the other half by the general public. The corporation is managed by a Board of Directors of fifteen, three of them appointed by the President.

The passage of this legislation has enabled the United States to exercise effective leadership in developing the international arrangements necessary for a world-wide communications system. It has been U.S. Government policy that the Communications Satellite Corporation should participate in an international arrangement in which all countries have an opportunity to participate in the ownership, management, and use of the system.

A number of considerations suggest the importance of developing a truly international venture. Since the satellites will be primarily useful for communicating with other countries, the United States must agree with those sovereign countries on the arrangements for talking with them. Much of the traffic will be between other countries, not involving the United States at all. In view of the importance that all countries attach to communications, many of them wish not merely to own and operate ground stations (either alone or together with other countries in the same region), but also to participate in the ownership and management of the satellites themselves. Countries that do not wish to invest in the satellite portion of the system will not share in management and profits but will want an opportunity to satisfy their communication needs by leasing channels.

The United States has sought mutually satisfactory arrangements along these lines with the countries principally concerned to assure the development of a single global system rather than competing systems. Economic, technical and political considerations all point clearly to the desirability of a single system: From the economic point of view, a single system would avoid wasteful duplication of expensive satellite and ground facilities; from the political point of view, a single system would enhance the possibility for the fruitful exchange of communication between all countries and would avoid destructive competition to tie different countries into the communication systems of political blocs; and from the technical point of view, a single system would facilitate technical compatibility between satellites and ground terminals, would assure the best use of the frequency spectrum, and would promote operational efficiency and flexibility in routing.

The objective of a single global system of satellite communications was brought measurably closer when, on August 20, 1964, an interim intergovernmental agreement worked out between the United States, Canada, Australia, Japan, and the European Conference on Satellite Communications (representing twenty-two countries) was signed. This agreement, to which some fifty countries are already parties, calls for the establishment of a basic global system by the end of 1967. It includes commitments to invest in the space segment of the system, and establishes an international committee (known as INTELSAT) to supervise day-to-day management by the U.S. corporation. The agreement is open for accession to all other members of the ITU that wish to invest in the satellite portion of the system. Moreover, it provides for an international conference of the parties early in 1970 to consider definitive arrangements to supersede these interim ones, including the possibilities of continuing the latter on a permanent basis or of establishing a permanent organization with a General Conference and an international administrative and technical staff.

Hopefully, the Soviet Union will eventually cooperate in the global communications system. The United States has already carried on communication experiments with the Soviet Union under the Dryden-Blagonravov agreement. In 1964, the Soviet Union made optical and photometrical observations of the Echo II satellite and provided the United States with analyses of them. Messages were transmitted via the satellite from Jodrell Bank in England to Zimenski Observatory in the Soviet Union. And although several U.S. invitations to discuss the subject had previously been ignored, preliminary discussions with the Soviet Union on its possible participation in the global satellite communications system were held in June, 1964. The Soviet representatives in these discussions did not indicate a desire to participate in the interim arrangements at the outset, but left the door open for future cooperation.

This four-point program of multilateral activity between governments in the development of law, scientific cooperation, meteorology, and communications is paralleled by a wide measure of cooperation within the world scientific community. Working through the Committee on Space Research (COSPAR) of the International Council of Scientific Unions, twenty-four nations pool space research, thus continuing the remarkable cooperation that characterized space activities of the International Geophysical Year.

COSPAR's World Data Centers for Rockets and Satellites, maintained at Washington, Moscow, and Slough, England, form the world's major repositories for analyzed data. The United Nations Space Committee has justly pointed to COSPAR and the Data Centers as a useful channel for the exchange of information.

COSPAR has pioneered in maintaining a registry of satellite launchings, upon which the U.N. registry is based. It has also established SPACEWARN—a system in which launching nations provide essential information within a few hours after the successful firing of a satellite or space probe. Today, the United States communicates all its launchings through this "hot line" of the scientific community. Within a few weeks, more detailed statements of the experiments aboard scientific satellites are made available, and are finally published in COSPAR's Information Bulletin, widely distributed throughout the world.

Beyond actively participating in COSPAR, the United States has stimulated the development of space cooperation through a growing network of bilateral arrangements. Through these arrangements, NASA has brought the benefits of the U.S. program in the peaceful uses of outer space to other nations of the world and has helped to stimulate their national programs. At the same time, the United States has greatly benefited as well, since much of its space program depends on the help it receives from other nations. More than sixty countries have worked with the United States in actual flight experiments, in ground-based activities, in direct support of orbiting experiments, or in cooperative training programs.

The experience gained in these bilateral arrangements has been invaluable for the world weather program, the global communications venture, and other multilateral arrangements. Without the foundation laid by NASA in its bilateral undertakings, the U.N.-sponsored program of multilateral cooperation would not have been possible.

The cooperative efforts of the United States and other countries on the frontiers of space serve the mutual interests of all. They provide a way, despite political differences, to explore the enormous possibilities which the space age opens for mankind. This approach is not based on faith or on a fuzzy idealism. We must recognize that the deep political differences of our time place an upper limit on cooperation. But if we cannot send Messrs. Glenn and Titov together on a single spaceship to the moon, we can cooperate with the Soviet Union in other ways. If we cannot form joint ventures, then at least we can coordinate activities for mutual benefit.

While political differences place an upper limit on coop

eration, considerations of self-interest place a lower limit as well. The Soviet Union for years resisted rules for frequency allocation and usage for radio communication facilities, but finally accepted the frequency allocations of the ITU in order to avoid interference in the operation of its radio circuits. Its cooperative attitude at the 1963 Space Radio conference of the ITU encourages the hope that its national interest will lead the Soviet Union to cooperate further in the development of space communications.

It is in the interest of all countries, whatever their ideology, that space and celestial bodies should not be subjected to competing national claims, that cooperative experiments be undertaken and information exchanged, that world-wide weather services be developed and that communications among nations be improved. Recent meetings have served to emphasize this common interest to Soviet scientists and technical experts and, through them, to the Soviet Government. While the United Nations and its Specialized Agencies are not the only institutions to promote cooperation, they do help to put cooperation between the United States and the Soviet Union into a broader framework that recognizes the interests of other countries. And, since the success of the U.N. programs is enhanced by U.S.-Soviet cooperation, the interest of other countries in such cooperation that is manifested in U.N. meetings may help to stimulate affirmative Soviet actions.

For the United States, cooperative efforts are an absolute necessity if certain space efforts are to be successful. In weather and communications, for example, the technology of the United States can yield maximum dividends to its own people and to others only if many nations join in allocating radio frequencies, in tracking and communicating with space vehicles, and in placing necessary ground installations on their territories. For certain activities, bilateral arrangements are most suitable; for others, cooperative projects may be easier to achieve if they are multilateral and bear United Nations endorsement.

Perhaps it is not too much to hope that, beyond these benefits, cooperative space ventures will strengthen the sense of world community. The new responsibilities of the United Nations for promoting scientific cooperation and information exchange and for assisting in the development of world-wide weather and communication services cannot fail to strengthen the organization as a force for peace by binding its members together through ties of common interest.

It was this conviction of the common interest in space cooperation which led President Kennedy to make his dramatic offer to the Soviet Union in his second appearance before the General Assembly on September 20, 1963:

> In a field where the United States and the Soviet Union have a special capacity—the field of space—there is room for new cooperation, for further joint efforts in the regulation and exploration of space. I include among these possibilities a joint expedition to the moon. . . . Why . . . should the United States and the Soviet Union, in preparing for such expeditions, become involved in immense duplications of research, construction and expenditure? Surely we should explore whether the scientists and astronauts of our two countries—indeed, of all the world—cannot work together in the conquest of space, sending some day in this decade to the moon not the representatives of a single nation but the representatives of all of our countries.

On December 2, 1963, while the world still mourned the fallen President, Ambassador Stevenson returned to this theme in opening the annual Assembly debate on space cooperation:

> President Johnson has instructed me to reaffirm that offer today. . . . If giant strides cannot be taken at once, we hope

that shorter steps can. We believe there are areas of work—short of integrating the two national programs—from which all could benefit. We should explore the opportunities for practical cooperation, beginning with small steps and hopefully leading to larger ones.

The proper goal of the United States in space is not national glory but a partnership befitting our common humanity. The experience gained today could form the basis for the kind of partnership we seek tomorrow. The potential benefits of such a partnership are perhaps as limitless as space itself.

Chapter 10

Human Rights:
The Ultimate Foundation

QUESTIONS OF HUMAN RIGHTS are now at the forefront of international attention. The wall in Berlin, anti-Semitism in the Soviet Union, the general deprivation of human rights in Communist countries, *apartheid* in South Africa, the setbacks for freedom in less developed areas, and the struggle for racial equality in the United States —all have stirred public opinion around the world and profoundly affected international relations.

During most of the first twenty years of the United Nations, the drive for freedom tended to be defined as the drive for national independence. But we know that history is studded with examples of unholy alliances between nationalism and tyranny. Now that freedom has been achieved for so many new nations, we are still faced with the previous question: What about freedom for individual men and women and children, the individual human persons whose dignity and worth is reaffirmed on the opening page of the United Nations Charter?

The world today offers a very far from satisfactory answer to this question. In some nations, fundamental freedoms are denied by governments as a matter of principle —through racial separation, political oppression, or religious persecution. In other nations, many freedoms are deliberately postponed, by government action, to concentrate on what are thought to be more urgent items of public business. In all nations in greater or lesser degree, freedoms are threatened by lust for unchallenged political power—by the animosities of tribe or class or caste or sect or party, by prejudice and bigotry and other evils that still divide the branches of humanity.

These facts pose a central challenge to United States foreign policy, particularly as prosecuted in international organizations. The United Nations and its affiliated agencies have developed increasingly effective measures to promote two of their great objectives—the maintenance of international peace and security and the promotion of economic and social cooperation. But the members of the United Nations have been not nearly so successful in devising methods to promote the third main objective laid down in the Charter—"respect for human rights and for fundamental freedoms for all."

Whether and by what means the United States should seek to rectify this imbalance in the achievements of the United Nations are questions which are at once urgent, controversial, and complex.

One of the important respects in which the Charter of the United Nations differs from the League of Nations Covenant is in its emphasis on human rights. The Charter makes the promotion of human rights one of the main purposes of the organization. In Articles 55 and 56, the members of the United Nations pledge themselves to take joint and separate action in cooperation with the organization to promote "universal respect for, and observance of, human rights and fundamental freedoms for all without distinction as to race, sex, language or religion." Moreover, Articles 13 and 62 of the Charter charge the General Assembly and the Economic and Social Council with responsibilities for making recommendations for the advancement of human rights.

These provisions have provided the legal basis for the consideration of human-rights questions by the General Assembly and other United Nations organs. It is true that another provision of the Charter, Article 2(7), forbids the United Nations to "intervene in matters which are essentially within the domestic jurisdiction of any state." But, when construed together with the human-rights provisions of the Charter, this paragraph does not preclude the Assembly and other United Nations organs from general discussions about the world-wide promotion of human rights that may include specific references to human-rights situations in particular countries. Moreover, the United Nations may consider and adopt recommendations about specific violations of human rights that are part of a member's official policy inconsistent with its obligations in Articles 55 and 56. This last qualification is important: It helps to explain why U.N. organs have passed recommendations concerning the enforcement of *apartheid* by the Government of South Africa and have not passed recommendations about racial discrimination in the United States—which is being vigorously attacked by the Federal Government. Of course, violations of human rights may be the occasion for mandatory sanctions against a member only when the Security Council determines that they constitute a threat to or breach of international peace.

The Charter of the United Nations also provides for a Commission on Human Rights. Under the chairmanship of Mrs. Eleanor Roosevelt, the Commission undertook as its first major task the drafting of the Universal Declaration of Human Rights, a statement of principles in nonbinding form to serve as a "common standard of achievement for all peoples and all nations." The Universal Declaration is a comprehensive affirmation of basic political and economic rights found in the Constitution and basic legislation of the United States as well as in the laws of other free countries—including the right to life, liberty, and property, fair trial, freedom of speech, assembly, and religion; the right to participate in government; the right to work, to equal pay for equal work, to just and favorable remuneration, and to form trade unions; and the right to an effective remedy if any violation of these rights occurs. It was approved by the General Assembly in 1948 without a single negative vote and with the abstention only of the Soviet bloc, Saudi Arabia, and South Africa.

The Universal Declaration has become the yardstick for measuring the progress of governments and peoples in their long struggle for freedom and dignity. The United Nations has published it in the native languages of all countries. The many nongovernmental organizations recognized under the U.N. Charter as consultants to the United Nations have given it wide publicity through educational and study programs. It helped to stimulate two regional conventions: the 1950 European Convention for the Protection of Human Rights and Fundamental Freedoms—the first comprehensive regional measure for incorporating human rights into law—and the Draft Inter-American Convention on Human Rights. It influenced the constitutions of at least seven states, including the Federal Republic of Germany, the peace treaty with Japan, and the Austrian State Treaty, treaties relating to at least four African states, and the legislation of many nations around the world. It has been cited by the International Court of Justice and by courts in a number of countries. While of no binding legal force itself, it has become a basic norm in the body of human-rights law now being slowly built up within nations. It has also become the working outline for the development of an international law of human rights through conventions which do have contractual force.

Following the adoption of the Universal Declaration, the members of the United Nations turned to the drafting of an international bill of rights in treaty form. In 1951, however, the General Assembly decided to divide the rights enumerated in the Declaration into two legal instruments: a Covenant on Political and Civil Rights embracing the traditional civil and political rights recognized in Western societies, which are generally amenable to legal enforcement; and a Covenant on Economic, Social and Cultural Rights, which have been emphasized more and more in recent years and which lend themselves less readily to enforcement than to long-range education, planning, and promotion. In view of existing differences between countries about human rights and the appropriate means for implementing them, it is hardly surprising that these instruments are still under negotiation.

Given the difficulties encountered in the negotiation of the comprehensive Covenants, it was natural that attention should turn to a more modest approach—the building of an international law of human rights step by step through specific conventions dealing with particular rights. The first such treaty instrument—the Genocide Convention, which has been in force since 1951—commits the parties to prevent and punish within their territories the destruction of any national, racial, religious, or ethnic group. Other United Nations conventions now in force deal with the rights of refugees, stateless persons, the political rights of women, the nationality of married women, and slavery. Also in force are ILO conventions on forced labor and discrimination in employment and a UNESCO Convention on discrimination in education. And in 1965, the General Assembly completed work on a Convention on Racial Discrimination. A number of other United Nations human-rights conventions are, as of this writing, at various stages of completion.

The United Nations and Specialized Agencies have also formulated declarations or recommendations to members on specific subjects, prior to their incorporation in conventions—such as the declaration on racial discrimination approved by the General Assembly in 1963 and one on religious intolerance now pending. And occasionally, declarations have been adopted without subsequent conventions (such as that on the social and physical well-being of children), where the subject matter was considered inappropriate for legal treatment.

Quite apart from the drafting of human-rights principles, the United Nations has sought to promote human rights in other ways. The most dramatic examples have come in the debates on world-wide progress in human rights in the General Assembly and in the Human Rights Commission, and in the Assembly's consideration of specific human-rights situations such as *apartheid* or the position of Buddhists in Viet Nam. The Trusteeship Council also regularly considers the situation—including observance of human rights—in three (originally eleven) territories placed under U.N. trusteeship. A committee established pursuant to the 1960 Declaration on the Granting of Independence to Colonial Countries and Peoples, which called for the granting of "all powers to the peoples of these territories . . . without any distinction as to race, creed, or color," examines conditions in other non-self-governing territories. And it should not be forgotten that the activities of the United Nations in peacekeeping and nation-building, even though not labelled "human rights," have become formidable instruments for the promotion of individual dignity.

Finally, a special "action" program for the promotion of human rights has been under way for more than a decade. This program has three main points:

1. *Reporting.* A system of periodic human-rights reporting, established in 1956, calls for governments to review progress and problems in their countries. The Secretary-General receives and summarizes these reports, and the Human Rights Commission prepares general comments, conclusions, and recommendations upon them. The first series of reports (1954–56) came from forty-one governments; the second (1957–59) came from sixty-seven. To overcome the inherent lack of objectivity in responses obtained solely from governments, a Committee on Periodic Reports, appointed by the Commission in 1961, recommended the nongovernmental organizations with consultative status at the United Nations as additional sources of information. Accordingly, they were invited to submit, for the third series of reports (1960–62), "comments and observations of an objective nature on the situation in the field of human rights."

2. *Research.* Global research has been conducted for the past ten years by the Commission on Human Rights, the Sub-Commission on Prevention of Discrimination and the Protection of Minorities, and other U.N. bodies. These bodies have studied particular rights listed in the Declaration, examining how they are observed in member states and suggesting areas for improvement. For example, the Commission has examined freedom from arbitrary arrest, detention, and exile. The Sub-Commission has explored discrimination in education, occupation, and employment, political rights, religious rights and practices, and the right to leave a country and to return. Recent studies look into the right of arrested persons to communicate with those necessary to their defense, discrimination against persons born out of wedlock, and equality in the administration of justice. The studies are based on submissions of nongovernmental organizations and the writings of recognized scholars, in addition to official government sources.

3. *Advisory Services.* A program of advisory services, approved in 1955 by the General Assembly, authorized the Secretary-General, at the request of governments, to organize regional seminars on human rights, award fellowships or scholarships, and provide services of experts to member states. The seminars have brought together government officials, lawyers, and scholars in a constructive exchange of ideas and experience. The topics discussed have included protection of human rights in criminal law and procedure, participation of women in public life, illegal exercise or abuse of administrative authority, freedom of information, and human rights in developing countries. Various suggestions for expanding the advisory services have been considered—including a larger budget for fellowships, encouragement of seminars on additional human-rights problems, and regional institutes for training civil servants in human-rights techniques.

What should be the position of the United States in this many-sided U.N. program in the field of human rights? The considerations for U.S. leadership are clear and compelling. They derive in part from the nature of American society. Since the Declaration of Independence, the United States has been dedicated to the pursuit of human rights and fundamental freedoms, not just for Americans but for "all men." Thomas Jefferson was expressing a deeply held faith of the Founding Fathers when he predicted that from American shores the "fire of freedom and human rights" would be "lighted up in other regions of the earth." Throughout American history, and still today, United States power in the world derives from its position not just as an arsenal of weapons or as a storehouse of commodities but as a base from which to seek the universal realization of the dignity of man.

Vigorous American support for human rights around the world is not only an essential and irreversible part of the American tradition: It serves to clarify the issues in the basic struggle for freedom in the world today. Communist leaders put human freedoms very low on their scale of priorities; they are prepared to violate them in their drive for world power and rapid economic growth. The same was true a generation ago of the leaders of the Axis powers. It is the belief in human rights, in the importance and worth of every individual, that distinguishes the United States and other countries of the free world from the totalitarians of the left and of the right.

It is not only affirmation of American support for human rights but also progress made in achieving them that serves the national interest. Peace and security, economic and social development, and human rights are the three sides of the triangle of world order. In the absence of any one of them, the triangle is not complete.

We have learned from hard experience of the intimate interdependence between human rights and peace and security. Nazi Germany should have taught everyone the lesson that internal suppression is often the handmaiden of external aggression, that the destruction of freedom at home can quickly lead to the destruction of freedom abroad. Dictators typically employ foreign adventures to solidify their domestic power; and the recklessness of their foreign policy is directly facilitated by the systematic destruction of domestic dissent. The other side of the coin is no less true: The more a country is threatened from without, the more dangerous it is for human rights within. Those concerned with the preservation and development of human rights in free societies cannot fail to be concerned with the promotion of human rights on a worldwide basis. The same is true for those concerned with the pursuit of peace and security. As President Kennedy asked so eloquently, "Is not peace, in the last analysis, basically a matter of human rights?" * World-wide progress in the vindication of human rights and fundamental freedoms

* Remarks at the American University, June 10, 1963.

will also be progress in creating a peaceful and stable world order.

Secretary Rusk recently summed up the intimate relation between American foreign policy and the promotion of human rights:

> One of the most compelling tasks before us today is to get on with the unfinished business of human rights. By doing so, we clarify the meaning of this world struggle between freedom and coercion for those who are still confused. Even more important, we move mankind closer to the decent world order in which we believe—and the only kind in which we and all other men who value freedom can live in security.*

But the international promotion of human rights is not a one-way street. World opinion is concerned not only with human-rights problems of other countries but also with human-rights problems in the United States, particularly with the struggle for racial equality. Some Americans fear that an attempt to assert United States leadership in the international promotion of human rights may result in unwanted international attention to our domestic problems. They raise the question: Are we prepared to "take the heat" ourselves as the price for "putting the heat" on others?

To a large extent, this question has already been answered for us. The United States is an open society with the world's most highly developed media of mass communication. Our domestic racial problems are widely advertised to every corner of the globe. So we are already "taking the heat" of intense international attention to our struggle for civil rights.

The same is not true for the closed societies of the world. In these countries, where the press is controlled and foreign newsmen are severely restricted in their freedom of

* Address before the American Jewish Committee, April 30, 1964.

movement, violations of human rights do not automatically succeed in impressing themselves on world opinion. Thus there tends to be a geographic imbalance in the focus of international attention to human-rights problems.

Nor is the imbalance one of geography alone. The current international preoccupation in human rights is on racial discrimination, specifically, on the struggle for Negro equality. The vindication of the rights of Negro communities in the United States and elsewhere is a matter of urgent public business. But there are other human-rights questions beside the question of Negro equality. In the preoccupation with how white men treat black men, the world must not lose sight of how white men treat white men, or how black men treat black men, or even how black men come to terms with white minorities in their midst.

Human rights, like the United States Constitution, should be color-blind in every sense of the word. In a world becoming increasingly race-conscious, there is a particular danger that violations of human rights within racial groups will tend to be ignored. The problem was poignantly illustrated in a recent cartoon which shows a smiling Mao Tse-tung telling an African leader: "Of course, there is no discrimination in China. Here we enslave everybody!"

The choice facing the United States in the field of human rights is now reasonably clear. On the one hand, it can take a defensive posture out of concern with its domestic difficulties. In this event, the world's concern with the racial issue in the United States will not go away; on the contrary, the present disparity between world attention on racial discrimination as manifested particularly in the United States and on other kinds of human-rights violations in other countries will probably increase.

On the other hand, the United States can assert its leadership in the world-wide promotion of human rights. It can focus international awareness and concern with human-rights problems on an objective examination of the state of human dignity in all countries, and thus place the struggle for equality in the United States in its total world setting.

The United States is already in the sun. Any additional light on human rights that can be generated through the United Nations will do more to illumine the deprivations of these rights in the dark corners of closed societies than in the open societies of the free world.

There are many different ways, of course, of promoting human rights. The United States has a powerful lever in its bilateral diplomacy. Increasing opportunities for action are becoming available in regional forums. In some cases, quiet representations to a government or an informal and *ad hoc* process of conciliation may produce the best results. But the experience of recent years also suggests the utility of exposing human-rights problems to world attention in the global forums of the United Nations, where they can be looked at by the community of nations as a whole.

The American interest in promoting the human-rights activities of the United Nations has already been reflected through vigorous leadership in a number of areas. The United States played the leading role, through the person of Mrs. Roosevelt, in the preparation of the Universal Declaration of Human Rights. It sponsored the "action" program to strengthen human rights through national reporting, research, and advisory services. It has left no doubt about its position when violations of human rights in countries such as South Africa and Tibet are brought before United Nations forums.

Yet the United States is now being challenged to take further leadership in two other areas of United Nations activity in human rights—the development of human-rights standards through the negotiation and ratification of human-rights conventions on the one hand, and the implementation of these standards through new international machinery on the other. Both of these raise serious policy issues for the United States.

United States policy on human-rights conventions has been a subject of particular controversy. The United States took a leading part in the negotiation of the Genocide Convention and other human-rights treaties in the early years of the United Nations, but in 1953, Secretary of State John Foster Dulles declared that, so far as the United States was concerned, these instruments were not appropriate means for the international promotion of human rights and that other non-treaty measures should be supported instead. Thereupon the United States ceased to participate in the drafting of human-rights treaties—including the two Covenants—and declined to ratify the Genocide Convention or any other convention in the field of human rights.

The Dulles policy was reversed shortly after the election of President Kennedy. The new Administration announced that the United States would henceforth consider each human-rights convention on its merits. As a first manifestation of the new policy, United States representatives participated in the drafting of the human-rights Covenants and the marriage convention. The Administration also reaffirmed support for ratification of the Genocide Convention. Then, in July, 1963, President Kennedy submitted to the Senate for advice and consent to ratification the conventions dealing with slavery, forced labor, and the political rights of women.

These three conventions—all of them now in force —seemed particularly appropriate for early U.S. participation. Each deals with a basic human right already guaranteed by the U.S. Constitution and existing federal law. They would thus impose no new obligation on the United States Government in respect to its own or foreign citizens. What they would do is to reaffirm these rights in an international context and with international effect.

What, precisely, do these Conventions provide?

The supplementary convention on slavery, thus far ratified by fifty-seven countries, supplements the 1926 slavery convention to which the United States is a party, by dealing with conditions akin to slavery. It requires contracting parties to take all practicable and necessary measures to bring about as soon as possible the complete abolition of such practices as debt bondage, serfdom, involuntary marriage or transfer of women for payment, transfer of widows as inherited property, and exploitation of children. It provides that contracting parties make participation in the slave trade a criminal offense and that any slave who takes refuge on board any vessel of a party be *ipso facto* free. It pledges the parties to make the mutilation, branding, or marking of a slave or person of servile status, and the act of enslaving or inducing another person into slavery, criminal offenses.

The convention concerning the abolition of forced labor, already ratified by sixty-seven countries, pledges each contracting party to suppress and not to make use of any form of forced or compulsory labor—as a means of political coercion or education, or as a punishment for holding or expressing political views ideologically opposed to the established system; as a method of mobilizing and using labor for purposes of economic development; as a means of labor discipline; as a punishment to those having participated in strikes; or as a means of racial, social, national, or religious discrimination.

The convention on the political rights of women, ratified by forty-three countries, provides that women be entitled to vote in all elections on equal terms with men and without discrimination; be eligible for election to all publicly elected bodies established by national law; and be entitled to hold public office and to exercise all public functions established by national law.

Obviously, however, words on paper are not enough.

Nobody believes that signing a human-rights convention in and of itself brings automatic improvement in the condition of people around the world. But United States participation in the great effort under U.N. auspices to define and clarify basic human rights of the kind embodied in these conventions can make a practical contribution to the national interest in promoting human rights in at least four ways:

First, United States ratification can stimulate other nations to adhere to these conventions and can augment their impact among countries already parties to them. The United States will thus encourage the implementation of these basic human-rights standards in foreign countries—particularly in newly independent countries that consciously take the United Nations conventions as a model.

Second, ratification will put the United States in a better legal and moral position to protest infringement of these human rights in countries that have ratified the conventions but failed to implement them in practice.

Third, ratification will increase United States influence in the continuing U.N. process of drafting legal norms in the field of human rights. As long as the United States fails to ratify any human-rights conventions, its views will carry less weight than they deserve.

Fourth, ratification will dissipate the embarrassing contradiction between our failure to ratify these conventions and our traditional support of the basic human rights with which they are concerned. As President Kennedy put it in sending the conventions to the Senate: "The United States cannot afford to renounce responsibility for support of the very fundamentals which distinguish our concept of government from all forms of tyranny."

These considerations, to be sure, will be met by other arguments of law and policy that have long been employed against any U.S. adherence to human-rights conventions. One of these arguments is that ratification of these conventions would alter in undesirable ways the laws of the United States. This argument is inapplicable to these conventions since they would involve no changes in American law. Another of these arguments is that ratification would alter the balance of federal-state power by placing in the federal domain the protection of certain human rights hitherto reserved for state action.* This argument is also inapplicable to these conventions since all of them deal with matters which the Constitution and legislation have already placed within the federal domain.

Still another argument employed against ratification of human-rights conventions is that they are not proper subjects for the exercise of the treaty-making power. Charles Evans Hughes articulated the generally accepted opinion on this matter when he declared that the treaty-making power must only be used "with regard to matters of international concern." † With the growing interdependence among nations, the application of this standard has inevitably made more and more subjects eligible for the exercise of the treaty-making power. Human rights are no exception, given the intimate relationship between human rights and U.S. foreign-policy goals. And the inclusion in treaties of human-rights matters is scarcely unprecedented: The United States concluded dozens of treaties regulating the slave trade in the nineteenth century.

Obviously, those who oppose the three human-rights conventions are not in favor of slavery and forced labor and do not oppose granting political rights to women; their basic fear is that, while these conventions are innocent in themselves, they will encourage the use of the treaty-making power in the human-rights sphere, and start the United States down a slippery slope to profound and

* In *Missouri v. Holland*, 252 U.S. 416 (1920), the Supreme Court held that the Constitution authorizes the Congress to pass legislation in implementation of valid treaty commitments on certain matters otherwise reserved to the states.

† 1929 *Proceedings of the American Society of International Law*, p. 194.

undesirable alterations in our constitutional system. But the common sense and good judgment of the President and of the Senate, without whose approval treaties cannot be ratified, are proof against this ominous possibility. It betrays scant confidence in our governmental process to say we should not accept a desirable treaty today because we may be tempted to accept an undesirable one tomorrow.

No right is effective without a remedy. This is true in the international no less than in the domestic sphere. It is no wonder, therefore, that measures for the implementation of international human-rights standards should be an urgent and important issue. Indeed, it is likely that discussions of human rights in the United Nations forums in the years ahead will focus very largely on this question.

The U.N. has already devoted a good deal of study to implementation measures in the field of human rights. In 1963, the General Assembly began consideration of the draft implementation provisions of the two human-rights Covenants. Because of the subject matter with which it deals, the Covenant on Economic, Social, and Cultural Rights requires only that the contracting states report their progress in living up to it. But the implementation articles of the Covenant on Civil and Political Rights provide for a nine-member Human Rights Committee to be chosen by the International Court of Justice and empowered to receive complaints from contracting states about alleged violations from other contracting states. The Committee would ascertain the facts of the dispute and make available its good offices to achieve an amicable solution on the basis of respect for the human rights concerned. Failing such a solution, it would issue a factual report including its opinion as to whether the facts disclosed a breach by the state concerned of its obligation under the Covenant. After such a proceeding, a contracting state could bring its case against another contracting state to the International Court of Justice.

The United States has already indicated its general agreement with the implementation procedures proposed in these Covenants, although it has questioned giving the Human Rights Committee the authority to issue opinions on the merits of cases brought before it, suggesting that this judicial function should be left to the International Court of Justice. Moreover, the United States would, by ratifying the three human-rights conventions described earlier, commit itself to the implementation provisions which each of them contains. In the case of the Conventions on Slavery and the Political Rights of Women, this would mean compulsory jurisdiction of the International Court of Justice in disputes concerning the interpretation of the Convention. In the case of the Convention on Forced Labor, it would mean regular reporting to the Committee on Compliance with Conventions of the International Labor Organization and, in the event of a dispute, resort to a special ILO Commission of Inquiry and thereafter to the International Court of Justice.

Some nongovernmental organizations and distinguished private citizens suggest that the provisions should go even further. They argue in favor of direct access to international judicial machinery, an International Court of Human Rights or an International Court of Habeas Corpus, by private persons who are unable to get an effective remedy against the violation of their human rights by their own governments. As a precedent for such ambitious proposals, they cite the European Commission and the European Court of Human Rights, which can consider individual petitions against alleged human-rights violations.

It should be noted, however, that France and Switzerland have declined to join the European Commission and

European Court of Human Rights and that a number of other European countries that accepted membership in these institutions have so far refused to accept the right of individual petition. Moreover, the considerable consensus on human-rights standards among non-Communist European nations hardly exists among the broader membership of the United Nations. Many U.N. members in recent General Assembly debates have called even the more modest implementation provisions of the human-rights Covenants too ambitious. The majority of U.N. members are clearly not prepared to permit their citizens to appeal over their heads to international judicial bodies. And, paradoxically, such a system of private petition would almost certainly work unequally against free as compared with totalitarian societies. For an international body of the kind proposed would be besieged with petitions from citizens of free societies having no fear of the consequences, while the citizens of totalitarian regimes, whose human-rights practices are most in need of examination, would hestitate to bring their case to an international body for fear of government reprisal.

Thus the right of individual petition to world-wide international bodies in human-rights cases is not a practical possibility at this time. And even the implementation provisions of the human-rights Covenants must await the completion of these instruments. For the immediate future, therefore, efforts must focus on less formal procedures for information and persuasion which do not have to be embodied in treaty instruments.

Much can be done with the existing resources of the United Nations—particularly through the opportunities for influencing international opinion in the General Assembly and the Human Rights Commission. The potentiality of the United Nations in this connection has been graphically illustrated on many occasions, but perhaps never more clearly than on the issue of anti-Semitism in the Soviet Union brought to the attention of the Human Rights Commission in March, 1964.

That session of the Commission met against a background of growing evidences of Soviet anti-Semitism. In a nation dedicated to atheism and nationalism, the 3 million Jews of the Soviet Union are suspect on two counts—as members of a religious group and as a national minority with ties to communities overseas. Far from opposing popular anti-Semitism, the Soviet Government has been willing to exploit it. It has discouraged Jewish religious observances by drastically reducing the number of synagogues, religious schools, and publications in Hebrew and Yiddish. It has deliberately advertised through the state-controlled press the Jewish identity of persons sentenced to death for so-called economic crimes. It has frustrated contact between Soviet Jews and their co-religionists overseas.

The particular event that focused the attention of the Human Rights Commission on Soviet anti-Semitism was the publication by the Ukrainian Academy of Sciences of a book called *Judaism Without Embellishment*. This so-called history of Judaism was reminiscent of the worst publications of Nazi Germany. The American Jewish Committee, a nongovernmental organization in a consultative status with the Human Rights Commission, sent copies of this poisonous publication to all the members of the Human Rights Commission with translations of key passages. But translations were hardly required. Members of the Commission had only to look at the crude drawings depicting hook-nosed men brawling in holy places.

As it happened, the Commission was considering at that very session the draft Convention on Racial Discrimination and the draft Declaration on Religious Intolerance. With the support of other delegations, Mrs. Marietta Tree, U.S. Representative on the Human Rights Commission, introduced an article to condemn and eradicate anti-Semitism.

The Soviet delegate then moved an amendment that associated anti-Semitism with Nazism and neo-Nazism—suggesting by implication that anti-Semitic practices did not exist in other kinds of societies.

But the Soviet Union was not permitted to succeed in this attempt to obscure the issue. Without mentioning the Soviet Union by name, Mrs. Tree drew the issue sharp and clear:

> Let us be honest here and recognize that anti-Semitism is a present as well as a past danger, that it exists in countries where Nazism is unknown and in forms which are infinitely cruel but may not be genocide, that it cannot be covered up forever by recalling the crimes of Hitler and the horrors of concentration camps, and that people everywhere must become freshly sensitive to its meaning and its reality. Let us be honest enough to realize how anti-Semitism has fed the evil purposes of dictators, Hitler included, and is being exploited even today to turn groups against each other and deflect attention from the failures of governments and the ineptitude of public administrators.
>
> We must deal with anti-Semitism even when it takes the forms of deprivation of the religious and cultural heritage which makes this group unique. We should make it clear that a state which makes provision for German-language schools for that ethnic group should not deny Yiddish or Hebrew schools to its Jews; that a state which can permit national and regional organizations of some ethnic groups should, under the principle of nondiscrimination, permit the same for Jews; that a state which permits recognized leaders of every other group to travel abroad to conferences and holy places should not be able to deny that right to Jewish leaders; that a state that finds facilities to publish textual materials in the language and traditions of some groups should not be able to deny this right to Jewish groups; that a state which is able to tolerate the differences in 100 nationalities should have no right whatever to extinguish those differences in the 101st.

This confrontation in the Human Rights Commission was one of several events that helped to focus international attention on Soviet anti-Semitism. Leading intellectuals and private groups in the United States and Europe issued vigorous protests—and were soon joined by the Communist parties of France, Britain, and the United States. The Soviet delegation to the United Nations distributed a long, hastily prepared critique of the controversial book, pointing out places where the author had made mistakes in fact and judgment. The Soviet Communist Party's Ideological Commission was hastily summoned to Moscow to repudiate "serious mistakes" in the work. Still later, Alexsei Adzhubei, editor of *Izvestia* and Khrushchev's son-in-law, announced that the book had been banned and all copies destroyed.

This episode does not suggest that the United Nations can solve the problem of the Jewish community in the Soviet Union or of other groups subject to persecution around the world. All it suggests is that existing resources of the organization can be used to call attention to human-rights violations by U.N. members and even, in some respects, to influence the policies of members. President Kennedy told the General Assembly in 1963 that "new efforts are needed" to strengthen those resources. In the words of Harlan Cleveland, "The problem we need to consider is how sharp beams of international light can be effectively poked into the world's darkest recesses of reaction—and how those beams, once inside, can be focused and intensified until, like the laser ray, they burn out the malignancy of man's inhumanity to man." *

At the present time, the beams of international light are not sharp and fully focused. The only comprehensive information received by the Commission on Human Rights is in annual surveys of different human rights based on

---

* "Switch on the Lights," Address before the American Jewish Committee, April 30, 1964; Department of State Press Release No. 199.

reports submitted by member governments. These reports are generally bland and incomplete; many countries fail to report at all. Moreover, the incoming material is not made available in original form; the document prepared for the Commission is merely a summary, so that governments are spared direct exposure of self-serving omissions and interpretations. The Human Rights Yearbook, published regularly three years after date, consists only of legislation, court decisions, and official documents. Discussion in the Human Rights Commission is further inhibited by the tradition that specific reference should not be made to a specific situation or a specific country.

The result of all of this is that the Human Rights Commission regularly bypasses discussions of current problems in specific countries. In the vacuum thus created, the General Assembly has tended to involve itself in political and emotional discussions of a few human-rights problems without the benefit of a broad analytic review of the entire subject. And the U.N. as a whole lacks an up-to-date, comprehensive, and professional analysis of the measures member states have taken to fulfill their Charter obligations.

One of the more interesting proposals to fill this gap has been made by Jacob Blaustein, a distinguished businessman and former U.S. Alternate Delegate to the United Nations General Assembly. Blaustein urged the appointment of a United Nations High Commissioner for Human Rights:

> Such a High Commissioner could, amongst other things, lend his good offices to governments and be available at their request to investigate situations where there have been alleged violations of human rights; he could assist underdeveloped countries in the organization of various institutions for the promotion of human rights; he could advise the Economic and Social Council on the human-rights aspects of the Development Decade; and he could assist the Commission

on Human Rights in its review of the periodic reports from governments on human rights.*

If such an office were established, the reports from governments might be made annually and the complete texts of them made available to the Commission. The Commissioner could supplement this material with an annual report of his own, based not only on the official submissions but also on public sources such as newspaper accounts, communications from nongovernmental organizations in consultative status with the U.N., and other information at his disposal. This report could be organized under headings to parallel the Universal Declaration of Human Rights and the various sections could include salient developments in member states during the preceding year. Governments could be informed in advance of such references and be permitted to comment on them. The Commissioner could present his report in person to the annual session of the Human Rights Commission which, on the basis of the report, could consider specific situations as well as general world trends. The same procedure could be repeated in the Third Committee of the General Assembly in its annual debate on the human-rights chapter in the report of the Economic and Social Council.

Most members of the United Nations would not be prepared to have such a Commissioner hold hearings, make on-the-spot investigations, or solicit additional information from them beyond what they had voluntarily supplied in their periodic reports. But they might accept the more modest features included in the Blaustein plan. In any case, the proposal has stimulated a search for new ways to strengthen the U.N.'s contribution to the promotion of human rights—in defining standards, in clarifying experience,

---

* "Human Rights—A Challenge to the United Nations and to Our Generation," Dag Hammarskjöld Memorial Lecture, Columbia University, December 4, 1963.

in reviewing government performance against Charter principles, and in exposing to the conscience of the world the denial of those rights that should be the heritage of all human beings.

At the 20th General Assembly, the Government of Costa Rica introduced a proposal to establish a U.N. High Commissioner for Human Rights. Ambassador Arthur J. Goldberg announced that the United States would give its "enthusiastic support" to the proposal. Just what the mandate of a High Commissioner would be and how he would gather his information is now the subject of careful study. Hopefully, U.N. deliberations on this subject will yield a sufficient consensus to permit the establishment of the High Commissioner's office in 1968, the twentieth anniversary of the Universal Declaration of Human Rights, which the General Assembly has decided to celebrate as Human Rights Year.

Thus new opportunities may be available in the international promotion of human rights, particularly through a process of publicity and persuasion. But such a process can work successfully only if the nations participating in it are genuinely devoted to the national pursuit of human rights —not the national pursuit of self-righteousness. We might well benefit from the application here of the familiar legal doctrine of "clean hands": Those who would call in question the practices of others should at least be making every effort to put their own house in order. For the real test of a nation's commitment to human rights is not what it says in the United Nations for all the world to hear, but what it does at home for all the world to see. Mrs. Roosevelt put the matter with her customary simplicity: "It is not just a question of getting the Covenants written and accepted. . . . It is a question of actually living and working in our

countries for freedom and justice for each human being." *
This truth applies to the United States as well as to other
U.N. members. With the passage in July, 1964, of the Civil
Rights Bill, the U.S. took a major step in the implementation of civil rights at home. It thus laid the foundation for
further American leadership in the promotion of human
rights abroad.

These are not times for easy optimism; neither are they
times for cynicism and despair. A genuine world community is waiting to be born—and we have it in our power to
hasten the event. The foundation of that community, if it
is to be acceptable to free men, must be respect for human
rights. As Ambassador Arthur J. Goldberg declared in his
first statement to the United Nations General Assembly:

> The ultimate object of U.N. activities, the ultimate object
> of any organized society, domestically or internationally, is
> man, the individual. The effect upon his lot, his fate, his
> well-being—that will remain the final measure of our success,
> and our failure. And if we talk about the competition be-
> tween states, that is the only worth-while competition—as
> to which system, which society, best improves the lot of man
> and upgrades human dignity.

* Statement in the Special Meeting of the General Assembly to Commemorate the Tenth Anniversary of the Adoption of the Universal Declaration of Human Rights, December 10, 1958, U.N. Doc. 58–30254.

Appendix

Adapting U.N. Procedures to Reflect Power Realities *

As THE United Nations develops an increasing capacity to act, there will be increasing concern with the procedures by which this capacity is exercised. The manifest disproportion between the voting power and real power of its members is now a central preoccupation of persons concerned with the future of the world organization. Unless we can find ways to allay the anxieties felt on this subject in the United States and in other countries, it will be increasingly difficult to use the United Nations in the years ahead for important tasks of peacekeeping and development.

The constitutional problem here involved is not unique to the United Nations. We have sometimes referred to these difficulties in the United Nations as the "international apportionment problem"—because the word apportionment has a very poignant meaning in our domestic political life, through the recent actions of our Supreme Court and state legislatures. Indeed, we are dealing here

* Based on a speech delivered by the author at the Annual Banquet of the American Society of International Law, April 23, 1965.

with problems in the management of power reminiscent of those which confronted our own Constitutional Convention in Philadelphia nearly 200 years ago. In Philadelphia then, as in the United Nations system today, the problem was how to reconcile the sovereign equality of states with the fact that some states are very small and other states are very large.

The sovereign equality of states is one of the fundamental principles of international law. In the words of a famous case decided many years ago by the U. S. Supreme Court: "Russia and Geneva have equal rights." Article 2, paragraph 1, of the United Nations Charter declares that the United Nations is based on the principle of sovereign equality. The sovereign equality of states, however, has never meant the equal right to participate in the decision-making process of international organizations. The composition of the Security Council and other Councils, the veto provision, the amendment process—these and other provisions of the Charter all accord special privileges to certain members. So the structure of the United Nations from the very beginning recognized the need to reconcile the principle of sovereign equality with the uneven disposition of real power and real responsibility for implementing U.N. decisions. Appropriate means of balancing these considerations were also incorporated in the constitutions of the Specialized Agencies.

Quite apart from Charter provisions, procedures have been developed over the years to adapt decision-making procedures to power realities. In the last several years, this central problem has occasioned a vast amount of staff work in our own and other governments—and a considerable amount of discussion and negotiation in the U.N. system. We have explored with other nations many different procedures for rationalizing the decision-making process. We recognize that no one procedure is appropriate for all cases: Certain procedures may be appropriate for the voting of General Assembly resolutions which merely manifest the views of members and have no binding legal effect; other procedures may be appropriate when the General Assembly is exercising its mandatory power to assess; still other procedures may be appropriate in Specialized Agencies lending substantial sums of money for exchange stabilization or economic development. So our search for adequate procedures has been undertaken on a case-by-case basis with special regard for the peculiarities of each case.

Before turning to a discussion of possible procedures, it may be useful to identify one solution to the problem which we have not considered. We have rejected the notion that most or all important United Nations operations should be subject to the "principle of unanimity." Specifically, we have rejected the Soviet Union's twenty-year-old demand that all peacekeeping operations of the United Nations be under the exclusive jurisdiction of the Security Council and thus subject to great-power veto. While recognizing that the Security Council has the exclusive right to initiate enforcement action, we have consistently recognized the complementary authority of the General Assembly to launch peacekeeping operations in which forces are voluntarily supplied and are stationed on the territory of a a country with its consent.

The United States has been prepared to take whatever risks are inherent in the principle that peacekeeping operations may be initiated and financed by the General Assembly free from great-power veto because we recognize a long-term interest in developing this means of containing violence in the nuclear age. We want to minimize these risks, of course, but not at the cost of crippling the capacity of the United Nations to act for peace and security. To put it another way, we are persuaded of the need to protect the interests of ourselves and other large and middle powers in the United Nations vehicle. But we do not want to do this by draining all the gasoline out of the motor. We prefer to keep the gasoline in and to keep the vehicle on the road through the introduction of "power steering."

How can "power steering" be built into the United Nations vehicle? Diplomats and scholars have explored six main approaches to this problem.

1. *Weighted Voting.* Most public discussion of the "international apportionment question" has focused on proposals to introduce weighted voting in the General Assembly and in the conferences of the major U.N. agencies. Weighted voting exists, of course, in the four financial agencies of the United Nations system—the International Monetary Fund, the International Bank for Reconstruction and Development, the International Finance Corporation, and the International Development Association. In each of these, voting power is roughly proportionate to financial contribution. Weighted voting is also employed in the main international commodity arrangements, where it is related to the size of participating countries' trade in the particular commodity. Execpt for these financial and trade arrangements, it is not otherwise employed in the United Nations system. But most U.N. members, while willing to employ weighted voting for decisions on the disbursement of loans or the administration of commodity agreements, are not prepared to introduce this system across the board to cover recommendations of the General Assembly and other bodies.

The obvious practical impediment to the introduction of weighted voting in the General Assembly is that it would require amendment of the U.N. Charter and therefore the approval not only of the Soviet Union, France, and other members of the Security Council, but also of two-thirds of the members of the General Assembly. In the present state of international relations, it is hard to imagine the permanent members of the Council and two-thirds of the Assembly agreeing on any formula that would assign different weights to their share in the decision-making process. The most likely consequence of pressing for a Charter review conference to consider weighted voting, as some have urged, would be to provide a golden opportunity for the Communist countries and others to press for amendments diminishing the powers that the United Nations has developed under the Charter during the last twenty years and that have generally promoted the objectives of U.S. foreign policy.

Even if it were possible to amend the Charter to provide for weighted voting, it is not at all certain that our national interest would be served by the result. No system of weighted voting could conceivably be negotiated that did not weight population as a major factor. It is questionable whether such an arrangement would suit a country like ours, which has only 6 per cent of the world's population and which, together with its NATO allies, has only 16 per cent. If population were a primary criterion, India with its 450 million people and China with its 700 million people might well end up with more votes that the United States.

Of course, it is always possible to construct hypothetical systems of weighted voting congenial to our interests, based mainly on such factors as literacy, per-capita income, and military power. But such systems are simply not negotiable —at least, not in the foreseeable future.

The Department of State in 1962 conducted a study of various weighted-voting formulas based on population and contributions to the U.N. budget. When these formulas were applied to 178 key votes that took place in the General Assembly between 1954 and 1961, it was found that, while they would have somewhat reduced the number of resolutions passed over U.S. opposition, they would have reduced much more the number of resolutions supported by the United States and passed over Communist opposition. The same conclusion was reached in projecting these formulas to 1970, having regard to further increases in membership. The results of this study reflect the fact that the desire for political independence and economic progress has put most U.N. members on the same side as the United States on most important matters, particularly where action is involved as well as talk.

We have therefore concluded that any system of weighted voting taking population substantially into account—and no weighted voting system would be negotiable that failed to do this—would help Communist countries more than ourselves, by making it easier for them to achieve a blocking one-third vote on U.N. actions for peace and welfare which are in the interest of the United States and other nations of the non-Communist world.

2. *Dual Voting.* Dual voting, or a system of double majorities, has recently been advanced by some commentators as a possible answer. Benjamin Cohen, for example, has proposed that General Assembly decisions on substantive matters be made in the future by a two-thirds majority of members present and voting, *provided* that the majority includes two-thirds of the members of the Security Council.

Dual voting has two great advantages as compared with weighted voting: It does not offend directly the one nation—one vote principle; and it does not require a complicated negotiation involving national prestige in which different weights have to be assigned to different members. But most members of the United Nations would probably feel that the introduction of dual voting on all substantive matters would require Charter amendment. It is doubtful that a sufficient consensus on the desirability of dual voting presently exists for such an amendment to be approved.

It is always possible, of course, that dual voting might be introduced in selected areas of U.N. decision-making. At the U.N. Conference on Trade and Development, the non-Communist industrial countries, in the closing weeks of the Conference, proposed a system of dual voting for the new U.N. trade machinery. Under this proposal, decisions on certain important matters in the periodic Trade and Development Conference were to be taken by a two-thirds majority, including a majority of developed countries and a majority of less developed countries; in the Trade and Development Board, such decisions would be taken by a plain majority, including a majority of developed countries and a majority of less developed countries.

This proposal found some support among not only developed but also less developed countries, some of whom recognized the futility of voting self-serving resolutions without the concurrence of at least a majority of those nations to whom the recommendations were addressed. But the idea involved too great a change in existing procedures to gain approval. And even some of the Western industrial countries had misgivings, on the grounds that special voting procedures of this kind might cause greater significance to be attached to U.N. recommendations than they were prepared to accept.

3. *Bicameralism.* Bicameralism in one form or other offers greater possibilities in the short run than either weighted or dual voting. In its extreme form, bicameralism would mean treating the Security Council and the General Assembly as an "Upper House" and a "Lower House" and requiring that decisions on some or all matters be passed by both of them. For example, the veto could continue to apply to enforcement action; but voluntary peacekeeping operations and perhaps recommendations in other areas could be adopted by two-thirds of the General Assembly and by nine of the fifteen members of the enlarged Security Council. Here again, this kind of proposal would probably require Charter amendment. It is therefore not a practical possibility in the foreseeable future. But more tentative and informal steps in the direction of bicameralism may be possible.

In September, 1964, the United States submitted to the Working Group of 21 a proposal covering arrangements for initiating and financing U.N. peacekeeping operations involving the use of military forces. We proposed that all proposals to initiate such peacekeeping operations be considered first in the Security Council; the General Assembly would not authorize or assume control of such operations unless the Council had demonstrated it was unable to take action. This proposal would work a change in present procedures. While, under the Charter, the Security Council would normally be expected to consider a threat to peace and security in the first instance, there is no requirement that the Security Council be the first to consider a particular peacekeeping operation. In the Suez crisis, for example, the Security Council met before the General Assembly convened in emergency special session, but it did not consider the proposal for the establishment of the United Nations Emergency Force. This proposal was initiated in the Assembly itself.

A new arrangement by which proposals for the establishment of peacekeeping forces would first be submitted to the Council would be a step in the direction of strengthening the primary responsibility of the Council in the peacekeeping field. It should commend itself not only to those U.N. members who are seeking to strengthen the Council's role, but to all members who want to work out a rational distribution of powers between the Council and the Assembly.

The UNEF, Congo, and Cyprus operations illustrated the importance of getting U.N. troops to world trouble spots without undue delay. Therefore, any proposal requiring prior resort to the Council should contain safeguards—perhaps a fixed time limit—to avoid jeopardizing the ability of the Assembly to take timely action under its residual powers.

4. *Committees With Selective Representation.* Probably the most promising method yet devised for building greater responsibility into United Nations decision-mak-

ing is that of committees with selective representation. The basic concept was provided in the Charter provision for a Security Council with eleven (now fifteen) members, including the five permanent members that bear the principal responsibility for the maintenance of peace and security. The same concept is embodied in the Charter of a number of the Specialized Agencies; for example, in the Governing Body of the International Labor Organization, the ten members of chief industrial importance have permanent seats.

Even where no specific provision is made for permanent seats for a certain category of members, elections to the executive boards of U.N. agencies have normally taken account of the special responsibilities of members in the particular functional area of cooperation, whether it be telecommunications, weather forecasting, or medical research. Presumably, this will continue to be true in the future as well.

In the case of the Security Council, the Charter itself declares that "due regard" should be "specially paid, in the first instance to the contribution of Members of the United Nations to the maintenance of international peace and security and to the other purposes of the Organization," as well as to equitable geographic distribution. This provision has not received the attention it deserves. It would enhance the effectiveness of an enlarged Council if it were adequately reflected in Council elections in the years ahead.

Members of the United Nations have found committees with selective representation to be particularly useful in the financial field. The General Assembly's Advisory Committee on Administration and Budgetary Questions bears responsibility for examining and reporting on the Secretary-General's U.N. budget estimates. The United States has supported the effective operation of this small, twelve-man body, which not merely is representative of the major geographic groups in the United Nations, but also reflects comparative contributions to the U.N. budget. We have sought to strengthen the authority of similar groups in the Specialized Agencies, and we believe members might usefully consider the possibility of creating such groups in agencies that do not have them.

We also favor use of a committee with selective representation in the peacekeeping field. Our working paper to the Committee of 21 proposed that the General Assembly establish a standing Special Finance Committee, the composition of which to be similar to that of the present Working Group of 21: the permanent members of the Security Council and a relatively high percentage of those member states in each geographic area that are large financial contributors. The General Assembly, in apportioning expenses for peacekeeping operations, would act only on a recommendation from the Committee passed by a two-thirds majority of its membership.

One great advantage of the committee approach is that it does not require amendment of the U.N. Charter or of the various Specialized Agencies' constitutions. The proposed Special Finance Committee for peacekeeping operations, for example, could be constituted under and governed by firm rules of procedure by the General Assembly. In effect, the Assembly would be adopting a self-denying ordinance to act only upon proposals first adopted in this new sub-organ.

5. *Informal Relations with International Secretariats.* Informal relations with the international secretariats may also provide a useful approach. Obviously, the Secretary-General of the United Nations and the heads of the Specialized and Affiliated Agencies engage in a continuous process of consultation with member states, and in these consultations, they naturally take account of the differing responsibilities the members have for supporting the work of their organizations.

During the United Nations operation in the Congo, for example, the Secretariat systematically consulted an advisory committee of countries that contributed military personnel. More informally, consultation was carried on with key contributors of services and money. For example, the United States and other major contributors were in frequent touch with the Secretary-General and his staff in New York and with the chief of the U.N. Congo operation in Léopoldville. This was a truly international undertaking; at the same time, its conduct reflected the views of the major supporters of the operation.

So far, the heads of U.N. agencies have generally paid close attention to the views of countries with special financial and other responsibilities. The main problem has been the inability of these countries to organize themselves effectively for the timely transmission of their viewpoints to the agency heads. In recent years, the United States Government has made special efforts to deal with this problem. We have sought to take a longer-range view of international organization activities and to develop our own position on programs and budgets far enough in advance so that the executive heads of the agencies can take them into account at the time when programs and budgets are being formulated—that is, early in the budget cycle before the proposals to executive boards and conferences are frozen. This is immeasurably better than having the programs and budgets formulated in the dark, only to be met suddenly at the general conference with the opposition of major contributors.

During the past year, the United States has begun a systematic series of consultations with some of the other major contributors in an effort to develop common positions on the programs and budgets of the international agencies. As governmental positions emerge on various issues facing the Specialized Agencies, they are presented informally to the Directors-General. We believe that, in the long run, this exchange of views among governments and with secretariats will make for more effective participation by the larger contributors in the international organizations and, consequently, for more realistic program proposals in the agencies.

6. *Conciliation.* The most recent, and perhaps the most original, procedural innovation in U.N. decision-making is the conciliation procedure established by the General Assembly for the new U.N. machinery in the field of trade and development. The need for this became apparent during the United Nations Conference on Trade and Development at Geneva. In the closing days of UNCTAD, there was an encouraging disposition to reach a consensus on some subjects, but there were also instances when the voting bloc of less developed countries passed resolutions over the opposition of the minority of industrial countries on matters involving important economic interests.

Some delegates argued that this was no cause for concern since the resolutions were recommendations only, and any resolutions of the new trade machinery would also be only recommendations. But the United States and other countries pointed out that the currency of such recommendations would be hopelessly debased if they failed to reflect a substantial consensus that included particularly the countries bearing principal responsibility for implementing them.

International trade questions have traditionally been dealt with by negotiation—not legislation. Undoubtedly, there is a constructive role for institutions whose primary purpose is to articulate through recommendations the measures that should be taken by developed and less developed countries to deal with the trade problems of the latter. But such institutions can only operate through a process of persuasion. Persuasion is assisted when delegates seek a consensus through conciliation and express that consensus in resolutions. If it is not assisted, it may even be set back by self-serving resolutions passed with automatic majorities. Public opinion in the industrial countries is likely to react adversely to recommendations that are passed over their opposition but that call for concessions from them.

What is wanted, in the last analysis, is not voting, but results. Because most delegations recognized this, a last-minute agreement was reached at Geneva that the new UNCTAD machinery should contain procedures "designed to establish a process of conciliation to take place before voting and to provide an adequate basis for the adoption of recommendations with regard to proposals of a specific nature for action substantially affecting economic or financial interests of particular countries."

The task of working out these procedures was left to a special committee appointed by the Secretary-General of the United Nations. The conciliation procedure the Committee devised will operate in the periodic Conference, in the Trade and Development Board, and in its committees. Under it, conciliation can be initiated and voting suspended on any resolution, upon the motion of a very small number of countries (ten in the Conference, five in the Board, and three in committees) or upon the motion of the President of the Conference or Chairman of the Board. The initiation of conciliation is automatic. However, guidelines are provided defining the kind of resolutions that are appropriate.

Following a motion for conciliation, a conciliation group is appointed with adequate representation of countries interested in the subject matter. If the group cannot reach agreement at the same session of the Conference or Board, it reports to the next session of the Conference or Board, whichever comes first. If the conciliation group reaches agreement, the agreed resolution can be voted; if it does not, a decision can be made to continue conciliation for a further period, or the original proposal (or some variant thereof) can be voted in the normal way.

In the event that a vote is taken after unsuccessful conciliation, the resolution must cite the conciliation group's report (which may contain minority as well as majority views), and the records of the United Nations must show how the members voted.

These procedures offer important benefits to all U.N. members: For the minority of developed countries, they provide some safeguard against the voting of unacceptable resolutions by automatic majorities, and a "cooling-off" period of six months or more during which efforts at compromise can be sought through quiet diplomacy; for the majority of less developed countries, they afford a means of engaging the developed countries in a sustained debate during which the latter explain the reasons for their opposition to proposals of the majority.

It is too early to see just how the conciliation procedures will work in practice, but we may hazard one prediction: The main value of the new procedures may be less in their actual use than in the subtle way in which their mere existence influences member governments in the direction of compromise rather than voting on disagreed proposals.

This catalog of procedures for coping with the international apportionment problem should serve to indicate four things: first, that the United States and other countries are very much aware of the need to adapt U.N. procedures to take account of power realities; second, that a wide variety of procedures can be developed to come to grips with the problem; third, that the most practical of them can be effected without amendment of the U.N. Charter or of the constitutions of other U.N. agencies; fourth, that a great process of procedural adaptation and innovation is already under way throughout the U.N. system.

Of course, procedures in and of themselves are only part

of the problem. What is really required is widespread recognition of the common interest in basing United Nations decisions on an adequate consensus—a consensus that includes the support of most of the countries bearing the principal responsibilities for action.

Will such a recognition be forthcoming? The cynic may ask why the majority of small countries should accept any restraint on the use of their voting power. The answer is clear enough. If United Nations procedures cannot be adapted to take account of power realities, the large and middle powers will increasingly pursue their national interests outside the United Nations system. If, on the other hand, the necessary procedural adjustments can be carried out, the United Nations and its agencies will be able to assume increasing responsibilities for action in both peacekeeping and development. This is the fundamental reason that the important procedural adjustments now under way in the United Nations serve the enlightened long-term interests of all its members.